# SPITFIRE DESERTER?

## THE AMERICAN PILOT WHO WENT MISSING

# SPITFIRE DESERTER?

## THE AMERICAN PILOT WHO WENT MISSING

BILL SIMPSON

AMBERLEY

First published 2018

Amberley Publishing
The Hill, Stroud
Gloucestershire, GL5 4EP

www.amberley-books.com

The right of Bill Simpson to be identified as
the Author of this work has been asserted in
accordance with the Copyrights, Designs and
Patents Act 1988.

ISBN 978 1 4456 7286 1 (hardback)
ISBN 978 1 4456 7287 8 (ebook)

British Library Cataloguing in Publication Data.
A catalogue record for this book is available
from the British Library.

Maps courtesy of David Martin of the Fairlop
Heritage Trust.

Typesetting and Origination by Amberley Publishing
Printed in the UK.

# CONTENTS

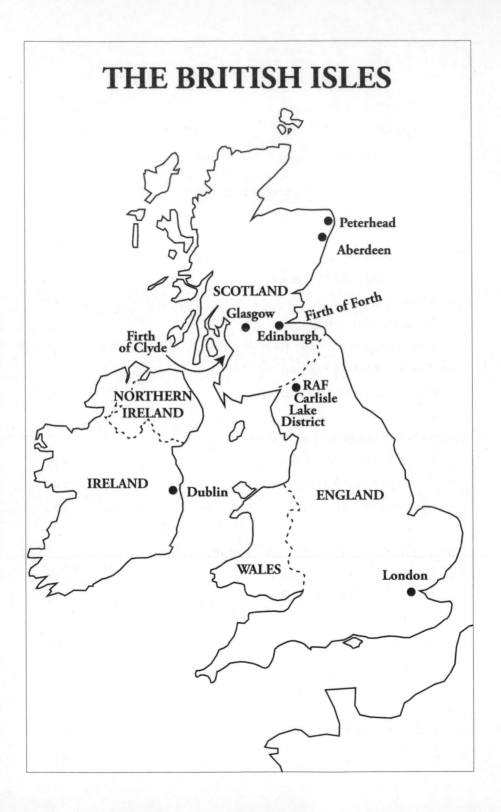

# THE BRITISH ISLES

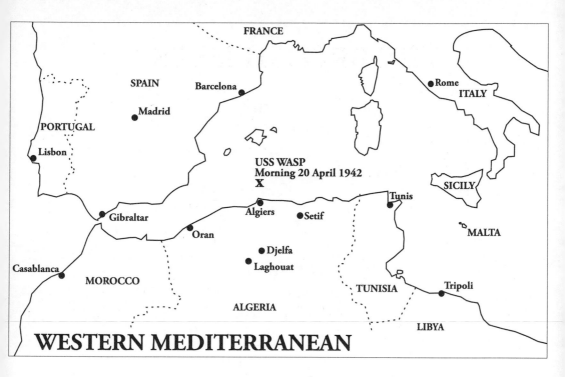

**WESTERN MEDITERRANEAN**

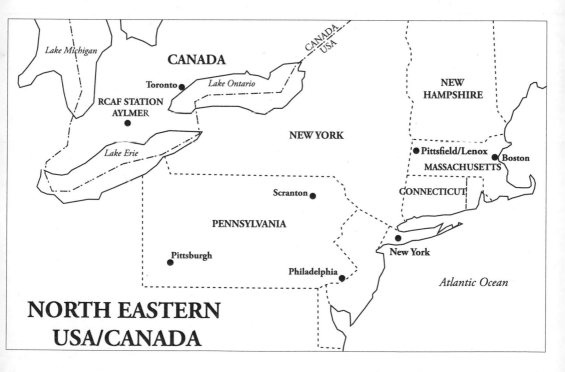

**NORTH EASTERN
USA/CANADA**

# PART 1

# THE ENIGMA

# AN INEXPLICABLE DEFECTION

Spitfire silhouettes, tiny, too small to count, filled the distant bright blue sky. At least that's how it seemed. And the heated air of mid-morning was filled with the faint but unmistakeable grumble of Merlin engines. The mass of aeroplanes seemed to confirm that the recent rumours about fighter reinforcements being sent to Malta were right after all. They were here at last, in sight, approaching the island. It was Monday 20 April 1942. Maltese and British alike stopped and squinted into the flare of the sky to try to see them as the sound of the many Rolls-Royce engines swelled, growing in intensity. The silhouettes grew larger, more visible, the immediately recognisable ellipses of the trailing edges of the wings against the brightness identifying them beyond any doubt as Spitfires and not the Messerschmitts or Cants or Macchis that were the more usual rulers of the sky. Some of the watchers could just make out that they were painted dark blue but most didn't care and pointed and smiled. Some hugged each other. Some just looked. Some had tears in their eyes. They were here at last.

The ragged masses of little aeroplanes split into two groups, one in tight formation making for the airfield at Ta'Qali in the centre of the island, the other dropping down towards Luqa, near the capital Valletta. There were forty-six Spitfires – most of the islanders dared to hope. The bombing of Malta had been going on for almost two years now. In June 1940, with Britain and its allies in full retreat in France and the Low Countries, and defeat seemingly unavoidable, Benito Mussolini, the Italian dictator, decided to throw in his lot with Adolf Hitler, the German Chancellor, to establish what became known as 'the Axis'. Within hours of Italy's declaration of war on Britain, the Italian air force, the *Regia Aeronautica,* from bases in Sicily a mere 50 or 60 miles away, attacked the Grand Harbour in the Maltese capital Valletta – a vital British naval base in the Mediterranean – and once started, the bombing never stopped. Even if the attacks were directed at military installations, the civilians suffered. They died in their thousands, with thousands more injured as their houses and the island's infrastructure were hit and the bombers sought to destroy their spirits and the will to fight. Close family links between some Maltese and Sicilians and other Italians made little difference – the bombing seemed endless.

Amid rumours that the Spitfires were coming, those defending the tiny island knew that Axis sympathisers passed information on to their enemies. The Germans and Italians were not unaware of the arrival of the Spitfires, and it wasn't long before they were being specifically targeted for destruction. For the forty-six pilots, it all had a nightmarish quality – they had been suddenly thrust into the middle of the most vicious and unforgiving air battle of the war. Some said it was worse than the desperate fighting of 1940 over the south of England, which stopped the German invasion of Britain and became known as 'the Battle of Britain'. Removed quickly from the airfields where they had just landed, and whisked off to basic billets and primitive accommodation, the newly arrived pilots came to terms with their situation and dwelt upon their deepest fear – that they might never leave Malta alive. Malta could accurately be described as the most bombed place on earth.

Forty-six Spitfires arrived on Malta but forty-seven had set off early that morning from the deck of the USS *Wasp*, an American aircraft carrier that had slipped into the western end of the Mediterranean in utmost secrecy after carrying the little British fighters and their pilots from the River Clyde in Britain to make the hazardous take-off from the carrier's deck. One Spitfire had failed to arrive. A signal from Malta to the Air Ministry in London[1] stated that the pilot

... INTENDED TO DESERT. HAD PREVIOUSLY LANDED FOR NO GOOD REASON IN IRISH FREE STATE BUT NOT INTERNED. IN CONVERSATION ON VOYAGE STATED MALTA WOULD NEVER SEE HIM.

And for some, this became a shameful incident in the RAF's now 100-year history. Long after the war was over, it was said that the pilot's fear of a death on Malta had preyed upon his mind, so he had chosen to desert rather than confront the enemy. His non-appearance was also described as an inexplicable defection. It was suggested that he had flown to North Africa deliberately, crashing his Spitfire and then, claiming to be a civilian pilot, finding a friendly American consul who would arrange for him to be repatriated back to the United States. And once the allegations appeared, they were repeated in publications and records.

The pilot in question was a young American called 'Bud' Walcott who joined the Canadian Air Force before the United States entered the war. In fact, on that fateful evening in April 1942, while his colleagues struggled to adapt to their new conditions in what was arguably the most dangerous fighting zone of the war at that time, Walcott was having to adapt himself to being a prisoner of the Vichy French in North Africa with just as uncertain a future ahead of him as those newly arrived on Malta. But unlike his erstwhile colleagues, he was having to rely utterly on his own resources in his solitary situation, without the support of the other members of the squadron.

While our lives are shaped by our actions and decisions, each of us has little control over the actions of politicians and national governments who enter into alliances and agreements with other nations that can have terrible consequences for us, often indirectly or even directly leading to the death or horrific maiming of those called upon to go to war. Some of these national relationships may have collapsed hundreds of years ago, and some more recently, but their consequences often last and while their lessons should be learnt, they rarely are.

Walcott's life, and his mentality, was influenced by a series of unlikely circumstances both within and without his control which arguably led to his tragic end. A minor actor in the immense theatre of violence convulsing much of the world, Walcott struggled through events which pushed him in all directions.

2

# CONVERGENCES

On Christmas Eve 1919, seventeen-year-old Alma Walcott, wife of John Walcott, two years her senior,[1] gave birth to a baby boy who was registered with the City of New York Health Department on 2 January 1920 as Salvator Bassi Walcott (later to be called Bud). Bud's Certificate and Record of Birth shows that both his parents were white, that they lived at 283 Central Avenue, New York City, and that he was born at home. The certificate should include the name of the borough along with the street but this piece of information has been omitted, although the birth of baby Salvator was supervised by a midwife whose residence is noted as Linden Street. There are several Central Avenues and Linden Streets in New York, but in the Bushwick neighbourhood of Brooklyn, the streets with these names are very near each other so it's safe to say Salvator was a Brooklyn boy. He is also described as being 'white' and his parents' occupations are given as 'Housewife' and 'Counterman', although the census records for the following year, 1920, give father Walcott's occupation as 'waiter'.

Coney Island fun fairs, Brighton Beach, the Navy Yard; all these have associations with the area of New York called Brooklyn, a name which derives from its original name *Breuckelen* when it was first settled by the Dutch. Bushwick, where Walcott was likely born, is in the north of the borough, bordered by the neighbouring district of Queens – indeed in the boundary area of Ridgewood, some of those who live there can't really decide if they come from Brooklyn or Queens.

In the 1920s, Brooklyn was expanding and developing links to nearby Manhattan Island via the subway and improved roads. The predominant group in Bushwick were Germans and the predominant industry was brewing. But prohibition was in force in 1920, and this had a dramatic effect on the breweries that either closed, turned to other types of manufacture or produced a very low-alcohol beer known as suds or near beer. Brooklyn was always the butt of jokes – in American movies later in the twentieth century, there was often at least one gum-chewing, wisecracking, cigarette-bumming, fly-by-night (but always lovable) rogue with the distinctive raw accent of Brooklyn. It had crime, but also a great sense of loyalty and community. The blocks were the primary focus of loyalty for the kids who played in the street – stick baseball games were played between the kids of different blocks, plus all the other games the kids played on sidewalks and stoops. Wide sidewalks had strips of earth between them and the roadway – sometimes planted with trees and plants, sometimes just bare earth where local dogs were taken to do their business.

Brooklyn is not short of famous sons and daughters: Mary Tyler Moore, Buddy Hackett, Lena Horne, Jackie Gleason, George Gershwyn and Phil Silvers – to mention just a few. And of course there were the famous Brooklyn Dodgers at Ebbets Field.

Life in Brooklyn was special, but also tough for poor families trying to make a living. John Walcott was born in California and came from Italian stock. Alma, whose maiden name was Roberts, had Scottish forebears but was born in Lee, a small town in Massachusetts about 200 miles west of Boston near to the New York state line in an area known as 'the Berkshires'. Her family had strong roots in the Berkshires and her mother and stepfather owned property there.

Some time before Bud's arrival, Alma's mother appears to have remarried to become Mrs Salvator Bassi and it is striking that Bud was given the name of his stepgrandfather. The young married couple seem to have suffered some catastrophic mishap, because by the time he started elementary school, aged five, Bud was living with his grandparents in the Berkshires; it was this place, and not Brooklyn, that would become the centre of his life. Quite what occurred isn't clear. Ten years on, the 1930 census shows a John Walcott living in the same area of Kings in Brooklyn but now married to Catherine, who is listed as born in Massachusetts but with her father and mother both born in Ireland, whereas the 1920 census had Alma born in New York to a Scottish father and a mother from Connecticut. Whether or not Alma died, or divorced John, henceforth she does not figure in Bud's life. He names his grandmother as his next-of-kin in many of his service documents, but he also mentions his father John. If Alma and John had remained together and the Catherine mentioned in the 1930 census is the same person, why would they send their son to live with his grandparents – unless they were unable to care for him in Brooklyn? The information about his parents gleaned from public documents is not consistent but it is not unreasonable to assume that Alma, his mother, died and his father had little to do with his son. To name the infant after Alma's stepfather – the infant's stepgrandfather – suggests that Alma had more affection for her mother's new husband than her own father, who had either died or divorced her mother.

For Bud, his new life couldn't have been more different from the bustling, cheek-by-jowl life that he would have experienced in Brooklyn. If Bud was older than a very young baby who would remember little if anything of his neighbourhood in Brooklyn, this new way of life would be what is now called a 'culture shock' – but then, Walcott would endure several culture shocks in the course of his life.

The drive from Boston along Interstate 90, the Massachusetts Turnpike, is breathtaking in its beauty, particularly in the autumn, when the leaves on the trees on the gently rolling hills are turning to the reds, golds, browns and yellows for which New England is so famous at that time of year. From Lee, coming off the interstate and onto Highway 7, a short drive to the north brings the traveller to Lenox and north of that, Pittsfield. However, if instead of coming off at Lenox you drive a few miles further along the interstate, to the south of it is Stockbridge, another beautiful little New England town famous as the home of the artist Norman Rockwell and the quaint but very comfortable and famous Red Lion Inn. This quartet of small communities provided a stability in Walcott's life.

Visitors are attracted by the beauty, but the Berkshires also boast Tanglewood, the world-famous venue for outdoor music concerts. It started in 1934 when some wealthy summer residents of the area invited the New York Philharmonic Orchestra to perform in the area – a successful enterprise that was repeated. In 1936, Mrs Gorham Brooks and Miss Mary Aspinwall offered to donate the Tappan family estate, the 210-acre Tanglewood, with all its buildings, to Serge Koussevitzky and the Boston Symphony Orchestra. It would have been difficult to refuse the gift and the venue has gone from strength to strength and is now one of the leading attractions for visitors to the area, with 350,000 coming annually these days to enjoy performances from such diverse performers as Earth Wind and Fire, John Williams and the Boston Pops Orchestra, James Taylor and the Mark Morris Dance Group. The story of Tanglewood provides clues to life in the Lenox area in the 1930s – specifically the wealth of the Tappan family and the influence of the summer residents who were able to entice the New York Philharmonic to come north to perform.

In some ways, the history of Lenox and the Berkshires reflects the history of the United States. It was originally a forest wilderness populated by natives of the Mahican tribe. White settlers were not welcomed by the indigenous population. The difficult geography, French-inspired incursions from the north and territorial disputes with New York State only a few miles to the west all discouraged incomers. In 1750, the Hinsdale family built a home in what is now Lenox and their daughter was born there the following year, although they were forced to flee from attacks by the native Americans. Significant settlement of the area by white colonists really commenced in the 1760s, and by 1791 the census recorded the number of residents in the Berkshires as 30,291. Lenox itself came into being in 1767, named after Charles Lenox, the Duke of Richmond in Britain who had spoken in support of the colonists seeking independence. Life was hard for the original settlers but the town gradually developed along with the others in the area. Iron was found under Lenox and its mining created a labyrinth of tunnels under the town and an ironworks. A longstanding rivalry between Stockbridge and Pittsfield grew up and the decision to site the local courthouse in Lenox was a coup; it brought members of the legal profession to the area and the town. Many were struck by the intrinsic beauty of the locality and returned with family and friends for holidays. In the nineteenth century, word spread and one family in particular, the Sedgwicks, helped build the town's reputation. Charles Sedgwick was clerk to the court; his wife Elizabeth established a school for young ladies but arguably the most famous of the Sedgwicks was Catharine, Charles's sister. She was born in 1789 in Stockbridge and had four brothers. She became an author and her work was popular and in demand from the 1820s to the 1850s. She was particularly interested in the role of women and the feminist movement. She never married. She took the part of minority groups – the Shakers, the Native Americans and black people – and wrote about them. Although there was a spell when her work was deprecated by male critics due to her gender, the feminist movement of the late twentieth century stimulated interest in her work and she is currently seen as an important contributor to American women's literature. She invited many of her influential friends to visit, helping the reputation of the Berkshires to grow.

During this period the area became known as 'the American Lake District', a reference to the area with the same name in the north-west of England. By the middle of the nineteenth century, many intellectuals, artists and writers had found the area and loved it. Herman Melville wrote his acclaimed book about the white whale *Moby Dick* in his house in Pittsfield and another resident, although only briefly, was Nathaniel Hawthorne, whose works include *The House of Seven Gables* and *Tanglewood Tales*.

As in many country towns, the locals and the incomers had perhaps not a great deal in common and wealthy folk coming from the big cities for a few months did not have much to do with those who carved out a living there. The iron industry and a glass furnace as well as farming were boosted by the building of the railroad in 1838 but the local companies found it increasingly difficult to compete with similar industries in the east – some said high freight charges contributed to this – and eventually they died away. Lenox also lost some status when the county seat moved to Pittsfield in 1868.

The intellectuals tired of Lenox and as they moved away, a different group moved in – the wealthy of the east coast cities discovered the beauty of the area, and what became known as 'the cottage era' ran its course with the creation of numerous large estates (one being owned by the Tappan family) as holiday retreats for those who were near enough and could afford to buy the land. To call their residences 'cottages' was clearly a misnomer! The decline in farming was exacerbated by the considerable sums being paid for the land to create these large estates. Local historians suggest that the first of these cottages was bought by a wealthy woman from New Orleans in 1838 but it was the period roughly from the 1860s to the 1920s that saw the high-water mark of the cottages. In 1880, there were about thirty-five mansions in the area but by 1900 this had increased significantly with the construction of another forty. Of course, with the wealthy came power and prestige and the Berkshires became part of an annual social season with the participants whiling away the late summer and early autumn – presumably to view the changing colours of the leaves. They competed to build expensive, luxurious and sometimes quite grotesque mansions on huge estates and held lavish parties, each trying to outdo the other. While this influx of the rich and famous brought economic advantages to the more humble locals who lived there all year round, and improvements to the town by those of the wealthy who had a philanthropic bent, it changed the character of the area. Land and property prices increased and became unaffordable for the ordinary person, resulting in little in the way of true social interaction between the two groups. Tensions occasionally surfaced – the creation of some estates prevented locals from walking on the land they loved and prevented them using it for recreation, and this was resented.

The arrival of the socialites was reported in national newspapers. In its 19 May 1895 edition, *The New York Times* was reporting on arrivals in Lenox and among them were Mr Anson Phelps Stokes, an entrepreneur and philanthropist, and his wife; Mr & Mrs John L. Kane at the cottage of Mrs Hartman, which 'they have taken for the season'; and Mr & Mrs George Westinghouse Jr and family, who had arrived in 'their private car' the previous week to occupy 'their beautiful place, Erskine Park'. Westinghouse needs little introduction. He was an engineer with particular interest in electricity and founded the Westinghouse Corporation. One of the other reports that day is of interest – that of Mrs Robert Winthrop, who was expected soon from New York to 'occupy the Tillotson cottage, which she has rented for the season'. Although not stated explicitly, it's likely that Mrs Winthrop was the widow of a successful New York banker who had died three years previously. Winthrop was a neighbour and friend of the father of Theodore Roosevelt. However, it isn't the Winthrops that are of primary interest, but the owners of the cottage, the Tillotsons, a local family who had been in Lenox for many years and who would become an integral part of Walcott's life when he married one of their daughters, Virginia, during the Second World War. In more modern times, the late Robin Williams maintained a summer home in the immediate area in Pittsfield.

The cottagers who came to Lenox for the summer and autumn held several horse shows while they were in residence. In the first show of the 1899 season, on 22 September, the Tillotsons did well. There were seventeen classes with a total of 162 entries. Horses owned by the Tillotson family made their mark in three of them. In Class 5, 'Pair of horses, with appropriate carriage for hire – [was] Won by Sidney W. Tillotson's brown geldings Duke and General'. The same Tillotson's roan mare Chillowee won Class 13, Horse and Buggy; F. S. Tillotson won the roadster class with a brown mare and a brown gelding, both unnamed. The success was perhaps not a surprise because the Tillotson livery stable was a fixture in Lenox for many years. It opened its doors in 1872 and annually boarded forty to sixty horses. The family also had a grain business, as well as woollen mills. In 1922, four mills owned by the W. E. Tillotson Manufacturing Company were sold to a consortium of men from New York and Pittsfield, known as the Berkshire Woollen Company, for $1.5 million by Louis Hollingsworth, for some time the head of the Tillotson company. With just under 1,000 employees, the mills had not been operating for some eight months – a considerable downturn for the local area.

On 2 October 1885, Alice, the wife of Sidney Tillotson, gave birth to a boy they called Robert, later known as 'Bob'. He married Marion Ferguson from Pittsfield on 16 December 1914 and they in turn had two daughters – the elder, Marion Roberta (known as 'Bobbie', presumably after her father), was born in 1915 and Virginia was born in 1918. Bob inherited entrepreneurial and hard work ethics from his father. Aged 10, he sold newspapers and later worked in the family livery and grain businesses, which stood him in good stead when Sidney, his father, died in an accident falling from a freight car unloading grain and Bob had to take over the businesses in short order. Photographs in middle age show him with a full, round face, thinning dark hair and wire-rimmed spectacles. With the advent of the automobile and the decline in the use of horses and horse-drawn vehicles, the need for the livery stable reduced but with an eye for opportunity, Bob Tillotson opened a car showroom. While not in the same league as the incoming cottagers, the Tillotsons were a relatively wealthy and influential local family, with their influence made even greater by Bob's political activities. He was an enthusiastic Republican and became an Assistant County Commissioner at the age of 29, in 1916, a post he held for four years before being elected a County Commissioner for the next twenty years until 1940, seven of them as chairman. He was said to be a close friend of Calvin Coolidge, the thirtieth President of the United States, and other political heavyweights. He seems to have been a gregarious and likeable man – he played baseball and American football as a youngster and had a good sense of humour, with a particular penchant for telling ghost stories. Apart from his political activities, as befits a man of his position, he played his part in local community activities. He had a particular interest in water supply and was the secretary and treasurer of the Lenox Water Company.

Salvator Bassi, Bud's grandfather, was in the restaurant and hotel business. Before moving to Lenox he had run restaurants in Brooklyn but in 1925 was running the Twin Maples Inn on the Pittsfield Road on the northern edge of Lenox, about half a mile from the town centre and this is where young Bud was brought up. His name changed and he became 'Salvatore Roberts Bassi' suggesting that, if anything, his grandmother wished to preserve the name of Bud's biological grandfather. However, Bud does not seem to have been legally adopted by his grandmother – on joining the Royal Canadian Air Force (RCAF) he reverts to Walcott. Whatever, the circumstances of his parents, young Bud, or 'Salvi' as he was known, was now firmly based in New England, ultimately marrying the Tillotsons' younger daughter Virginia and living and eventually dying there. He and Virginia are both buried in the graveyard of 'the Church on the Hill', which is at the top of the hill travelling north on Main Street. Around a slight bend to the left, past a wood and a hundred yards or so further on is what was 'Twin Maples' and in 2013 was 'the Cornell Inn'. This is where young Bud grew up with his grandmother and stepgrandfather.

In the early 1930s, the Bassi and Tillotson families both owned a great deal of property and land, some of which may have had common boundaries. On Main Street, the Tillotsons owned four houses, a garage, two bungalows, a shed, a storehouse and an ice house (in addition to other property elsewhere). The Bassi family also owned property on Main Street – two acres of land valued at $1,000, two houses, a garage and an ice house. Clearly, both families could rent property as a source of income and it is more than likely that they knew each other and were possibly neighbours. Their property holdings would help them survive the worst effects of the Depression, which started in 1928.

Salvi seems to have been happy here. Bill and Irene Roche lived diagonally across the road from the Inn and Bud formed a firm friendship with the family. Bill Roche was born in 1908 and, according to his son Dave, was the first person in Berkshire County to gain a pilot's licence. Bud was in and out of the Roche family house as he grew up and his love of flying was encouraged, if not triggered, by Bill. By the time Bud joined the Canadian Air Force he had logged some flying hours, and with aviation all the rage in 1920s and 30s, the bug he caught from his neighbour grew.

The Tillotson girls attended Lenox High School; Bobbie graduated in 1933, with her younger sister Virginia graduating two years later in 1935. Salvi started at Lenox High in 1934, graduating in 1938 and so it is unlikely that he would have been particularly friendly with the sisters at the school. Virginia was a year older than Salvi and while he graduated aged 18, she was only 16 when she graduated but this would have been normal for the time. Following in the footsteps of Bobbie, who had studied there in 1933 and 1934, Virginia went on to Lasell Junior College at Auburndale in Newton Massachusetts, about 8 miles from the centre of Boston. Until 1932, it was called Auburndale Female Seminary and was somewhat of a trailblazer in the field of women's education in the United States being the first college to offer a two year course – although it was more in the style of a European finishing school than a scholarly academic institution. After completing her studies, Virginia worked for the General Electric Company (GE) in their Pittsfield plant, which operated there (not always owned by GE) from the end of the nineteenth century until 1986, manufacturing electrical transformers. When the plant closed, it did so in the midst of some controversy regarding the release of possibly carcinogenic material into nearby watercourses.

Bobbie subsequently married into the Hollingsworth family.

The youngsters' three high school class photos give some idea as to their appearance. Bobbie has fair hair with a confident smile; Virginia is dark with more than a passing resemblance to her father and looks somewhat serious – perhaps wondering what lay ahead. Salvi is a solemn young man, neatly turned out in collar and striped tie with a light-coloured jacket and the quiff of hair that would become something of a trademark. He wasn't a tall man, his stature probably best described as medium – neither slight nor heavily built – and in some photographs he wears either a rather enigmatic smile or what appears to be a worried expression. But by most accounts he was a likeable young man, although whether or not his classmates agreed with this is not known. With regard to his studies, he opted for a range of scientific subjects that would stand him in good stead later in life with his interest in aviation.

The class motto – 'Ever Upward' – was eminently suitable for Walcott, and uncannily expressed a similar philosophy to that of the RAF whose motto is '*Per ardua ad astra*' or 'By hard work to the stars'. The class colours were blue and white (again appropriate) while the flower was the white carnation. He graduated on Monday 20 June 1938 along with the thirty-seven members of his class. His diploma, in the name of 'Salvatore Roberts Bassi', does not mention any special honours or awards so presumably his results were average. It is of passing interest that on his High School Diploma his name is spelt 'Salvatore', with the 'e', but on his Certificate and Record of Birth it is spelt without the 'e'.

Bud's graduation marked the end of another era in his life as the wider world, and the problems of making a living, beckoned. The towns in the Berkshires are small, close-knit communities and the opportunities for newly graduated students were limited. Some would, no doubt, move on to college but this required money, and despite his grandmother's ownership of property and apparent prosperity, his future did not include further study – indeed, he struggled to find a stable career.

He was an accomplished magician and by definition must have been comfortable in front of an audience. In 1938 he was placed third in a talent contest in Pittsfield, demonstrating his 'sleight of hand' tricks. He became an entertainer on the cabaret circuit, which took him away from Lenox, operating on his own, going from one engagement to another in towns and cities not too far from where he was brought up. At this stage in his life he was known to the Tillotsons but the extent of the relationship with Robert and his daughters isn't clear. Certainly in the future he became very close to Virginia, but whether the friendship started and ripened at school isn't known but it seems unlikely. By 1938, Virginia had already graduated from Lasell and was working at the transformer plant, which doesn't suggest a ready compatibility for the pair.

# 3

# PERHAPS THE ROMANTIC?

As Walcott graduated from high school, in Europe the Second World War was becoming more and more inevitable – even if relatively little fighting had taken place. The events that would shape Walcott's life were drawing together little by little. In particular, the actions and relationships between Britain, the United States, France and Germany and their respective leaders, seemingly distant and unconnected, were slowly producing inevitable consequences for their citizens and individuals across the world. Walcott was only one of millions caught up in this way as his life took him down difficult paths.

The event that brought Britain into the war was the German invasion of Poland on 1 September 1939. This was but part of another series of peculiar alliances culminating in the so-called Molotov–Ribbentrop Pact, or more formally the Treaty of Non-Aggression between Germany and the Soviet Union, of August 1939, signed by the two foreign ministers. Poland's history is peppered with invasions by its neighbours, who coveted what Poland possessed. This vividly illustrated Poland's historical and unenviable geographic situation, between two powerful states. Germany and the Soviet Union had signed several non-aggression and co-operation pacts since the end of the First World War, which in hindsight resulted in some bizarre consequences, such as German pilots training for service with the new *Luftwaffe* at Soviet airfields. As ever, the relationship between the two countries was complex, but, again with the benefit of hindsight, it is clear that once the National Socialists gained power in Germany, war between the two was inevitable. Simplistically, Hitler believed that a strong country was quite within its rights to take whatever resources it might need from another and also that a country gained inner strength by being tested in war. Further, his philosophy of the superiority of the Aryan races meant that many of those in the Soviet Union were regarded as inferior with no place in the Germanic future – the so-called *untermenschen*, or subhumans.

In the late 1930s Hitler's rhetoric was decidedly anti-Soviet, but following the Munich Agreement in 1938, for both countries some sort of non-belligerency pact became desirable. Importantly for Germany, a war with Britain would create uncertainty over the supply of raw materials, which could be obtained from the Soviet Union. For the Soviet Union, a pact would reduce the threat of war. Following Stalin's purges of the Red Army officer corps in the late 1930s, the outcome of a war would be highly uncertain. Stalin harboured a pathological fear of those who might create opposition to him, and an unforgiving hatred for those who had opposed him in the past. Even those who had supported him on his rise to power were not spared. In Stalin's eyes, anyone who was in a position to be a threat, no matter how loyal they had been to him in the past, or how loyal they continued to be, had to be eliminated. Clearly, Stalin's position would become untenable if he lost the support of the Red Army and he decided to excise any potential for future opposition by removing many of the army's officers from their positions and killing large numbers of them. In addition to the arrest and execution of men such as Marshal M. N. Tukhachevky, the Deputy Commissar for Defence, and others at the highest levels, three of five marshals, all three high-level army commanders, twelve second-ranked army commanders and sixty out of sixty-seven corps commanders, and more than 70 per cent of divisional and regimental commanders had disappeared, leaving the Red Army without an adequate command to fight a major war.[1] And this was recognised in Germany.

There was a fear that the western allies (Britain, France) would welcome a war between Germany and the Soviet Union as it would weaken both antagonists. Germany and the Soviet Union were both ruled by tyrannical dictators and the violence, misery and death perpetrated by them almost defies belief. Hitler's atrocities have tended to gain more attention than those of Stalin, but the Soviets killed many more people than the Germans. The great Soviet dissident Aleksandr Solzhenitsyn wrote of Stalin's regime:

That no other regime on earth could compare with it either in the number of those it had done to death, in hardiness, in the range of its ambitions, in its thoroughgoing and unmitigated totalitarianism – no, not even the regime of its pupil Hitler, which at that time blinded Western eyes to all else.[2]

With great irony, Solzhenitsyn remarked: 'Hitler was a mere disciple, but he had all the luck: his murder camps have made him famous, whereas no one has any interest in ours.'

Britain and France undertook to support Poland, Belgium, Romania, Greece and Turkey in the event of an attack by Germany but not by the Soviet Union, which, on 21 August 1939, agreed with Germany that certain parts of eastern Europe would fall to the Soviet sphere of influence, including the eastern half of Poland. It is well known that Germany invaded Poland on 1 September 1939, but the invasion of Poland by the Soviets two and a half weeks later, on 17 September, is less well known. A cartoon by David Low in the *Evening Standard* on 20 September shows Hitler and Stalin meeting over the body of a defeated Poland. Hitler is doffing his cap as he says to the Soviet dictator, 'The scum of the earth, I believe?' to which Stalin replies, 'The bloody assassin of the workers, I presume?'

Although Britain and France declared war on Germany (even if the support given was only moral), they did not declare war on the Soviet Union. At the same time, in the Far East, the Japanese were fighting their way through China. Much of the world stared into the abyss.

Despite war being declared, not a great deal happened. Britain sent an army to the Continent – the British Expeditionary Force (BEF) – anticipating a German attack but it stagnated into what became known as 'the Phoney War' until April 1940, when Germany invaded Norway and Denmark. Britain and France sent an expeditionary force comprising ground, naval and air force elements to assist the Norwegians but were defeated and forced to withdraw. In particular, the loss of the aircraft carrier HMS *Glorious* shocked the Royal Navy. With German naval bases in

Norwegian ports, the North Sea became a threat to British maritime interests. The British Prime Minister Neville Chamberlain resigned, to be replaced by Winston Churchill just as the long-expected German invasion of the Low Countries started on 10 May. It was disastrous for the Allies as the German *blitzkreig* swept all before them. At the end of May, the BEF found itself encircled at the French channel port of Dunkirk and had to be evacuated off the beaches and the port facilities by the Royal Navy and a host of civilian ships of all sizes, crucially leaving all its heavy weapons and transport behind. Portrayed at the time as a deliverance, it was in reality a resounding defeat. The British public did not know then that Hitler had likely ordered his troops to stop on the outskirts of the town because he still harboured hopes that he could come to some sort of accommodation with the British and did not want to outrage them.

The fighting continued, and in mid-June Churchill flew to Paris for talks with the French Prime Minister Paul Reynaud to shore up resistance against the common enemy, but the talks came to nothing. Reynaud resigned to be replaced by Marshall Henri-Philippe Pétain, the popular hero of the First World War but now to become regarded as a traitor and collaborator when, shortly afterwards, France surrendered to Germany on 22 June in the most humiliating fashion, signing the document of surrender in the railway carriage at Compiègne where they had made Germany sign the Armistice in 1918 after the First World War.

Germany, however, occupied only a part of France – broadly the north and west of the country – and it allowed the remaining two-thirds, and the colonies, to be supposedly neutral with a French government based in Vichy in the central region. In reality, Vichy France, as it came to be known, was not truly independent but more of a puppet state subservient to its conquerors, although it continued to operate its own military. The consequences of these events would significantly affect the life of Salvi Walcott – at this time touring the cabaret circuit in the USA and unaware of what the future held in store for him.

After the fall of France, Britain stood alone with only the support of its Empire and Commonwealth countries. While the American President Franklin D. Roosevelt was sympathetic to Britain's situation, much of America remained isolationist, determined that this latest European war remain just that – a European war – and there were many who would not countenance a war that necessitated the death and injury of American servicemen in defence of the British Empire, which they considered abhorrent. Had Americans not fought for independence from British domination a century and a half before? The American ambassador to the United Kingdom, Joseph Kennedy, father of the future President John F. Kennedy, reinforced the view to Roosevelt that America should stay out of a fight that was only going to end in Britain's defeat.

The situation for Britain was extremely serious, and it is perhaps understandable that some Americans and Britons would see no hope of victory, only defeat or, at best, accommodation with Hitler as the inevitable outcome. But many Americans did not fully explore the issues. Although Hitler might have been placated for a number of years while Germany settled the British and Soviet problems, it seemed inevitable that he would turn his attention to the American continent, and, like it or not, America would have to fight Germany and its allies. Many Americans perceived the main threat to their country as coming from Japan and its expansionism in the Pacific, but in reality, Japan alone could never have posed the same threat to the mainland of the United

States as would Germany (or Germany and Japan operating as allies). After the Japanese attack on Pearl Harbor on 7 December 1941, significantly, Germany declared war on the USA – not the opposite – and the western allies agreed that Germany should be dealt with before Japan because of the greater threat posed by the Nazis.

Kennedy was not alone in anticipating a British defeat – some in the British government thought the same. As Winston Churchill said in Parliament on 18 June, 'What General Weygand called the Battle of France is over. I expect that the Battle of Britain is about to begin.' While Churchill may have had fears about Britain's ability to resist a German invasion, his fierce speeches strengthened the resolve of his countrymen, providing the inspiration to resist the aggressor.

It seemed inevitable that the next step would be a German invasion of Britain, and Britons steeled themselves for this. Winston Churchill, who had an American mother, looked to the United States for help – but it was not readily available. The Royal Navy needed ships and there were fifty obsolete American destroyers that Churchill wished to acquire. But fears of a British defeat, with the destroyers as well as the rest of the Royal Navy falling into German hands and being used against America, made it difficult for the United States to release them. Of more immediate concern for Churchill was the possibility that the French fleet, now supposedly neutral, might be used against Britain alongside the German Navy, the *Kriegsmarine*. The French armistice with Germany placed many of its fighting men in an invidious position. Having been at war for ten months alongside their British allies, they now found themselves expected to cease fighting and become neutral while their country became a puppet state of the Third Reich.

This resulted in a severe deterioration of relations between Britain and France. While some Frenchmen threw in their lot with Britain, many others considered that Britain had abandoned France in its hour of need – a feeling that turned to hatred after the Royal Navy shelled ships of the French Mediterranean fleet at anchor in Mers-el-Kebir in North Africa to keep them from the Germans. But a more positive consequence of this action for the British was the sending of a signal to President Roosevelt and the United States that Britain was prepared to fight on. Britain may have been fearful that the French fleet might join with the German *Kriegsmarine* but the Americans had the additional fear that if Germany prevailed, or if Britain decided to seek an accommodation with Germany (as some in the British government, notably Lord Halifax, thought was the sensible way forward), then they might in the future have to contend with an enemy fleet that also included ships of the Royal Navy. Further, with Britain hoping to obtain the fifty obsolete destroyers from the United States it would have been difficult for the President if these had been supplied, only to be turned against the US Navy later in the war. As ever, the consequences of the actions being taken then were numerous and far-reaching.

The deterioration of relations between France and Britain, and the hatred felt by some Frenchmen for the British following these incidents (and others) would affect Walcott directly and intimately – as will be explained.

The anticipated invasion of Britain did not come – nor did Britain come to an accommodation with Germany. The United States could hand over the fifty destroyers to the Royal Navy. Having failed to destroy the RAF's Fighter Command during the summer of 1940, Hitler turned his attention to the Soviet Union and postponed the invasion of Britain indefinitely. Indeed, there are those who believe that Hitler was always lukewarm about invading Britain with the risks that it entailed. While some of the German generals viewed the crossing of the English Channel as a rather glorified river crossing, there were also those who realised that it amounted to much more than this. Without allies, Britain could be contained, although it would have been preferable if it sided with Germany. It is relevant to note that a few Americans fought with Fighter Command during the Battle of Britain, and this is explored later.

In the autumn of 1940, it wasn't clear that the Battle of Britain had been fought and won. For the weary airmen of Fighter Command, the German attacks reduced as the days shortened to give them some respite, but they couldn't know whether or not the spring of 1941 would see a resumption. The German airmen involved in what they called the *kanalkampf,* or Channel war, did not recognise that there had been a 'Battle of Britain'. Many of the more prescient appreciated that they had not managed to defeat Fighter Command, but for them, like their opponents in the RAF, the winter brought some respite from the constant operations over the English Channel. Many expected a resumption of the attacks in the spring of 1941 when the weather improved and the daylight hours lengthened. As it transpired, this did not happen, at least on the same scale, and the RAF thus took the offensive on a daily basis, carrying out 'sweeps' attacking targets in France.

In December 1940, Walcott joined the RCAF. His motives for doing this aren't known but there is one intriguing factor in the mix: a letter of recommendation to the RCAF from Robert Tillotson. Walcott's motive would have been one of the following – or a mixture of them. He might have felt that for reasons of principle he had to become involved in the war, he might have just been seeking adventure, he might have been running away from something, or he might have been trying to prove himself.

Salvi did not have long-term success as a vaudeville magician. He began when he graduated in June 1938, but by September 1939 bookings had dried up and he became a night soda manager in Providence, Rhode Island, having returned to his grandmother. He also worked as a soda man in New York and it was from New York that he signed up for the RCAF. His home address in December 1939 was West 56th Street in Manhattan. This is an apartment block east south east of Central Park and near Columbus Circle between 8th and 9th Avenues and not far from Broadway so it was pretty much in a lively part of town. In his air force attestation paper, Walcott gives the name of a woman at the Hotel Tudor as a referee so it is possible that this is where he worked. It was situated in East 42nd Street between 2nd and 1st Avenues, which would be a reasonable walk from the apartment but no problem for a fit young man, which he clearly was. He enjoyed swimming and playing American football and wasn't averse to baseball. However, he must have found life as a soda man not to his liking.

Having started this employment in October, only two months later, at the beginning of December, he completed his attestation form for the RCAF. He states that he had twelve hours of flying experience – eight hours dual and four hours solo – none as a simple passenger. It could be assumed his flying time was with Bill Roche, the family friend back in Lenox. By way of comparison, a renowned British RAF fighter pilot, Robert Stanford Tuck, spent more than twelve hours in dual instruction before going solo in 1935, flying the same sort of aircraft available to Walcott. If

Walcott flew solo after eight hours, it is reasonable to assume that he had the necessary aptitude to be a good pilot.

Thus, we have a picture of a young man who is twenty years old with an unsuccessful career as a nightclub magician behind and not much of a future ahead of him. By now his mother is dead and he has lost touch with his father. His grandmother is his next-of-kin but living in a small town in New England while he is in New York. His career prospects are limited. He is clearly an outgoing, independent and by all accounts pleasant young man with an interest and some experience in flying. As he contemplates his future, perhaps he sees aviation as an exciting and fruitful career. The US Army is not mobilising for war – indeed the USA seems determined to keep out of the fighting in Europe – but Britain is desperate for aircrew and actively seeking trainees and so the Royal Canadian Air Force presents opportunities for him to fly.

There is nothing to suggest that Walcott harboured any great political or moral concerns about the war and what was happening in Europe; it seems unlikely he was driven by any sense of morality or a desire to help destroy the evil that was Nazi Germany. In later life, he showed a little political awareness – but this appears to have been to support his politically engaged wife, not for any intrinsic reason of his own. There is a greater likelihood that he wished to escape some overwhelming personal problem. As a not-so-successful cabaret magician he may have had money problems or fallen in with a bad lot and felt that he was in some sort of danger, and one solution would be to go to Europe to fight. His relationship with the Tillotsons, or more particularly Virginia Tillotson, might also have been a factor.

It is difficult not to see Walcott as a happy-go-lucky sort of man, a bit of a Jack the Lad who might have seen Canada as an escape route from an uninspiring future and a mediocre career as a magician. He may have started training with the US Army and been 'washed out', but wherever he received his training, it provided a base for him to build on. Therefore, his motivations to enlist were probably the possibility of a career as a pilot along with the adventure of fighting in a war in Europe and all that this entailed.

He provided the RCAF with the names of two referees. In addition to the woman at the Hotel Tudor, he also suggests Henry L. Smith, the Superintendent of Lenox Public Schools who, in a letter dated 2 December, states that Salvi was 'a willing and conscientious worker' and 'popular with the students and faculty alike'. He also states that his 'character was above reproach'. As mentioned, it is interesting that the other letter of recommendation comes from Robert Tillotson rather than the woman at the hotel. It is dated 11 December 1940 and is addressed to the Commanding Officer of the RCAF Recruiting Centre at 90 O'Connor Street in Ottawa and it reads:

> I have received your letter of December 9th, in which you state that Salvator Bassi Walcott has made application for enlistment in the Royal Air Force.
>
> I have known this young man ever since he was a child, and I can recommend him most strongly. He has unusual ability; is energetic and capable. I consider him to be an excellent type of young man for this service, and believe that he merits your consideration.

Tillotson styles himself 'Berkshire County Commissioner'.

Bud's relationship with Robert Tillotson is intriguing considering that he would marry into the family within a few years. If the supposition that Walcott was in a rather dead-end job with no real prospects is correct, then it seems unlikely that in December 1940 the wealthy and influential Tillotson would wish to have much to do with him. With Lee and Lenox being small communities, with the Tillotson daughters attending the same school as young Salvi and with Walcott's grandmother owning property near to the Tillotsons, Robert Tillotson would know the young man but it is difficult to imagine that the relationship would have been close; unless perhaps there was an expectation that Bud would inherit from his grandmother and become wealthy in his own right. But Tillotson would have been able to write a genuine reference nonetheless. It is tempting to imagine that Salvi was in a relationship with Tillotson's daughter and her father was more than happy to help the young man move away from her (and he couldn't have moved much further or into a more dangerous situation) but there is nothing to confirm this, and it seems that Tillotson's only motive was in his role as county commissioner to help one of the young men in the neighbourhood improve himself.

On the other hand, perhaps Bud was just a romantic who went to war with the simple aim of proving to his girl that he was worthy of her affections.

# 4

# CITIZENSHIP AND OTHER ISSUES

Although America has at times tried to retain a distance from European wars, its citizens have a proud history of volunteering to fight for what they see as right. Walcott was by no means the first to volunteer, and he has not been the last. The relationship between the United States and its former colonial master has been a factor in allowing volunteers from the United States join British forces through Canada, although, as will be seen, Americans have fought for other countries too.

At the end of the First World War, when Walcott was born in 1919, the USA was still a relatively young and developing country. However, events in the distant past had an effect on the life of the young American. Only 143 years had elapsed since the Declaration of Independence from Great Britain had been made in 1776, and only fifty-four years since the end of the Civil War and the assassination of Abraham Lincoln, the sixteenth President, in 1865. Links with Britain were generally strong, if perhaps somewhat ambivalent. A number of European countries, including Holland, Spain, France and England (prior to the union of the Scottish and

English Parliaments in 1707) had attempted to colonise the 'New World', one of the more significant colonies being established by English settlers at Plymouth in New England in 1620. By 1650, the number of colonists from all countries had reached about 50,000, mainly down the east coast, including a Dutch settlement at New Amsterdam, now New York, although they were ejected by the English in 1664.

Prior to independence, France and Britain vied for control of the American colonies, and some years before the colonists declared their independence the French, based in Canada, attempted to gain ground in what was British colonial territory, to the great concern of the British settlers. This resulted in what became known as the French and Indian Wars and culminated in Quebec and Montreal being captured by the British, with the French effectively being removed from North America by ceding parts of their territory to Britain and some to Spain. All of this was agreed in the Treaty of Paris of 1763, signed by the three countries. However, shortly after this, the American colonists took up arms against the British because of their perceived inequitable treatment by the London Parliament – 'No taxation without representation' – which resulted in the Declaration of Independence by the thirteen Atlantic coast states from New Hampshire in the north to Georgia in the south. But the desire for independence was not held by all the settlers, and many of those who were not in favour of a complete break with Britain moved to Canada, which was not part of the independence movement and whose colonists wished to retain their links with Britain and have done so until the present day. Indeed, when it came to the final vote of approval by the Continental Congress of the thirteen states in 1776, it was not unanimous – New York abstained and John Dickinson, a Pennsylvania lawyer who had drafted out a declaration of rights but nonetheless held moderate views, together with others of a like mind, was not present when the vote was taken.

Declaring independence in 1776 did not end conflict between Britain and the United States – nationhood had to be wrested from the British, and it was only in 1783 when Britain signed another Treaty of Paris (not to be confused with the 1763 treaty) that it acknowledged American independence, causing about 50,000 American colonists, known as 'United Empire Loyalists', to migrate to the north, settling mainly in Nova Scotia and to the north of Lake Ontario. In June 1812, the USA declared war on Britain while the latter was engaged in the Napoleonic Wars with France. America was initially neutral but the British considered that the Americans were taking advantage of this because the way the Americans carried out shipping commerce infringed neutrality rules. On the other hand, the practice of the Royal Navy to press allegedly British-born sailors from intercepted American ships into service caused much upset, and this, linked with suspicions that the British were actively and practically encouraging native Americans to resist the movement of settlers westward, led to the declaration of war after many years of failed diplomacy and increasing frustration.

Americans advanced north to Canada, hoping that it would fall quickly and easily, but these hopes were dashed when Canadians defeated an American force commanded by General William Hull at Detroit only two months after the declaration of hostilities. The American Navy fared better, inflicting a number of defeats on the British as the fighting continued into 1814. Perhaps one of the more memorable actions took place in August 1814 when a British expedition to Chesapeake Bay managed to capture Washington and destroyed the Capitol Building and the White House. However, after the American victory at the battle of

Plattsburgh in 1814, peace negotiations commenced and although they proved to be difficult and complex, the war ostensibly came to end with the signing of the Treaty of Ghent on Christmas Eve 1814. Fighting did not quite cease. On 8 January the following year, at New Orleans, Andrew Jackson defeated the British and this finally ended the war. For the Americans, the Battle of New Orleans restored confidence and faith in themselves as a nation and it opened the way to the settlement of the west and a turning inwards as the country grew.

It also resulted in a new relationship between the United States, the United Kingdom and Canada. While Canada retained close ties with the United Kingdom, the USA was now an independent country and free to pursue its own agenda and foreign policies, and this was clearly expressed in the USA's actions during the First World War. It is interesting, although admittedly pointless, to ponder on what the situation might have been if the Confederate south had not been defeated during the American Civil War in the 1860s. Britain and France were sympathetic to the ambitions of the Confederate States of America – a separate union – with the British even having a military observer, Lieutenant Colonel Arthur Fremantle of the Coldstream Guards, travelling with Robert E. Lee's Army of Northern Virginia as it neared Gettysburg in Pennsylvania in 1863.

The confederacy would have gained significant credibility if it had been endorsed by the British government, but this was not likely to happen. Although many of those whose allegiances were with the south saw the Civil War as a struggle against an unwelcome and oppressive government in the north and did not see slavery as being the main reason for the fight, in Britain, which had only banned slavery through the struggles of William Wilberforce thirty years before in 1833, many saw the struggle in America as being solely about slavery. However much it might have suited Britain to have an independent southern United States as an ally, it would have been unacceptable to have endorsed the motives of a country struggling for independence while vowing to retain slavery. Less than 100 years before, Britain had been at war with those Americans seeking independence, now another American rebellion was taking place, with the tacit approval of Britain, the enemy of such a short time before.[1] The world would have been quite different if after the American Civil War the mainland of North America had three nations – Canada, the United States of America and the Confederate States of America; perhaps even more intriguing if the Confederacy had won the Civil War.

But this didn't come to pass; the north prevailed and the United States of America took a different path to its past colonial masters, especially in the role it took in the First World War, which started in 1914.

The assassination of the Austrian Archduke Franz Ferdinand by Serbian dissidents in Sarajevo on 28 June 1914 set in train a complex series of events that resulted in Great Britain declaring war on Germany and its allies on 4 August. The origins of the First World War have been well covered elsewhere. With Germany invading through Belgium, the war was fluid and the BEF, hastily sent to the Continent on the declaration of war, forced westwards following the Battle of Mons but shortly thereafter the fighting stagnated into trench warfare and what became the horror and slaughter of the Western Front. For Canada, as one of Britain's dominions,[2] it meant an immediate entry into the fighting in France; Canadians would perform with considerable valour, and at great cost. The United States attempted to remain neutral.

Still expanding, America had looked to the south, to Mexico, for territorial gain and viewed the carnage in the old world as something to be avoided if at all possible. President Woodrow Wilson declared America neutral when Britain declared war. He had lofty ideals and hoped the United States could act as a moderating influence, not merely as a disinterested neutral. This proved difficult, although America tried to operate an even-handed policy towards the main belligerents – for example, allowing American banks to lend to both sides. And the influence of the European immigrants to the country was sure to be another factor to take into account. In a population of 105 million, 8 million had strong German connections and more than 4 million had similar Irish connections, and both groups harboured strong desires to see Britain brought down. Further, adopting the even-handed policy was complicated by Britain and France dominating exports from America while those to Germany declined. America had an economic interest, if nothing else, in the success of the Allies.

Germany at this time possessed a fleet of submarines, U-boats, which threatened to choke off Britain's sea supply lanes. In the early afternoon of 7 May 1915, *U-20* sighted the 32,000-ton Cunard liner *Lusitania* in clear weather, just off the south coast of Eire as it neared the end of a voyage from New York to Liverpool. It was considered to be a fast ship and thus able to outrun any submarines. The Admiralty had issued a warning the previous evening that German submarines were active to the south of Ireland, but nonetheless the ship sailed into the danger area in sight of land.

At 14.09, *U-20* fired a single torpedo, which caused, in the opinion of the submarine commander, an unusually large explosion, to be followed shortly afterwards by a second. It is reported that within a mere eighteen minutes, the four-funnelled liner slid beneath the waves, bow first. In all, 1,153 passengers died, of whom 128 were Americans, and it caused an outrage in the United States not unlike that following the destruction of the World Trade Center in New York in 2001. The President, too, found it almost inconceivable, and five days later made a speech in Philadelphia in which he extolled America's position as different to other countries with its desire to bring peace to the world rather than war. He said: 'There is such a thing as a man being too proud to fight. There is such a thing as a nation being so right that it does not need to convince others by force that it is right.' But he spoke with the briefest of notes and his words came back to haunt him. He acknowledged later that he had not spoken with sufficient clarity and, as is the way, rather than being seen as idealistic, in some quarters it was taken that America was frightened to fight. Indeed in the British trenches on the Western Front, shells which failed to explode were sometimes known unkindly as 'Wilsons'. In mitigation, the Germans claimed, probably correctly, that the ship had been carrying munitions; however, after protests from President Wilson, they gave assurances that the indiscriminate nature of their submarine operations would be stopped.

This state of affairs didn't last long. In early 1917 Germany decided once again to declare all-out war on any ship making for Britain or France, and its U-boats sank a number of American ships. This hardened American public opinion and forced the President into a corner. Matters became worse with the emergence of a telegram sent to Mexico by German Foreign Minister Arthur Zimmermann inviting that country to join the war on the side of Germany and its allies. Mexico was smarting from losses of territory to the United States dating back to mid-1800s. The telegram translates as:

> We intend to begin on the 1st of February unrestricted submarine warfare. We shall endeavour in spite of this to keep the United States of America neutral. In the event of this not succeeding, we make Mexico a proposal of alliance on the following basis: make war together, make peace together, generous financial support and an understanding on our part that Mexico is to reconquer the lost territory in Texas, New Mexico and Arizona. The settlement in detail is left to you. You will inform the President of the above most secretly as soon as the outbreak of war with the United States of America is certain and add the suggestion that he should, on his own initiative, invite Japan to immediate adherence and at the same time mediate between Japan and ourselves. Please call the President's attention to the fact that the ruthless employment of our submarines now offers the prospect of compelling England in a few months to make peace.
>
> Signed, Zimmermann

On 6 April 1917 the American President signed a declaration of war against Germany, much to the relief of the western allies. Nonetheless, he still insisted that America would not become one of the allies but would be an 'associate power', working for peace when suitable circumstances prevailed. The American army was small, only 190,000 strong and ill-prepared for war, and so it would be into 1918 before it started to make an impact on the war. Initially, and somewhat ironically, the first soldiers to arrive were equipped by the British and French. In the spring of 1918 there was only one American division in the front line, although once the numbers built up the American contribution would be welcomed –

and the fighting prowess of the Doughboys admired – by the time the Armistice came into effect in November 1918.

However, these were not the first American citizens to join the battle. Apart from those who would enlist in the French Foreign Legion, a couple hundred Americans had joined the French Air Force or *Aéronautique Militaire* before the USA formally declared war. Two Americans – Dr Edmund L. Gros, who was director of the American Ambulance Service, and Norman Prince, already flying for France – managed to convince the French government that it would help the Allied cause in the United States to be able to demonstrate that Americans were already fighting. The government agreed, and in April 1916 the *Escadrille Américaine* formed as a squadron with a French commanding officer, Captain Georges Thenault, wearing French uniforms and with French mechanics but a preponderance of American pilots – thirty-eight in all. It quickly found action, and took part in the Battle of Verdun a month after forming. Perhaps not surprisingly, Germany protested to America that such a unit with such a provocative name flew in the face of the declared American neutrality and the squadron changed its name to *Lafayette Escadrille*. Other Americans flew with France under the banner of the Lafayette Flying Corps and they gained a romantic and legendary status. After the war, several films enhanced the romance of the unit – *The Legion of the Condemned* in 1928, *Lafayette Escadrille* starring Tab Hunter in 1958 and, more recently in 2006, *Flyboys* – albeit with poor reviews for the latter. The Americans fought with toughness and several of them are well known to military historians – Norman Hall and Raoul Lufbery to name but two. Of the original thirty-eight American pilots, ten lost their lives but were replaced by others.

The reasons they chose to fight for a foreign country are probably many – a sense of adventure, the need to escape from a situation at home, a desire to fight for what is right – who knows? These fliers created a precedent – there was no equivalent squadron in the British Royal Flying Corps, although Americans did join the British forces as well.

In 1917 in Russia, the communist October Revolution swept away the old monarchy and replaced it with what would become one of the most repressive and totalitarian regimes in history. Some of the leaders hoped that the example of a workers' socialist state seen in Russia would encourage workers in other countries to throw off the yoke of repression, but this didn't happen in just such a way. Historically, Russia and Germany had always harboured designs on Poland, which was often occupied by one or the other. Following the end of the First World War, Poland invaded Russia in an attempt to regain territory in the Ukraine lost during partitions of the eighteenth century, and initially they made good progress, capturing Kiev. But the Red Army regrouped and reversed the Polish gains until it was about to enter Poland itself. This created a dilemma for the Soviet leaders – Trotsky took the view that a Polish revolution should be the result of the efforts of the workers themselves, without assistance from the Red Army, which, it was suggested, would be seen merely as occupiers once again. In the event, the Red Army failed to capture Warsaw and Poland enjoyed a brief period of independence.

Early on in this Polish/Russian war, an American, Captain Merian C. Cooper, was instrumental in forming a squadron of mainly American pilots to fight on the side of the Poles against the Soviets. It wasn't exclusively American, though, with a Canadian member and four Poles. But why would Americans want to fight for a small European country against its historic enemy?

It is said that it was to repay a moral debt to Poland arising from the help given to the American revolutionaries by Tadeusz Kościusko, a Pole who fought on the side of the colonists. Born in 1746 to a family with modest landholdings, Kościusko attended the Warsaw military academy then moved to Paris in 1770 to continue his studies. He remained there for six years before moving to North America in 1776 where he became involved in the revolution against the British as a military engineer of some brilliance. He fought in a number of battles, including Saratoga in 1777, considered by some to have been the turning point in the conflict, until in 1783 he entered New York with the commander-in-chief, George Washington. As a memorial to him, a bridge bearing his name was opened in 1939 spanning the Newtown Creek which separates Brooklyn and Queens – coincidentally, the very locale of Walcott's birth. It isn't the most attractive of bridges, but its existence demonstrates the high esteem in which Kościusko is still held in the United States. There is also a street in Brooklyn named after Kościusko.

Kościusko returned to Poland in 1784, taking part in fighting against the Russians, and in 1794 was appointed commander-in-chief of the armed forces, which gave him almost dictatorial powers. Desiring to draw on the manpower of the Polish peasantry to join the fight, he radically changed the land laws to give serfs much more freedom and liberalise their relationship with the landowners. In 1794, Polish forces suffered a major defeat at Maciejowice, which resulted in the Third Partition of Poland by Russia. Kościusko was injured and captured, remaining in Russia until 1796 when he was released. He died in Switzerland in 1817.

During the Revolution, another Pole, Kazimierz Pulaski, also made a distinctive impression. Born in 1745, he came from a line of minor Polish nobility and, with a love of horseriding, joined the Polish army with a commission, aged only 15. He fought against the Russians, becoming a national hero in 1771 after victories in Poland. However, shortly afterwards he was accused of attempting to abduct the king and was sentenced to death. He managed to flee to Turkey and, unable to return to Poland, moved to Paris, where in 1777 he met Benjamin Franklin, who was at that time seeking experienced military leaders to help the revolutionary colonists in America. Appointed General of Cavalry by the Continental Congress, he fought and died at the Battle of Savannah in 1779.

According to legend, one of Merian Cooper's ancestors fought alongside Pulaski at Savannah – hence the perceived debt. The squadron, *7. Eskadra Lotnicza* or the 7th Air Escadrille, adopted the name 'Kościuszko Squadron' with a badge including thirteen blue stars and vertical red and white 'bars' to acknowledge its American origins together with a peasant cap and crossed scythes representing the Polish origins. After the war, the squadron number changed but it continued to be known as 'the Kościuszko Squadron', even during the Second World War when it reformed as 303 Squadron of the RAF, now a 'free Polish' unit but retaining its old name. A derivation of the original badge was carried by 303 Squadron aircraft during the war against Germany, although at that time 303 did not have an official badge. However, recently, a group of concerned ex-RAF and RAF Volunteer Reserve (RAFVR) airmen decided that something should be done. Working with the Polish ambassador in London and the defence attaché, they had a badge, based on the same design, created by the College of Arms Inspector of Royal Air Force badges. The RAF Club in London has the badges of most RAF squadrons on their walls, and now they have the official badge of the wartime 303 (Polish) Squadron.

Merian Cooper was an adventurer. He was born in 1893 in Jacksonville, Florida, and at an early age decided to become an explorer. He attended the US Naval Academy but was expelled. After service with the Georgia National Guard, in 1917 he trained as a pilot in Atlanta and in October of that year was in France and served as a bomber pilot with the US Army Air Service. In 1919 he became a member of the Kościuszko Squadron and for his trouble was shot down in July 1919 to become a prisoner of war of the Soviet Union for nine months. But he escaped to find freedom in Latvia, and subsequently was awarded the *Virtuti Militari*, which is the highest Polish award for bravery. As might be expected, he did not rest but had a flamboyant and interesting life as an explorer – more intriguingly, he came up with the idea for the film *King Kong*. He was heavily involved in all aspects of the film, including the final 'killing' of the beast when he piloted the plane that appears to achieve this.

Many Americans had joined the RCAF before the USA came into the Second World War after Pearl Harbor in December 1941, but the various relationships were complex and even unlikely.

On 4 November 1939, Congress passed the Neutrality Act, which was intended 'to preserve the neutrality and the peace of the United States and to secure the safety of its citizens and their interests' and established laws restricting the activities of American nationals and belligerent countries. Section 3, headed 'Combat Areas', paragraph (a) states:

> ... it shall be unlawful ... for any citizen of the United States or any American vessel to proceed into or through any ... combat area.

The expression 'combat area' was defined earlier in the document. In paragraph (b), provision is made for a passenger on a vessel travelling in violation of the Act to be fined 'not more than $10,000 or imprisoned for not more than two years, or both'.

But the Act does not make mention of Americans joining the armed forces of foreign countries and the wording of the Act mentions only passengers travelling in combat areas, not combatants.

Of much greater relevance is the US Nationality Act of 1940, passed by Congress on 14 October of that year and thus very relevant to Walcott signing up less than two months later. As is the way with such Acts, it is complex and repeals provisions of previous Acts going back as far as 1900. This Act contains five chapters, the fourth being headed 'Loss of Nationality'. Again, it requires some study to understand the provisions, but as regards Americans joining the RCAF, the following are the key extracts:

Sec. 401. A person who is a national of the United States, whether by birth or naturalization, shall lose his nationality by:

(b) Taking an oath or making an affirmation or other formal declaration of allegiance to a foreign state, or
(c) Entering, or serving in, the armed forces of a foreign state unless expressly authorized by the laws of the United States, if he has or acquires nationality of such foreign state, or ...

Section 401 runs to paragraph (h), which covers treason, with a series of other actions mentioned in previous paragraphs, including employment by foreign governments, formal renunciation of nationality, etc.

Clearly, though, the issues are straightforward – Walcott could place his American citizenship in jeopardy by joining the RCAF and then taking an oath of allegiance to Canada, Britain or its monarch. The statute is quite clear. There is no ambiguity in the drafting of the provision – the person 'shall lose his nationality'.

Walcott joined the RCAF after this Act was passed by Congress, which again raises the interesting question as to why Robert Tillotson, a respected, publicly elected official, and Henry Smith, an employed public official, would actively encourage the young man to act in such a way that he would possibly forfeit his American citizenship. Perhaps they did not appreciate the consequences of the action being taken – but if they did not, the Canadian and US governments were only too aware of the ramifications of the flow of Americans joining the Canadian Air Force.

William A. 'Billy' Bishop was a renowned Canadian fighter pilot of the First World War, being credited with seventy-two aerial victories (including two balloons). By 1938, Bishop was an Honorary Air Marshal of the RCAF with responsibilities for recruitment. He appreciated that a war in Europe was becoming increasingly likely, that when it came it would significantly increase the requirement for trained aircrew, and that a potential source of aircrew would be the United States – as it had been in the First World War. As early as March 1939, Bishop visited Washington and returned to Canada believing that the American laws against recruitment into foreign military services might not be insurmountable. He spoke to Clayton Knight, an American pilot who flew with the British over the Western Front and became an artist specialising in aviation subjects. With excellent links to the American aviation community, Clayton Knight could report on opinion about the war within the community. Bishop also spoke to Homer Smith, a Canadian who had flown with the British Royal Naval Air Service but in the intervening years had become very wealthy and was willing to help fund initiatives to recruit Americans into the RCAF. The day after Britain declared war on Germany, Bishop set to work against a general background of enthusiasm for the idea among colleagues as well as caution that as far as the US was concerned, the recruitment of Americans would be quite definitely illegal. It seemed appropriate to canvass the opinions of Americans going through the flying schools, and on 9 September, while the government – at least officially – remained very cool, the Defence Minister, Ian Mackenzie, granted Homer Smith a commission as a wing commander in the RCAF tasking him to carry out the survey. Smith rented a suite of rooms at the Waldorf Astoria Hotel in New York as a base; then he and Clayton Knight toured the schools.

As in Britain during the so-called Phoney War, little happened. Although Clayton Knight and Homer Smith established an organisation and identified several hundred potential American recruits with flying experience, the Canadian authorities showed little interest until the German assault on the Low Countries in May 1940. Billy Bishop had also been setting up the British Commonwealth Air Training Plan, a scheme whereby British pupil pilots would be trained in Canada before being sent to the RAF, but this resulted in an increased demand for instructors, which could not be met from the normal sources. However, the possibility that Smith and Knight might be able to supply several hundred American pilots presented a means of overcoming the immediate problem, which the authorities were happy to grasp – provided that the pilots could be employed without upsetting the US government. The Clayton Knight Committee came into existence with the remit to find and recruit American pilots to serve with the RCAF as instructors. The signals coming from US government sources were encouraging. Provided this was being done discreetly, there would be no opposition. But the situation was delicate. While many in the US supported the concept of giving assistance to Britain and France, the isolationist lobby was considerable and opposed any measures that might see the US drawn, again, into a European war. Apart from anything else, as mentioned before, some held the view that America should not be drawn into a fight perceived to preserve the British Empire. For others, Britain's defeat seemed inevitable – epitomised by the attitude of American ambassador to London, Joseph Kennedy, and the famous pioneer flier, Charles Lindbergh. If the Clayton Knight Committee was to be successful, it was essential that those holding these views should not be gifted reasons to strengthen their arguments.

None of the US laws about foreign recruitment were rescinded.

The State Department asked that US nationals should not be asked to swear an oath of allegiance to a foreign state that could place them at risk of losing their citizenship (as discussed above) but this was solved by requiring recruits to take an oath of obedience to their superior officers instead, although it seems that some of the first recruits did take an oath of allegiance to the British king.[3] Later, American authorities agreed that all Americans serving with the British and Commonwealth services would have the right to transfer to the US military should America be drawn into the war.

Of course, some Americans joined the Royal Air Force directly and independently. Many went on to form 'Eagle Squadrons' composed of Americans and widely publicised, although with the risk that the American isolationists and others might object in a similar way to the objections raised about the French *Escadrille Américaine* during the First World War. These Americans were independent of Clayton Knight and his committee. Some were 'thoroughbred' Americans, born and raised in the States, but some who have been described as 'Americans' come from more mixed backgrounds.

As an example, Carl Raymond Davis, who flew during the Battle of Britain with 601 Squadron, was born in South Africa to American parents but reportedly became a British citizen in 1932. In one source he is described as an American who flew in the Battle of Britain[4] and in another as a South African.[5] He did not survive the war.

'Jimmy' Davies was born in New Jersey in 1913 but his family moved to Wales and he joined the RAF in 1936. In 1940 he was flying Hurricanes with 79 Squadron but was killed on 27 June carrying out a reconnaissance over St Valery in France with two others. The three Hurricanes were attacked by German fighters and only one pilot survived. By then Davies had racked up an impressive score of enemy aircraft shot down and was both Mentioned in Dispatches and awarded the Distinguished Flying Cross.

Walcott's only operational unit was 603 Squadron. On 16 October 1939 the *Luftwaffe* carried out its first attack in British airspace over the Firth of Forth near Edinburgh. Three of its aircraft were lost and the first was credited to Flight Lieutenant Patrick Gifford, one of 603's flight commanders. Although Gifford has never been considered as anything other than a Scot, his mother was American, from New Jersey, but spent her married life in Castle Douglas in south-west Scotland.

A handful of so-called thoroughbred Americans served with Fighter Command during the Battle of Britain. Probably the most celebrated were 'Billy' Fiske, 'Shorty' Keough, 'Andy' Mamedoff and 'Red' Tobin. Of these, Billy Fiske was colourful and flamboyant. He was born in 1911 in Brooklyn. His full name was William Meade Lindsley Fiske III, and he was the son of a wealthy banker. His life reflected the family wealth. After education in Chicago, Fiske moved to Europe and, after further education in France, went up to Cambridge to read economics and history. He discovered bobsledding while in France and represented the USA in the 1928 Winter Olympics at St Moritz as the driver of the American five-man bobsled team, becoming the youngest competitor to win a gold medal. He carried the Stars and Stripes at the opening of the 1932 Winter Olympics at Lake Placid and once again, as driver of the four-man bob team, took another gold medal. He worked in London for a firm of American bankers and married the Countess of Warwick in 1938, almost exactly a year before the outbreak of war. In 1939, work took him back to the States but he returned to the United Kingdom in the *Aquitania* on 30 August 1939. He joined the RAFVR but to do this, claimed to be a Canadian. He took an oath of allegiance to King George VI, which of course would put his American citizenship at risk. Having qualified as a pilot, he was posted to 601 (County of London) Squadron of the Auxiliary Air Force[6] (AuxAF), known as 'the millionaires' squadron' because of the wealth of so many of the officers. With his own wealthy parents and his affinity for Europe and Britain, Fiske would feel quite comfortable. The squadron was equipped with Hawker Hurricanes. Sadly, on 16 August his plane was hit. With his aircraft damaged by German fire and burning, Fiske attempted to return to his base at Tangmere and brought the plane down safely. Taken to Chichester for hospital treatment, he died of shock. He was twenty-nine years old.

It is notable that both Fiske and Walcott, as will be seen, served with AuxAF squadrons, but their experiences were quite different. Fiske was a commissioned officer of the RAFVR, while Walcott was a non-commissioned officer of the RCAF. The AuxAF and the RAFVR were both reservist organisations but with significant differences. The AuxAF came into being in the mid-1920s based on the format of the existing Territorial Army. Full squadrons were created in or near cities and population centres, and drew on local resources. The majority of squadron personnel were reservists assisted by a small core of regulars with the objective that each squadron would be trained and equipped to the same level as the regular squadrons so that if an emergency arose, they would all take their place in the order of battle on an equal footing. The RAFVR first started training aircrew in 1937 but it provided a reservoir of trained airmen, not just aircrew, who would be used to fill gaps on an individual basis rather than full squadrons. It was said that auxiliaries were gentlemen trying to be pilots and those in the RAFVR were pilots trying to be gentlemen! As a colourful, wealthy adventurer, Fiske appears to have fitted in well with his fellows in 601 Squadron, while Walcott did not fit in well and had a quite different experience. Walcott was posted to 603 (City of Edinburgh) Squadron and it is of passing interest that when 603 made the flight to Malta during which Walcott disappeared, the other squadron to make the journey at the same time was 601.

Of the other Americans, Vernon Keough, like Fiske and Walcott, was born in Brooklyn. He gained his civil pilot's licence in the US and was a professional parachute jumper. He was small in stature, apparently 4 foot 10 inches tall, hence his nickname Shorty, and he needed a cushion to allow him to see over the instrument panel of the aircraft he flew! Mamedoff was born in Connecticut in 1912 and was an accomplished pilot in the United States. He had Russian ancestors and intended to come to Europe to fight for Finland against the Soviet Union. The last of the trio, Eugene Tobin, was born in Utah in 1917. He and Mamedoff had become friends in California and Tobin had hoped to fight for Finland alongside his friend, but before they left Canada, the fighting was over. In Canada they met up with Keough and the three sailed to France intending to join up there, but with France having been invaded and in turmoil, they couldn't enlist so made their way to Britain. They signed up for the RAF at the same time and had consecutive service numbers. On completion of their training, they all flew with 609 (West Riding of Yorkshire) Squadron, yet another auxiliary unit.

Clearly, American fighter pilots had a glamorous and romantic image and unsurprisingly the British were quick to realise this. Americans fighting in RAF squadrons were one thing, but to have a full squadron made up of Americans was another. The propaganda opportunities were huge. Imitating the French before them in the First World War, on 19 September 1940 at RAF Church Fenton, 71 Squadron, which had disbanded in 1918, reformed as an 'all-American' unit initially flying Brewster Buffalo aircraft but in 1941 converting to Hurricanes. Keough, Mamedoff and Tobin were all posted to 71 Squadron on its reformation. To be absolutely clear, these were Americans who were members of the Royal Air Force and could conceivably be regarded as 'soldiers of fortune'.

In the early months, Britain was supported by countries of the Commonwealth. Canada and Australia, in particular, sent squadrons from their respective air forces to join the fight but, in addition, a large number of airmen arrived in Britain from the countries occupied by Germany. With aircrew in short supply it would have been foolish not to tap up these refugee airmen, and where there were enough of them, separate squadrons were established – Free French, Dutch, Poles, Czechoslovak, etc. The Commonwealth squadrons had their own numbers, which sometimes duplicated an RAF squadron, so it was decided that Commonwealth squadrons should be renumbered to avoid any confusion; for them, the 400 number series was used. For squadrons made up of airmen of the occupied nations, the 300 series was used so that, for example, 303 Squadron was a Polish unit. In this vein, the 500 and 600 series of numbers were allocated to auxiliary and/or reserve units, as we have seen, or special squadrons. Perhaps the best-known special squadron was 617 – the 'Dam Busters' – but as another example, 618 Squadron was a sister unit of 617 developing spherical bouncing bombs that, it was hoped, might be used against German capital ships like *Tirpitz*. Unfortunately this was not a success.

To distinguish them from RAF personnel, airmen from these other countries wore shoulder flashes with the name of their country of origin. Over the years of the war, a series of Air Ministry orders permitted the use of shoulder titles for those coming from Commonwealth countries but not, it seems for those from the USA. Many of the Americans wore 'USA' titles – it is said that one wore a 'Texas' title in honour of his home state but these were not official.' However, the Americans in the Eagle Squadrons were able to wear a shoulder patch based on the design of the Great Seal of the United States and with the letters 'ES' to denote the status of the wearer; of course, this – and the very existence of the Eagle Squadrons – was encouraged for its propaganda value.

As the numbers of Americans in the RAF increased as the war progressed, two other Eagle Squadrons were formed: 121 and 133. These Americans fought with valour and distinction for Britain and many died in operations over occupied Europe. They may have been a source of propaganda but their contribution to Britain's survival was real and costly for them. They are rightly celebrated for their brave deeds. Once America was drawn into the war and became a vital ally for the British, the reasons for the existence of the three squadrons were much less compelling. America softened its hard attitude towards its citizens who were flying with British and Commonwealth air forces and accepted that they could be transferred to the US Army Air Corps (USAAC) without any sanctions. The threat of losing citizenship was rescinded. The three Eagle Squadrons transferred lock, stock and barrel to the 4th Fighter Group of the USAAC on 29 September 1942 as the 334th, 335th and 336th Squadrons. By now they were all equipped with Spitfires, which they continued to fly but in American markings until they were issued with American aircraft.

So as a general point, 'Americans' served in the RAF and with the British air forces in different capacities. The more celebrated were those who made their own way to Britain and joined up directly, but others, like Walcott, were less celebrated because they enlisted in the Canadian Air Force and did not receive the adulation given to the Eagle Squadron pilots, even though many served with equal distinction and also transferred to the USAAC.

To return to the work of the Clayton Knight Committee, the air arms of the American army and navy gave their help with some enthusiasm. Knight soon discovered that the standard required by the Americans for their trainee pilots was considerably higher than in the RCAF and those who failed the US training might very well suit the Canadians – indeed US Army Major General 'Hap' Arnold promised to give Knight the names of those students who had failed.

The committee operated with discretion. Applicants underwent medical examinations and ideally should have held a US Civil Aviation Authority Certificate and logged a minimum of 300 hours. By the end of 1940, 321 volunteers had been accepted.[7]

Walcott, of course, had some flying experience but nothing like the 300 hours desired by the Clayton Knight Committee, and it's likely that he found his way to the RCAF independently. In Ottawa on 6 December 1940, Walcott underwent the normal interview that would map out his future and signed the RCAF attestation paper. Generally, his assessment is 'average' and the interviewing officer concludes that he is suitable for flying as a pilot or observer but not for commissioned rank. Walcott is 6 foot 1 inch in height and weighs 156lbs, with medium physique. Neatly dressed and upright in bearing, he is deemed to be confident, sincere and quick in response; very intelligent, calm, and eager to fly – but with only a 'fair' personality and being only a 'fairly pleasant young man', which seems to be rather at odds with the character one would expect of a cabaret magician. Other descriptions of Walcott during his military career differ with this one; all such descriptions and conclusions are essentially subjective.

Three weeks later, on 27 December, in Montreal and in the presence of a Justice of the Peace, Bud signed an affidavit that he, 'Salvator Bassi Walcott', was the same person as the 'Salvatore Roberts Bassi' referred to on his high school certificate and the two letters of reference. The following day he formally joined the RCAF with the rank of AC2,[8] the lowest rank in the service, and service number R79006.

# 5

# THE ROAD TO OPERATIONS

All recruits into the Royal Air Force followed a similar path to qualification as an operational pilot – essentially an initial course of 'square bashing' (what Americans would call 'boot camp') as an introduction to the service, then elementary flying training followed by service flying training before going to an Operational Training Unit (OTU) for conversion on to the type of aeroplane that would be flown with a squadron in combat.

Walcott did his square bashing at No. 3 Initial Training School (known as 'wings' in Britain) at Victoriaville in Quebec, from 24 March 1941 to 4 May. A contemporary publication of the time[1] describes the RAF initial training wings as:

> ... the reception departments into which flows the raw material, the young men who, coming straight from civil life, feel for the first time the growing meaning of comradeship and pride in the service. Day after day these recruits drill, march, and attend lectures. It is a strenuous time, in which muscles, nerve and brain are brought up to concert pitch.

Stirring stuff, and no doubt a glorified description of the reality – strict discipline, long hours of what appear to be pointless activities and punishments, the accent on 'spit and polish' or 'bull', and, for many, initial homesickness while new friends are made. Of course, the harsh discipline could turn to outright bullying in the hands of the non-commisioned officers (NCO) who were instructors and many recruits found the regime hard and unpleasant and experienced great relief (and pride in their success) once it was over. Others, of course, relished the new challenges that military life posed and found the whole process stimulating and exciting. Walcott was assessed as being 'keen and intelligent and cheerful' but his disciplinary record was not unblemished. During his time at Victoriaville he was sentenced to seven days' confinement to barracks with the forfeiture of a day's pay for being absent without leave for thirteen hours and fifteen minutes and failing to report to the service police on his return from leave. This would not be the last of Walcott's transgressions.

The six-week course finished on 4 May with promotion to LAC.[2] Walcott graduated seventy-fourth in the class of 370 and was recommended for training as a pilot but, again, not for a commission.

Immediately on finishing at Victoriaville, he transferred to No. 13 Elementary Flying Training School (EFTS) at St Eugene near Ottawa for his introduction to flying on course number 27. The basic training programme for pilots has not changed much over the years, rather it has become lengthier and increasingly demanding as the complexity of the aeroplanes has grown. There is an initial phase during which the trainee learns how an aeroplane flies, along with practical instruction in how to fly. The aeroplanes used are small and forgiving so that students may make mistakes without them necessarily being catastrophic. The trainer in use at 13 EFTS was the Fleet Finch. Like the Tiger Moth in common use in Britain and in Canada, the Finch was a biplane with a fixed undercarriage. The RCAF examined the Fleet 10D model and found that it didn't have the capability for aerobatics that were needed, so, with appropriate modifications, it entered service as the Model 16 or 'Finch'. Initially with an open cockpit, in service a sliding cockpit hood was added. The Finch was regarded as a sturdy, dependable elementary trainer, which remained in service with the RCAF until 1947.

General handling – taxiing on the ground, control of the engine, flying straight and level, turns, etc. – are all taught and then incorporated into flying circuits. A circuit involves taking off, turning 90° on to a crosswind leg, turning another 90° on to the downwind leg (flying parallel to the take-off runway but in the opposite direction), turning again onto the base leg and, finally, into the final leg and approach to land back on the runway – more or less a rectangle in the sky.

In addition, before being allowed to fly solo, pilots were taught how to deal with stalls, spins and other potentially dangerous situations they might encounter on any flight. One of the most critical is an engine failure on take-off. If this happens it is natural to try to turn and land back on the airfield, but without power a turn can become a stall, which often results in a fatal crash if attempted at low level. It depends just how high the aeroplane is – at low altitudes it is better to land straight ahead, but if there is sufficient height it might be possible to turn and land back although clearly the pilot needs to be knowledgeable enough to make the judgement. Often turning back is not the solution, and, of course, the ability to deal with such events comes with experience.

Having mastered these basics in the opinion of the instructor, the pupil pilot flies a circuit without supervision – the first solo, which is always a most memorable day for the pilot. Traditionally, having flown a number of faultless circuits, the instructor tells the pupil to taxi the aeroplane back to the flight line, then jumps out and says, 'Ok. Off you go – you're on your own,' with the pupil nervously realising that the time has come. Then the instructor watches his charge make his or her first faltering solo – usually successfully. Most pilots are generally considered suitable after about ten to fifteen hours' dual instruction.

The course ran until mid-June. By the end, Walcott had clocked up a total of forty-nine hours forty-five minutes' flying time, of which twenty-four hours forty-five minutes was solo. Walcott was assessed as generally average but uncomfortable with aerobatics. It was recorded that he had a 'good personality', a reflection on his gregarious and outgoing attitude to life. Right at the end of the course, Walcott failed to report for duty in the morning and received a day confined to barracks and one day of drill. His misdemeanour did not affect his training, and on 4 July 1941 he was transferred to 14 Service Flying Training School (SFTS) at Aylmer, Ontario. Aylmer has a proud place in the history of the RCAF during the Second World War, and many British and Commonwealth pilots passed through the school on their way to operations. It opened on 3 July 1941 and Walcott must have been one of the first trainees to pass through the school although his course was numbered 32. The purpose of the SFTS was to bring the trainees to a level of general competence as pilots when they would receive their flying badge or wings. The aircraft used was the North American Harvard, a low-wing monoplane with a retractable undercarriage and enclosed cockpit – still very forgiving but rather more looking the part of a modern aircraft. Having to deal with a retractable undercarriage made life slightly more complicated for the budding pilot and it wasn't unknown for trainees to forget that they no longer had a fixed undercarriage and land their aircraft on its belly with all the damage that this entailed.

Many Harvards survive to this day – including one with the registration number 3222. This aeroplane served at Aylmer, and on 26 July 1941 Walcott was flying solo in it when he suffered an engine failure and crash-landed. The accident occurred mid-morning. Walcott was practising aerobatics at 5,000 feet. Aerobatics were usually performed in a safe area away from the main airfield but Walcott was near enough to try to glide the Harvard back and land on the airfield. Unfortunately, he undershot and landed wheels-up short of the runway on the south side of the aerodrome. He suffered no injury but was taken to the hospital for observation because of a high temperature.

The aeroplane he flew was built by North American Aviation at Inglewood in California as part of an order for 100 Harvard Mk IIs for the RCAF. This particular type was known as the NA-75, and the batch was given RCAF serial numbers 3134 to 3233 – Walcott's was 3222 with the buzz number 53. It was brought on charge on 8 July 1941 and so had only been operating for eighteen days before the incident with Walcott, who was considered blameless. In fact, the young pilot had probably reacted well to a dangerous, potentially fatal situation.

Interestingly, this aircraft survived and in 2013 was still flying in a beautifully restored condition in the markings that it would have worn when Walcott made his forced landing. After Aylmer, it served with No. 1 Flight Instructors School at Trenton, Ontario, and then post-war at the Primary Training School at Centralia, also in Ontario. The RCAF relinquished ownership on 25 August 1960 and it was sold off as surplus. It changed hands a couple times before being bought by Norman F. Beckman of Woodstock in Ontario in 1969 and flown with the civil registration CF-MKA. It was flown as one of four privately owned Harvards that launched the Canadian Harvard Aircraft Association at Woodstock in 1985. In 1988, she was repainted in the original RCAF training colours and re-registered as C-FMKA. In 2011, Norman Beckman's son Kent took ownership and he has been flying it from Woodstock since 2001 as part of the Canadian Harvard Aerobatic Team.

The course ended on Thursday 25 September, on which day Walcott, along with the other graduates, received his wings and a promotion to sergeant. He was now a qualified pilot. His flying time totalled 156 hours 15 minutes, of which 86 hours 10 minutes were solo. His flying assessments are similar to those at the EFTS – an average flyer but specifically 'weak in Navigation' – which may be relevant to incidents yet to happen. But his character assessments are far more upbeat than before. He is considered to have a somewhat easy-going nature but was full of energy and apparently well liked. His skills as a magician were much appreciated and he seems to have been a popular member of the course. Once again, though, he has been disciplined for being absent without leave for two and a half days during August and punished with seven days' confinement to barracks, forfeiting three days' pay and a forty-eight-hour pass.

Significantly, he was recommended for a commission and perceived to have a bright future once he had obtained experience. He was granted a week-and-a-half's embarkation leave before being required to report to Halifax to leave for Britain.

While Bud progressed through his training in 1941, the outlook for Britain remained bleak. Fears of another summer of heavy air fighting over southern England proved groundless, although the *Luftwaffe* continued to raid cities, and industrial and military targets. But Britain was determined to take some offensive action despite only having limited capability to do so. The RAF was the only arm able to sustain a campaign. Bomber Command strived to mount raids against targets in Germany while Fighter Command carried out sweep operations over northern France from bases in southern England, aiming to entice German fighters into combat. Some of these operations were massive, involving a few bombers acting as bait escorted by as many as a dozen fighter squadrons in various escort roles. Ironically, to carry out these sweeps the British fighter pilots' predicament in 1941 was the mirror image of the German pilots' issues in 1940, with British pilots nursing damaged or fuel-starved aeroplanes across the English Channel to return home while downed German pilots were landing in 'friendly' territory. Otherwise, nothing seemed to stop the advance of German forces. After German invasions in Greece and the Balkans in support of the Italians, British forces were forced to surrender Crete and withdraw to eastern North Africa where, once again, the fighting was not going well.

In the Atlantic the vital convoys from the United States and Canada were coming under increasing attack by German U-boats, and although in May the Royal Navy managed to sink the enemy battleship *Bismarck*, it lost the battle cruiser HMS *Hood* – a sinking which rocked confidence. *Hood* was a potent symbol of British naval power and its loss a blow for British pride as well as its naval capability. A lucky shot from a German gun apparently dropped a shell down one of *Hood*'s funnels, which blew up an ammunition magazine. (There are suggestions that at some time the armour plating on the deck was reduced at the Rosyth Dockyard in Fife, creating a weak spot, which the German shell hit.) The sinking of *Hood* was quick and shocking. Having captured Crete using paratroopers and airborne forces, the Axis siege of Malta intensified. Hitler came under pressure from his military commanders to order an attack on Malta using airborne forces in a similar operation to the attack on Crete, but the landscape of Malta was different. Since ancient times the land was farmed using low walls to divide adjacent fields, and these became effective anti-glider obstacles for the German *Wehrmacht* as well as being a danger to British aircraft force-landing after combat. Left with bases at each end of the Mediterranean, the Royal Navy had to run the gauntlet of German and Italian aircraft and fighting ships to supply the tiny island with the essentials it needed.

With hindsight there was one tiny glimmer of hope, although it may not have been recognised as such by many: the German invasion of the Soviet Union in June. For Britain there were two consequences: the likelihood of a German invasion reduced enormously, and Britain gained an ally – albeit one that was unlikely, demanding and surly.

Joseph Stalin, the Soviet dictator, completely misjudged the intentions of his erstwhile and uneasy ally Hitler. After the purges of the officer classes in the late 1930s, the Red Army was poorly led and not in a position to undertake a conflict with the *Wehrmacht*. The German/Soviet alliance was one of convenience. It allowed Germany to concentrate on its campaigns in the west of Europe without worrying about a Soviet attack in the east, while for Stalin it provided time to rebuild the Red Army to a point where it could undertake a war with Germany, possibly in 1942. Such a war was almost inevitable at some point. Although the two dictators operated in similar ways, they would never be able to coexist in the long run. In 1940, Hitler was already looking to an invasion of the Soviet Union while Stalin intended to maintain good relations with his western neighbour and avoid doing anything to precipitate a conflict before he was ready for it.

During the summer of 1941, there were signs that Germany was preparing to attack. Despite reports of the massing of German troops on the border with the preparation of pontoons and boats to cross rivers, Stalin steadfastly refused to accept that an attack was likely and ordered that no actions should be taken to provoke the Germans. When the attack came Stalin was quite stunned and took some time to come to terms with Hitler's duplicity and the inability of the Red Army to push back the attacks. He took to his *dacha* for several days, leaving the country effectively leaderless and paralysed – much to the consternation of those in government with him, many of whom were unwilling to take the lead because of fears that any actions would result in dreadful retribution from the paranoid dictator they served if and when he took control again.

While Britain now had an ally, the relationship would always be uncomfortable. Winston Churchill abhorred all that the Soviet dictator stood for, but recognised that if Britain was to survive then pragmatism was needed and, in simplistic terms, it was better to have the Soviet Union as an ally than have none. Demanding, treacherous and ruled by his paranoia, Stalin sought only to advance his own cause. Despite Britain's parlous economy, he demanded to be supplied with war matériel, which could only be transported by sea – the notorious Arctic convoys.

These Allied convoys formed in lochs and harbours on the west coast of Britain or at Iceland before making the hazardous voyage around the North Cape of Norway to Murmansk at the Kola Peninsula. As if it wasn't enough to be shadowed and attacked by German U-boats and bombed and torpedoed by *Luftwaffe* aircraft based in Norway, the freezing weather made conditions almost intolerable. Ships became overloaded with ice. Decks became so slippery as to be almost impassable and an unprotected hand inadvertently touching bare metal would stick to it. For those sailors who found themselves in the icy water, the chances of survival were almost nil.

The shock to the human body of being suddenly immersed in the cold water produces several effects, all of which can be fatal. Firstly, there is a massive increase in the heart rate combined with a rise in blood pressure as the blood vessels on the surface of the skin constrict. This can result in a heart attack or a stroke. Then there is loss of breathing control, which results in involuntary gasping. If the mouth is underwater then the result is drowning. If this does not kill, the next phase is hyperventilation, which makes it difficult to remain on the surface or swim. It can result in a decrease of carbon dioxide in the bloodstream which can have several effects – dizziness, faintness, numbness in the extremities and their cramping. And if the water temperature is below 5°C there will be pain. If the body survives the initial shock, a general weakness sets in with numbness, which leads to a lack of use of the hands and feet – a loss of sensation, motor control and a stiffening that makes it difficult to keep the mouth above the water if there is no lifejacket. With each breath, a small quantity of water may be ingested into the lungs with eventual fatal consequences. After this, the chilling will result in hypothermia, defined as a core body temperature of less than 35°C, and the individual will die. For those who survived the initial shock, death would come within a matter of minutes from the cold. Both the merchant ships and their naval escorts were ordered not to stop dead in the water to carry out rescues because they became sitting targets for the German submarines. And even then, Allied sailors who reached Murmansk were treated with suspicion and hostility, on occasions not being allowed off their ships after having fought their way through.

As the war progressed, Churchill's influence waned and he was increasingly ignored by Stalin and President Roosevelt until, when the final division of Europe was agreed at the end of the war at the Yalta conference, his desire for the restoration of an independent Poland, which had been Britain's original reason for declaring war, was unachievable in the face of the Soviet Union's expansionism.

Bud Walcott departed Canada on Wednesday 12 November 1941 on a voyage across the Atlantic that took eleven days and ran all the risks of the ship being sunk, with a potential terrible death in the icy water. However, he arrived in Britain on 23 November and was posted to 59 Operational Training Unit (OTU) Crosby-on-Eden in Cumberland on Tuesday 9 December.

Leaving Canadian shores and arriving in Britain brought the reality of the war much closer. The United States was still at peace and many British airmen sent there to train in the constant sunshine of the southern states commented on the richness of the food and the bright lights of the cities, which contrasted sharply with the shortages back home and the blackout. Canada was similar. There was no immediate threat from bombing or any serious enemy action, although German submarines did venture into American and Canadian territorial waters – some going into the Gulf of Mexico and into the mouth of the Mississippi. There the lack of a blackout allowed ships sailing close to the shore to become silhouetted targets for the U-boats out at sea. While Bud's life had been changed by joining the RCAF, the war had remained several thousand miles away and in the future. The long, uncomfortable and risky sea trip would start to bring home to him that his life was potentially in danger and travelling around a blacked-out and blitzed Britain with its rationing and other hardships would starkly bring home that this was no game and that the stakes were high.

Crosby-on-Eden is in the north-west of England near the ancient city of Carlisle and the beautiful English Lake District just south of the border with Scotland. The airfield still exists, and like many ex-wartime aerodromes has been used for private flying; it is now Carlisle airport. The OTUs represented the final formal stage of a pilot's training, with the next posting usually to an operational squadron. The OTUs trained the pilots to fly the type of aircraft they would be flying operationally, although the final judgement as to whether a pilot was ready for operations rested with the OC of the squadron to which they were posted. The pilots' final polishing was carried out on the squadrons.

The RAF operated using a 'command' structure, e.g. Fighter Command, Bomber Command, Training Command, Coastal Command, etc. Although elementary training was carried out by Training Command, the conversion to operations was the responsibility of the relevant command so that in Bud's case, as he was to be a fighter pilot, his operational training was the responsibility of Fighter Command. The next level in the operational structure were the 'groups'. For example, in Fighter Command in 1940, 11 and 12 Groups were responsible for protecting the south of England and were most heavily engaged in the Battle of Britain. These groups were geographically defined but within Fighter Command, 81 Group was responsible for operational conversion training and was formed on 16 December 1940. At that time, 59 OTU flew Hawker Hurricanes – single-engine fighters comparable to the legendary Spitfire made by Supermarine.

Up until the middle of the 1930s, while the RAF introduced new aircraft, their planes lacked significant technical improvement, and, being biplanes with open cockpits and fixed undercarriages, looked much like the aeroplanes used during the First World War. Germany was re-arming and, strictly in violation of the terms of the Treaty of Versailles, secretly formed a new air force, the *Luftwaffe*. To equip the new air force, German aircraft companies developed types that were, for the time, cutting edge technology. Particularly impressive was the fighter designed by Willi Messerchmitt, the Bf109 a low-wing, single-engine cantilever monoplane. (It is also somewhat ironic that some pilots of the clandestine new German air force were secretly trained in the Soviet Union.) But the RAF was not unaware of the deficiencies in their operational types and they introduced two similar low-winged, single-engine monoplanes: the Supermarine Spitfire and the Hawker Hurricane. All three new aircraft were in service with their respective air forces at the end of the 1930s. As a very general comment, they all possessed similar performance characteristics with each being slightly better than the other within certain parameters – turning circles, speed to altitude, etc. – although the Bf109 was significantly superior in a dive with the advantage provided to their Daimler Benz engines by petrol injection, whereas the Rolls-Royce Merlin engines of the Spitfires and Hurricanes were gravity fed.

On the British side, the Hurricane was recognised as a stable gun platform while the Spitfire was considered to be more manoeuvrable. As a result, the aim during the Battle of Britain in 1940 was to have the Hurricanes attack the German bombers while the Spitfires kept the Bf109s at bay. With its graceful lines, the Spitfire became the iconic symbol of the Fighter Command and the Battle of Britain, although more Hurricanes actually operated during the battle.

But apart from the aeroplanes employed, the Bf109 pilots enjoyed other advantages. While the British Hurricanes and Spitfires were equipped with four .303 machine guns in each wing, the Bf109E in use during the Battle of Britain employed 20mm cannon, far more destructive than the British machine guns. Further, the German fighting tactics had been learned from experience gained during the Spanish Civil War when elements of the *Luftwaffe* operated as the Condor Legion on the side of General Franco. The British typically flew in tight vics of three, which meant that the two wingmen were concentrating on holding formation rather than looking out for the enemy, while the Germans operated in pairs, a *rotte*, or pairs of pairs, a *schwarme*, flying in a much more flexible way that allowed each pilot to cover his comrade. And with regard to the weapons, the Air Ministry required that the eight guns of the Spitfires and Hurricanes be harmonised so that the bullets came together 400 yards ahead of the aircraft to create a concentrated area of damage on a target. The Germans, however, realised that the key to combat success was to get as close as possible to the target – 400 yards was much too far. Many British pilots appreciated this, but the Air Ministry took months to change the official rule. Some squadron commanders took it upon themselves to make the change unofficially, and to change the basic flying tactics, but such initiative was not, as a rule, welcomed by officialdom.

As the war continued, improved variants of each type were introduced in response to improvements in the enemy's aircraft although ultimately the Hurricane dropped out of the race and gradually became obsolete as a fighter, although it was still employed for ground attack and other roles. Eventually even the Bf109 was supplanted by the Focke Wulf 190, which was pitted against the later marks of Spitfire, although the 109 flew until the German surrender.

When Bud Walcott arrived at Crosby-on-Eden the whole aspect of the war had changed. Two days before, on Sunday 7 December, the Japanese attacked Pearl Harbor in what a shocked President Roosevelt called a 'day of infamy'; for the British this meant, at last, a long desired and powerful ally. The British reaction can be summarised in the words of its Prime Minister, Winston Churchill:

> No American will think it wrong of me if I proclaim that to have the United States at our side was to me the greatest joy. I could not foretell the course of events. I do not pretend to have measured accurately the martial might of Japan. But now at this very moment I knew the United States was in the war, up to the neck and in to the death. So we had won after all![3]

And later: 'We had won the war.'

Within the space of six months, Britain had acquired two potentially powerful allies. But while Churchill might have believed that victory was now a certainty, the road ahead remained hard and uncertain. Indeed, it would be a full year before he could feel confident enough to say: 'Now this is not the end. It is not even the beginning of the end. But it is, perhaps, the end of the beginning.'

And so the major players were now in place – on the Axis side Germany, Italy and Japan, on the Allied side Britain and its Commonwealth, the Soviet Union and the United States of America. The war was global and each alliance gained the support of other, smaller countries.

With no diaries or letters to fall back on, Walcott's views on this turn of events are unknown. He may have wished that he had remained at home to join the American forces, but whether he did or not, at this time it was not an option for him. However, it was an incident during his training at 59 OTU that would be used to first raise questions about his courage and commitment to Britain and its air force.

Coming from his upbringing in the Berkshires of Massachusetts, Walcott was fortunate that his first posting in this new country took him to the English Lake District – one of the most beautiful parts of the United Kingdom and in many ways not dissimilar to the Berkshires, which as noted earlier are sometimes called the American Lake District. Crosby-on-Eden is a few miles to the north-east of the ancient city of Carlisle, with the Lake District to the south and west, easily accessible from Crosby. Certainly, Walcott could have spent leave periods there if he so wished. Rugged hills called fells and spectacular scenery are hallmarks of the area, with many walks covering the full spectrum of difficulty as well as climbs. The country to the east of Crosby is less rugged but still beautiful, and not unlike the rolling hills of home for Bud. It could only confirm any preconception that an American might have of 'England'. And only a couple of miles along the road lay Crosby-on-Eden – a small, quaint, rural village that has been there for centuries and has witnessed much passing history. Lying on the old Roman road, the Stanegate, it was on the main road out of Carlisle for travellers going to Tyneside to the east. If he suffered from culture shock, as well he might, the surroundings could have been far worse than Cumberland. But this was his first experience of the RAF proper, and he was now in a country that was enduring rationing, the privations of a wartime economy and a threat of invasion.

In February 1942, 59 OTU reported personnel strengths of eighty-one RAF officers and 2,061 other ranks, along with six officers of the Women's Auxiliary Air Force (WAAFs) and 270 other ranks. With regard to aircraft, it had an eclectic and interesting mix of trainers and obsolescent operational types: seventy-eight Hurricanes, eighteen Miles Masters, three Fairey Battles, one de Havilland Dominie, one Tiger Moth and a single Lysander. It was not a small station, but as a new home for the young American now in a war zone, with his own country just entering the conflict and Christmas only a couple of weeks away, inwardly he might have begun to question his situation and his future at this point.

As discussed above, Spitfires and Hurricanes were both single-engine, single-seat fighters designed to do much the same job and, initially at least, with broadly similar performance characteristics. Although the exact dimensions vary from mark to mark, the Hurricane's wingspan was 40 feet with a fuselage of 32 feet while the Spitfire's wingspan was 37 feet and with a length of 30 feet. Both aircraft used the Rolls-Royce Merlin engine, making their cockpits very similar. At this time, directly in front of the pilot, all RAF aircraft used a basic flying panel of six instruments all in the same places, so it was the same in a Spitfire, a Hurricane or a Lancaster, etc. On the top were the airspeed indicator, the artificial horizon, the rate of climb and descent indicator, with the lower row incorporating the altimeter, a direction indicator and a bank and slip indicator. Each had a compass mounted centrally below the panel. In the event of the failure of one or even several instruments, the others could be used to fly the aeroplane. For example, if the artificial horizon failed so that the pilot didn't know the attitude of the aircraft, an unwinding altimeter combined with an increasing airspeed indicates that the machine is diving. Of course, at that time no dual trainers existed (nor were there any simulators) for these fighters so a pilot's first flight in either of these aircraft was solo without the benefit of an instructor to correct any errors. For trainees whose previous experience did not include aircraft with retractable undercarriages, forgetting to lower the undercarriage for landing was common – usually signified by a red Verey light being fired from the control tower or watch office. Of course, the Harvard had a retractable undercarriage so Walcott would have been familiar with this configuration, although, as will be seen, he had his issues when landing.

Soon after arriving in Britain, Bud took off on a training flight in poor weather.[4] He was flying the more powerful Mark II Hurricane, and once aloft several of his instruments became unserviceable. Instead of landing he continued the flight, perhaps trying to fly on the instruments that were still functioning. He flew into cloud and eventually just managed to pull the Hurricane out from a dive shortly before it would have hit the ground. Walcott was said to be impulsive and a risk-taker, and this incident may have been compounded by his own lack of experience and his natural instinct to press on. The ex-operational aeroplanes used as trainers tended to be a bit war weary, and subject to breakdown as well as suffering at the hands of the trainees. Although considered a rest posting for operational pilots, many instructors found the flying at the OTUs more stressful and dangerous than sorties against the enemy. But this wasn't his only black mark while at Crosby.

Once competency in general handling was achieved the course moved on to navigation exercises, and in the early afternoon of Wednesday 28 January 1942, at 14.15, Bud took off in Hurricane Mk I V6573 with the identity number 29 on the fuselage to carry out a local flight which went somewhat awry. An hour and a half later, a lost, cold and anxious Sergeant Walcott, low on fuel, spotted an airfield, which he circled before landing. It turned out to be Collinstown aerodrome, Dublin's airport, in neutral Eire roughly 180 miles the crow flies from Crosby. Irish authorities first sighted the errant Hurricane over County Louth, heading west at 15.36 and then south near the coast at Balbriggan before landing at 15.51 at Dublin. They noted that the aeroplane only had about 12 gallons of fuel left in the tanks, which were showing 'Empty', and that the pilot was 'suffering from the severe cold'.[5] The Irish authorities held Walcott overnight because the decision to release him came after dark.

Dublin Airport opened officially on 19 January 1940, with an iconic terminal building on several floors designed to create the impression of an ocean liner. In those days air travel was out of the ordinary, mainly for the wealthy, and had a romance about it, perhaps not unlike sea travel. The first flight from Dublin was a short hop by Aer Lingus, the Irish national airline, to Liverpool. Because of the war the airport was hardly used, and Walcott would have landed on an airfield that was less than busy, with the only regular activity a twice a week flight to Liverpool. In 1945, flights were resumed to Croydon and gradually extended to the continent and further afield.

The following morning, having had the Hurricane refuelled, Walcott was allowed to depart at 10.20, making for home via the RAF station at Aldergrove in Northern Ireland. A report made by the Irish authorities noted that he did not have a map, a fact that seems quite incredible given he was supposedly on a navigation exercise but again may have been an indicator of Walcott's impulsive, possibly negligent attitude to flying if the report is correct. What these incidents do not suggest is any sense of fear – if anything, he displays a lack of sensible fear, which is dangerous in itself and borders on the reckless. Controlled fear heightens awareness and reaction. Those who claim to have no fear are probably lying, but if not they are placing themselves and their colleagues in real danger if they do not appreciate when discretion should become the better part of valour.

Eire, of course, was neutral and there are conventions as to how members of the armed forces of countries actively at war should be dealt with by neutral states into whose hands they fall. Essentially, aircraft which are armed are held – with their crews – until the end of hostilities, while (as in this case) training aircraft and crew are returned. And this did not apply only to the Second World War. In June 1982 during the British/Argentine war over the Falkland Islands, a Royal Air Force Vulcan bomber was impounded by Brazil after having to make an emergency landing at Rio de Janeiro. The 'Black Buck' operations, as they were called, required the British aircraft to make the long return flight from Ascension Island off the west coast of Africa to the Falklands. This involved multiple mid-air refuellings from multiple tanker aircraft – not easy at the best of times – and on the return trip, the refuelling probe of one of the Vulcans broke so that it could not take on the fuel needed to reach base. Accordingly it diverted into Rio, where it landed safely. However, it had not delivered all its weapons and still had a SHRIKE anti-radar missile on board. (The SHRIKE tracks its way to enemy radars using the radar's own emissions to identify the location of the emission source and destroy it.) Accordingly, the aeroplane was impounded briefly and the missile confiscated. The aircraft, without the missile, returned to the UK but was not cleared to take further part in the conflict.

With the violence of war in the twentieth century, it is ironic that the major powers signed agreements as to how war should be conducted in codes of practice known popularly as 'the Geneva Convention'. In fact, prior to the Second World War, three Conventions had been agreed – in 1864, 1906 and 1929. A fourth was agreed in 1949 after the war ended, together with three subsequent protocols. These agreements and protocols do not deal with the conduct of war but with the treatment of individuals uninvolved in the fighting, including prisoners of war (POWs). One of the best known provisions of the Convention is that a POW should only be required to state name, rank and number and should not be forced to supply military information to his or her captors. The custodian of these agreements is the International Committee of the Red Cross (ICRC), based in Switzerland. Agreements about the use of weapons were set out in the Hague Conventions of 1899 and 1907, with a subsequent protocol. With the general introduction of aircraft into warfare during the First World War, a commission was established at The Hague to draw up rules regarding their use. The commission sat from December 1922 to February 1923 and after due consideration published a set of rules which, although never formally adopted, have been used to provide guidance as to how air power should be exerted. These rules include advice as to how aircraft from belligerent countries are to be treated if they intrude into a neutral country's airspace.

Article 42 includes the paragraph:

A neutral government is bound to employ the means at its disposal to intern every belligerent military aircraft which is found within its jurisdiction after landing or watering for whatever cause, as well as its crew and its passengers, if any.

And included in Article 46:

> A neutral government is bound to use the means at its disposal to:
>
> 1. Prevent the departure from its jurisdiction of an aircraft capable of perpetrating an attack against a belligerent Power, or carrying or accompanied by apparatus or material which could be assembled or utilized in such a way to enable it to perpetrate an attack, if there are reasons to believe that such an aircraft is intended to be utilized against a belligerent Power;
>
> 2. Prevent the departure of an aircraft the crew of which includes any member of the fighting forces of a belligerent Power;

In Walcott's case, he is clearly a 'member of the fighting forces of a belligerent Power' and his aircraft is clearly 'capable of perpetrating an attack against a belligerent Power' because it was equipped with eight Browning machine guns (but without ammunition). However, this might be countered by the fact that it was marked as a trainer and it could be argued that there were no 'reasons to believe that such an aircraft is intended to be utilized against a belligerent Power' although with provision of ammunition it could be employed against the enemy despite its age. There was mention earlier that citizens of other countries wore shoulder flashes denoting where they were from. The Irish report states specifically that Walcott was wearing 'RAF uniform with "U.S.A." on shoulder straps', so clearly he was not afraid to be known as an American.

Again, the changing relationships between countries is relevant; in this case regarding the United Kingdom and Eire (once part of the United Kingdom) but also the United States.

Bitterness engendered by the treatment of the Irish by the British, particularly during the potato famines of the mid-nineteenth century, gave rise to a hatred of the 'English' (probably mistakenly rather than the 'British') and the forming of a significant republican movement in the south, which resulted in the violence of the Easter Rising in 1916. While many Irishmen fought as part of the British Army during the First World War, others fought against it and proclaimed Irish independence. The republican insurgents came from several different groups but the main two were the Irish Volunteers and the Irish Citizen Army. The groups came together under the Military Council of the Irish Republican Brotherhood to organise the rising. Significantly, they gained support in the form of encouragement and the supply of arms from Germany.

In April 1916, a large consignment of weapons, ammunition and explosives intended for the rebels was intercepted by the Royal Navy and the offending ship, *Aud*, escorted to Cork where the crew scuttled it. One of those involved in the enterprise was Sir Roger Casement, born near Dublin in 1864, who served in the British Foreign Office as a consul but became disillusioned because of the ill treatment of the native populations he witnessed at the hands of the British and other colonial powers, particularly Belgium (in the Congo) and by a British-registered rubber company in Peru in South America. He joined the independence movement in Ireland and after the declaration of war between Britain and Germany in 1914 spent some time in Germany negotiating German assistance and trying (unsuccessfully) to raise an army of Irish volunteers from those who had been captured while fighting for the British Army on the Western Front and now languished in POW camps. Despite harbouring doubts about the German commitment to his cause, Casement was put ashore on 21 April 1916 by a German

U-boat at Banna Strand, County Kerry, but was captured soon after by the British and charged with treason, espionage and sabotage. Incarcerated in the Tower of London, he was tried, sentenced to death and ultimately hanged on 3 August 1916. As a member of the 'establishment', his actions and execution caused considerable shock in Britain.

Casement had not, however, been involved in plans that were being made for a major rising in a number of places by the rebels, which was scheduled to start at the end of April 1916. Despite some confusion, which resulted in only minor risings in the hinterland, Dublin was wracked by violence, with several locations being taken over by armed rebels who fought the police and army. The best known was the occupation of the General Post Office (GPO) on Sackville Street at noon on Easter Monday – 24 April – and the Proclamation of Independence read out from the front of the building by Padraig Pearse. One of the other leaders was Éamonn De Valera who commanded the 3rd Battalion, which occupied an area around Lansdowne Road and Northumberland Road. The fighting over the GPO became the stuff of legend.

After days of bitter fighting, the rising was crushed. More than 3,000 men and about eighty women were arrested and, ultimately, sixteen men were executed by the British authorities. One of those who escaped the death penalty was Éamonn De Valera – one reason at least being because he had been born in America and was an American citizen. Britain hoped that the USA would enter the war and did not want to create more anti-British sentiment in its former possession.

But the crushing of the Easter Rising did not crush the desire for independence and the struggle, intensified after the Armistice in 1918. The British employed ex-soldiers to augment the forces of law and order. They became known as the 'Black and Tans' because of the mixture of dark police and khaki army uniforms issued to them. They carried out their work with vicious enthusiasm, their violence creating more and more dissent among those sympathetic to the republican cause until eventually even the king found it necessary to express concern. The result was the creation of the Irish Free State on 6 December 1922, but the country remained a member of the British Commonwealth. Under the agreement with the British government, the six counties in the north of Ireland opted not to become independent but to remain with the United Kingdom, leading to a partition of the island. The relationship between the two 'Irelands' has been uneasy over the years, with a great deal of violence in Northern Ireland as Republicans and Unionists fought in a guerrilla style against each other, with British forces deployed there in 1969 to assist the police keep control. The violence spilled over to the British mainland, with Irish Republican terrorist bombings in London and other English cities, which caused the death and maiming of many innocent civilians. The recent so-called 'peace process' has brought stability and a great reduction in the violence but has not ended the sectarian tensions in the north of Ireland.

When war broke out in 1939, Eire remained neutral, a decision that disappointed the British but hardly came as a surprise. The Irish *Taoiseach* (equivalent to the British Prime Minister) was Éamonn De Valera, the commander of the 3rd Battalion of the rebels during the Easter Rising in 1916. He desired that the policy of neutrality be adopted by the *Oireachtas* (a collective term for the two houses of the legislature which form the parliament) and this came to pass. De Valera considered that neutrality sent a signal to the rest of the world community that Eire was a sovereign state and not just a subsidiary of the United Kingdom. However, in 1939 the bitter civil war was only seventeen years past, and feelings still ran strongly. There was a genuine fear that if Eire allied itself to Britain, another civil war might break out. It wasn't until 1949, when it became a republic, that Eire truly separated from the United Kingdom. In 1939, it still maintained some links with the British Crown and some Britons took the view that Eire should be joining with them in fighting Germany. Within the Irish population, however, there were mixed feelings about the position to be adopted. Despite the violence that had led to independence, many Irish people had sympathies for the British cause and many travelled to Britain to work, with tens of thousands fighting in the British armed forces – although those who left the Irish Army to fight for the British were classified by the government as deserters. After the war, they were denied employment in State organisations and deprived of their pension rights. One famous fighting Irishman was Brendan 'Paddy' Finucane, killed in 1942 as a fighter pilot with the RAF but born in Dublin in 1920.[6] But some Republicans, conscious of the support given to their cause during the First World War, harboured hopes that Germany might once again lend support to the cause of a united Ireland.

Should Eire have decided to side with the Axis, then the threat to Britain from enemy forces based there would have been unacceptable. Plans were drawn up to invade Eire, or at least key parts of it, to deny Germany naval bases and airfields there and to give the British forces improved access to the Atlantic, which would become a major battle zone as the vital convoys moved back and forth between Britain and the American continent. In 1940, the United Kingdom offered the North and the South the guarantee of a united Ireland should neutral Eire join the British cause, but this offer was rejected by the governments of both Irelands.

De Valera appreciated that maintaining absolute neutrality would be difficult. A minority of the population favoured joining the British cause but the majority favoured neutrality. However, in late 1939, Sir John Maffey, born in 1877 and a career civil servant, was appointed as Britain's representative in Dublin – not ambassador for legal reasons – and immediately formed good relations with the *Taoiseach*. Over the years, he would gain small concessions for the British, which chipped away at Eire's neutrality while not compromising it in a major way, although Germany did complain about Irish concessions to the British. The *Luftwaffe* dropped bombs on various locations in Eire during 1940 and 1941, and although they could be attributed to navigational errors, some wondered if they might be warnings against making too many concessions to the United Kingdom. The hard line taken against the Irish Army deserters contrasts with the nods to the British cause given by the Irish administration.

While the immediate concern of this book is Walcott and the actions taken against British military aircraft, many British seafarers found themselves in neutral Eire as well. On the air side, the Irish authorities agreed that British aircraft could fly down what became known as 'the Donegal corridor', a 4-mile strip connecting County Fermanagh in the north to the sea, across County Donegal in the south, saving them the need to make the much longer flight across Northern Ireland's territory to reach the Atlantic Ocean to protect the vital convoys from the USA and Canada.

Incursions into Irish airspace by British and German military aircraft occurred frequently once the war started. The first two British aircraft, both flying boats, a Short Sunderland

and a Saro (Saunders Roe) Lerwick, landed separately in Irish waters on 3 September 1939, the day war was declared by the United Kingdom, and both were allowed to leave unhindered – apparently they were considered to be mariners! In September 1940, a Hurricane of 79 Squadron based at RAF Pembrey in Wales crash-landed in County Wexford after intercepting some Heinkel 111s and its pilot, Flying Officer Paul Mayhew, was interned – he was the first. When Walcott arrived in January 1942 piloting a training aircraft which landed intact, as opposed to crashing, he was allowed to return to Britain.

But Walcott was not a run-of-the-mill British airman. He was American and with the recent entry of America into the war just a few weeks before, the relationship between Eire and Walcott's mother country may have been a factor in how the Irish authorities dealt with the wayward pilot. He was not the only American to find himself in Eire at that time. At 10.30 on 30 November 1941, Spitfire II serial P8074 took off from RAF Eglinton near Londonderry on a convoy patrol. It never returned. The engine overheated to such an extent that the pilot was forced to abandon the aeroplane with the message, 'I'm going over the side.' He landed in the Inishowen peninsula of County Donegal in Eire and was interned. The pilot was twenty-three-year-old Nebraskan Roland Wolfe, a member of 133 Squadron – which, it will be recalled, was one of the Eagle squadrons.

The airmen of all nations who were interned by the Irish authorities were housed in the Curragh Internment Camp and were treated more as 'guests of the State' than prisoners. They were allowed out of the camp if they gave their parole – a promise that they would return and not use their freedom to escape. They were allowed into Dublin once a week. Some were married. Some joined local golf and rugby clubs. German and Allied internees were kept in separate sections but probably met outside the camp, with interesting results!

Wolfe returned to the north while apparently under parole and the British authorities eventually (after two years) decided that he should be returned to the Republic because he was thought to have broken his parole although he maintained that he had not.

Wolfe's situation was markedly different to Walcott's. Firstly, he was on operations. Secondly, his aircraft was destroyed when it came down in Eire and was not flyable. And thirdly, although both were American, Wolfe came down a week before America came into the war while Walcott arrived several weeks after Pearl Harbor.

The relations between Eire and the USA were somewhat strained during the war. In April 1940, David Gray came to Dublin to oversee American interests. Gray was a distant relative of President Roosevelt, his wife Maude being an aunt of the President's wife Eleanor, which gave him an easier access to Roosevelt. Gray was a forceful man who took the view that it was only a matter of time before America was engaged in the struggle against Germany and also that Eire should join the war too or at least actively give its support to the Allies. There was always a desire that ports and airfields in Eire be opened up for use by Allied forces, but, of course, this was unacceptable and led to thoughts on both sides that they might be taken by force. But De Valera continued, at least in public, to expound Eire's neutrality – even if there were concessions to the Allied cause.

Once America came into the war, its interests regarding Eire coincided with those of the British and again pressure was being brought to bear for Eire to become more overtly involved. But again, De Valera could not do this. On 26 January 1942, the first

American troops landed in Northern Ireland. The Irish protested and demanded to know what they would be used for – some fearing they might invade the south, and some expressing Eire's view that Northern Ireland was their territory. The protest was dismissed. Some on the British side had thought that the replacement of British troops in Northern Ireland with Americans might make relations easier, but this does not seem to have been the case.

Two days after the American troops landed in the north, Bud Walcott landed at Dublin. There is a suggestion that the decision to release Bud was taken by De Valera himself,[7] but this has not been independently verified. It has been interpreted by some as a signal that De Valera did not wish to unduly upset the Americans following the landing of their troops in the north two days before.

Walcott's service records do not mention the incident, nor do the Operations Record Books of 59 OTU or other stations to which he may have returned, such as RAF Aldergrove. No records of a court of inquiry have been found, nor anything to suggest that Walcott was sanctioned, although it seems likely that he would receive at least a 'dressing down'. It is of note that the incident had been treated as merely an unfortunate mistake – a navigational error – and in conjunction with the comment at Aylmer he had been 'weak in Navigation' there is nothing to imply any dishonourable motive in his actions. Certainly, on the point of being sent to an operational squadron after more than a year of training, there would be no question of him being 'scrubbed' or re-mustered on the strength of what appears to have been a genuine mistake.

It was reported that Walcott landed at Collinstown at 15.52. At 20.10 that night, Colonel Liam Archer, the Assistant Chief of Staff, phoned Commandant William Delemere, the Officer Commanding Baldonnel airfield, which was the headquarters of the Air Corps.

He instructed that the pilot and the aircraft be released 'first thing' the following morning. The Hurricane was to be refuelled and serviced and the pilot provided with a map, a course to Aldergrove in Northern Ireland and a weather forecast. The map was on loan from the Irish authorities and was to be returned by post![8] It isn't known if it ever was.

Walcott was detained overnight in Portobello Barracks (now Cathal Brugha Barracks) in Dublin. It had been intended that he would be escorted to the Curragh Internment Camp by Captain Fitzpatrick of G2 Staff Eastern Command, to be detained but it was noted that later instructions were requested from a higher authority – possibly because Walcott was American. It therefore seems likely that De Valera might very well have been consulted on what was to be done and gave the necessary instructions.

Yet again, and in a very personal way, Walcott's life and future had been affected by factors out of his control and possibly with the direct influence of presidents and governments.

The Irish authorities produced a formal internal report[9] which is appended, but it is worthwhile quoting the relevant section:

He [Walcott] stated that he had been on a local flight from Cumberland from 14.15 hrs. and had lost his bearings. He also stated that he was running short of petrol, (there was approximately 12 gallons left in the tanks at the time of landing and the tank indicators were already pointing to zero) and suffering from the severe cold when he landed at Dublin Airport.

The airman was detained overnight and after refuelling was permitted to depart...

There is nothing in the report to suggest that Walcott requested any sort of asylum or appealed to be returned to the United States. If he had, it would have been recorded and discussed at length. Irish military intelligence, G2, took a great interest in the morale of the fighting aircrew and such a request would have been noted.

RAF pilots (including those of other nationalities serving with the RAF or other air forces associated with Britain) whose aircraft were flyable were clearly allowed to return from Ireland, while those whose aircraft proved inoperable were detained. Americans flying with American military units were not detained and German airmen were all detained. It was deemed that Americans were not likely to have been on operational flights, while Germans would have been. Most British internees were released before the war ended, while the German internees were only released after the war ended. The difference in the treatment of the airmen illustrates the attitude of the Irish government towards the three belligerent countries whose personnel were involved.

As far as the RAF was concerned, Bud's landing at Dublin appears to have been taken as nothing other than an unfortunate mistake and was quickly forgotten as Bud continued with his training, completing it a few weeks later.

On 14 March 1942 Bud Walcott was posted to his first operational squadron – 603 (City of Edinburgh) Squadron, Auxiliary Air Force, then flying Spitfire Vs and coming to the end of a rest period at RAF Peterhead on Scotland's north-east coast. He didn't stay long. Thirty-seven days later, he departed the squadron with his reputation badly damaged.

# 6

# OPERATIONS AND CONTROVERSY

The Royal Air Force formed on 1 April 1918 with the amalgamation of the British Army's Royal Flying Corps and the Navy's Royal Naval Air Service, both essentially tactical forces acting in support of their parent services rather than in strategic roles. With technological advances in flying towards the end of the First World War, the opportunities (and dangers) posed by heavy bombers were becoming clearer and the value of an independent air arm more apparent.

To bolster its regular regiments, the British Army used reservists, Territorials, and had done so for some time. The Territorial and Reserve Forces Act passed through Parliament in 1907 and the Air Force (Constitution) Act of November 1917, which established the Royal Air Force, included a provision to allow the creation of an auxiliary air force. Over the following years, the pros and cons of establishing a reserve-based supplement to the RAF were argued but in July 1924, The Auxiliary Air Force and Air Force Reserves Act extended the provisions of the Territorial and Reserve Forces Act to include an Auxiliary Air Force and the first squadrons formed the following year, 1925.

The Act made provision for two types of units: special reserve squadrons and auxiliary squadrons. The former were to be numbered in the 500 series and the latter in the 600 series. The two types of squadrons were structured differently, with the special reserve squadrons having a significantly greater number of regular personnel than the auxiliary units, which had only a small nucleus of regular staff with by far the greater being reservists – including the commanding officers. As discussed earlier, the concept was that the squadrons would be sited near centres of population from which they would recruit their members and they would be trained to the same standard as regular squadrons. In the early days, an aspiring auxiliary pilot had to hold a private pilot's licence. The conditions of service for other ranks gave them the assurance that they would never be called upon to serve further than 5 miles from their home airfield – a condition that seems incredibly optimistic even in 1925 – and also that they would have to give their permission to be posted away from their unit.

Officers and airmen signed up for a minimum of four years, during which time they were trained at weekends and during evening drill nights. The officers were drawn from the professional and landed classes, with other ranks from the so-called working classes. While territorial units of the army operated from compact drill halls in the towns, it almost goes without saying that as operational flying units, the squadrons each needed an airfield, usually on the outskirts of the town or city to which the squadron had its affiliation. However, this created a problem in that for the drill nights, travelling to the squadron airfield was time-consuming and costly. Few had cars and for the ordinary airmen in particular it meant using public transport that might not even extend as far as the airfield, costing money and impinging on working hours.

Accordingly, each squadron acquired a town headquarters near the centre of the city, far more accessible and thus convenient for the evening training periods but also put to use at weekends.

The plans envisaged eventually twenty auxiliary squadrons but to start with, only five – two based in the London area, one in the Midlands and two in Scotland located near to Edinburgh and Glasgow. The first of the new part-time units formed on 15 May 1925; it was 502 (Ulster) Squadron, a special reserve unit. Four months later, on 15 September 1925, the first of the auxiliary squadrons formed – 602 (City of Glasgow) Squadron – and a month later, on 14 October 1925, three others formed: 600 (City of London), 601 (County of London) and 603 (City of Edinburgh) Squadron. The latter was the squadron Walcott was about to join.

Over many years Edinburgh, which is Scotland's capital, and Glasgow, which is Scotland's largest city, have enjoyed a rivalry, and this was taken up by the two squadrons although without real rancour. Of course, 602 stole a march on 603 by being the first auxiliary squadron to form, but over the years 603 has had its moments as well – as will be seen. Until just before the start of the Second World War the squadrons flew light bombers, with 603 based at Turnhouse, an existing RAF airfield just to the west of Edinburgh and which, in an expanded form, is now Edinburgh Airport. RAF Turnhouse closed following the end of the Cold War and its facilities were used to handle cargo. Sadly, most of the military buildings have been demolished and virtually nothing remains of the historic station.

Despite the horrors of the First World War, young men flocked to join. For some it was 'the thing to do' but it also provided an interest with the opportunity to travel and of course, for the airmen, the opportunity of a trip – rather than load ballast to keep the aeroplane's centre of gravity within safe limits, pilots would sometimes order a passing erk (a male member of the RAF of the lowest rank) to hop in while the aeroplane was tested. In the 1920s and 30s, flying was fashionable and glamorous. The exploits of aviators such as Amy Johnson, Jim Mollison (a Scot) and Charles Lindbergh, who flew the Atlantic solo in 1927, captured the imagination of the general public and generated interest in the RAF and of course the reservists too. The populations of Edinburgh and Glasgow saw the silver aircraft of their squadrons flying over their cities and identified with them and felt they owned them. But for these two squadrons of the AuxAF, as well as their close relationship with the cities, there was an added dimension – their 'Scottishness', which was stimulated and encouraged by the pedigreed Douglas-Hamilton family and the Dukes of Hamilton.

The Duke of Hamilton is the senior Scottish peer, traditionally the bearer of the monarch's crown and the 'Keeper of the Palace of Holyroodhouse', the official residence of the monarch in Scotland. Alfred, the 13th Duke of Hamilton, and his wife Nina had seven children – four boys and three girls. The boys were Douglas, born in 1903; Geordie, born in 1906; Malcolm, born in 1909; and David, born in 1912, and they hold a unique position in Scottish and indeed British history in that they all served with the RAF during the Second World War with the rank of squadron leader or above. Douglas was the Marquis of Douglas and Clydesdale, known as 'Lord Clydesdale', but on the death of his father in 1940 became the 14th Duke of Hamilton and the 11th Duke of Brandon. As a young man, he became fascinated by flying, became an officer and a pilot in the Auxiliary Air Force and the Commanding Officer of 602 (City of Glasgow) Squadron from 1932 until 1936. During his tenure of command, in 1933, he led an expedition to be the first to fly over Mount Everest in an especially designed Westland PV-3 aircraft. Despite immense difficulties and dangers, the expedition was successful.

The family left its mark on 602 and 603 Squadrons. Douglas's three brothers were also intensely interested in aviation and all qualified as pilots. As well as Lord Clydesdale's command of 602 Squadron, between 1934 and 1938, the second son Geordie served as OC of 603. Both squadrons had pipe bands, and in 1933 King George V gave permission for the bands to wear the kilt and full regalia, the 13th Duke having given permission for them to wear the Grey Douglas tartan. But many of the squadron officers – particularly those in 602 and Lord Clydesdale – wished to adopt the kilt as part of their mess dress and application was made for this to be permitted. On 8 July 1936, His Majesty King Edward VIII, himself a qualified pilot, agreed that 'Officers of the Scottish Auxiliary Air Force Squadrons' could wear kilts with mess dress although it was optional and the uniform firmly specified: jackets and waistcoats were to be normal RAF pattern and the kilt 'Grey Douglas Tartan – military pleating'. 602 Squadron officers first wore their new mess kit in 1937.

Later in the war, in May 1941, Douglas, by now the Duke of Hamilton, was involved in the rather curious affair of Rudolf Hess, Hitler's deputy. In 1936, Douglas, as one of a group of British Members of Parliament, attended the Berlin Olympic Games where he met many of the German leaders, although not Hess. However, Hess decided, apparently on his own initiative, to try to reach some sort of a peace agreement with Britain and decided that the Duke of Hamilton should be his first contact. Also a qualified pilot, Hess unofficially flew a *Luftwaffe* Messerschmitt Bf110 to west central Scotland, bailing out near Eaglesham in

Lanarkshire and the Duke's residence at Dungavel. His mission was unsuccessful. He was held as a prisoner for the duration of the war and was eventually tried at Nuremburg along with the other surviving Nazi leaders. Found guilty, he was sentenced to life imprisonment and died in Spandau prison in Berlin in 1987 – its only remaining inmate.

For 603 Squadron, the 1930s were somewhat of a golden era. The squadron was performing well and the town headquarters saw much socialising – dinners, dances and parties. Indeed, on New Year's Eve 1933, it hosted a party with 200 guests – it must have been a glittering occasion. Of course, there were domestic facilities at Turnhouse so the members of the unit had the best of both worlds. Parties and dances were not limited to the officers but were held by the sergeants' mess and the junior ranks as well. But despite this, there was a strong social divide between the officers and the other ranks and the two rarely mixed. For some, their civilian lives were poles apart. It is fair to say that an AC2 working as a labourer living in Leith, Edinburgh's ancient port, and a flying officer lawyer working and living in Edinburgh's gracious New Town would probably have little idea as to how the other lived. And in the earlier days, some of the officers were part of the landed gentry. Even after the social levelling of the Second World War, when former members of the squadron met, the old ranks remained very much in their consciousness with officers calling the airmen by their last names and the airmen standing straight when being addressed. Of course, the social divisions within the squadron only reflected the social divisions prevalent in the society of the time. Individuals tended to 'know their place' and it was difficult to move from one social stratum to another. This does not mean that the officers had no concern for their men – in most cases quite the reverse. For example, George Denholm was 603's OC during the Battle of Britain and was affectionately known as 'Uncle George' on account of his age and his concern for the men under his command. But there was little social intercourse between the officers and the airmen. Only a few months before Walcott joined 603, when the squadron was based in the south of England, some pubs near the station were earmarked for officers and others for the other ranks and as late as 1945, one officer pilot, himself a former NCO, said that the only time he mixed with NCO pilots was 'down at the flights', that is when they were on duty.

On the outbreak of war in September 1939, the officers included five members of the legal profession, five employed in accountancy, a surgeon, two bankers, a timber merchant and a sheep farmer – all relatively well off. The other ranks also had an interesting range of occupations – a chemist, a joiner, a baker, a brass finisher, an optician and an ink maker, to name only a few. In a small town like Edinburgh with a population of less than one million, it is likely that members of the same profession would have professional contact away from the squadron – particularly the lawyers. And many of the airmen knew each other because they lived in the same parts of the town. Because the airmen auxiliaries did not routinely transfer to other units, they developed a closeness and *esprit de corps* that was enhanced for 602 and 603 by the official acknowledgement of their Scottishness with the wearing of the tartan. Consequently once the original auxiliary officers of the pre-war era had either been killed, injured or posted away to be replaced by others with no direct connection to the units, the essential character and spirit of the squadrons was maintained by the other ranks, the ground crews or as they were known, service echelons, who nourished it until matters normalised after the end of the war. 603 experienced a period of several months in 1942 when it had no pilots or aircraft and consisted of only the service echelon, which for that time *was* the squadron. But those who were posted into the squadrons readily adopted the auxiliary values and connections. One pilot of 602 Squadron – the Glasgow squadron – said that in 1945, they sang 'I belong to Glasgow' with gusto despite the fact that few of them had ever been there.

They were units proud of their origins. By the outbreak of the war, both were fighter squadrons. 602 again pipped the 603 by being equipped with the latest fighter, the Spitfire, before 603, which received its Spitfires shortly after war was declared. But in the early afternoon of 16 October 1939, both squadrons were involved in repulsing the first attack by the *Luftwaffe* against Britain when each shot down a Junkers Ju88 attempting to bomb Royal Navy ships moored in the Firth of Forth just east of the iconic rail bridge – the first two German aircraft to be brought down in British airspace. Both Ju88s came down at much the same time and there has been controversy over the years as to which was the first, with 603 generally being credited with this honour – although this is fiercely disputed by 602 to this day. Two weeks later, the two reservist squadrons were both involved in the bringing down of the first enemy aircraft onto British soil – a Heinkel He111, which crashed in East Lothian near Edinburgh and became known as 'the Humbie Heinkel'. Flight Lieutenant Patrick Gifford, mentioned previously as having an American mother, was involved in both these operations.

Both squadrons fought in the Battle of Britain in 1940, and in the summer and autumn of 1941 603 took part in many operations across the English Channel to France. These involved several squadrons of fighters escorting small numbers of bombers against industrial targets – power stations and the like. The squadrons were primarily intended to draw up enemy fighters and some tough fighting ensued. Of course, the British fighters found themselves in a role reversal to the previous summer when they had been on the defensive and the *Luftwaffe* the attackers. On an operation in December 1941, 603 Squadron lost three pilots – one killed and two taken prisoner – and it was decided that it should be sent north for recuperation to a less active sector at RAF Dyce near Aberdeen, now Aberdeen airport, in the north-east of Scotland. Only two days after arriving at Dyce, the OC Squadron Leader Roger Forshaw was killed during an attempted dusk interception over the North Sea, to be replaced by one of the flight commanders – Squadron Leader Lord David Douglas-Hamilton, the youngest of the four sons of the 13th Duke of Hamilton and the second of the four brothers to command 603.

By the summer of 1941, all of the pilots who had been on the squadron strength in 1939 were gone – killed, injured or posted elsewhere. The only pilot in 1941 who had been with 603 in 1939 was Flight Lieutenant Bill Douglas, and at that time he had been only a trainee. The remainder of the current complement were replacements new to the squadron. Some were regulars and some reservists. Some, like Walcott, came from other countries. But the service echelon – the ground crews – was relatively unchanged and the essential spirit of the squadron resided with them and would do until the end of the war in 1945. Having fought over the Channel for many months over the summer and autumn of 1941, when it moved north, 603 was a battle-hardened and tough unit – albeit resting. But rather than resting as one, many of the pilots were posted elsewhere and replaced, in some cases by inexperienced newcomers. Lord David himself was relatively inexperienced in combat, having only flown his first operational sortie a few weeks before the move north. He was a tall, powerful man with an air of authority. He had been a Scottish heavyweight boxing international and captain of the Oxford University boxing team. Having qualified as a pilot, he suffered disappointment in being posted to instructor's duties and was only posted to 603 as a flight commander on 20 November 1941 with no operational experience. A week later, he took part in his first operation in flak suppression support of Hurricanes of 607 Squadron attacking a German convoy in the English Channel. There was plenty of action and Lord David at last enjoyed the feelings of exhilaration and satisfaction experienced after such activity. He would rise superbly to the demands of unexpected command.

603 Squadron moved to RAF Peterhead from Dyce on 14 March 1941 – the day that Walcott was posted. In a bleak and windswept corner of Scotland, Peterhead is primarily a fishing port. In the latter half of twentieth century, with fishing in decline, it became a base for servicing the North Sea oil and gas industry and in the early 1980s an oil/gas power station was built just outside the town and near the Victorian prison, to which the town also lends its name. The land to the west is flat, allowing the chilly east winds from Scandinavia and further afield to whip across it all the way to the mountains of the central Highlands. In winter, when the weather includes sleet and snow, it can be quite miserable. The airfield, RAF Peterhead, lies a few miles to the west of the town on the coastal plain near the village of Longside and was opened incomplete on 19 July 1941, built to the austere requirements of

wartime – that is, basic brick-built buildings with few luxuries. It had a complement of more than seventy officers (including nine WAAFs) and almost 1,400 airmen and women, responsible for keeping about forty aircraft flying. Although many of the buildings were demolished, in 1999 it was still being used by helicopters and it is still quite clearly seen.

Quite what Bud made of his first operational appointment can only be surmised. The weather was cold and uncomfortable. At the beginning of March, 'A bitterly cold wind and periodical falls of snow made Dyce a very unpleasant place.' And on the day of the squadron move, although the service echelon arrived, only five of the squadron's Spitfires managed to land because of thick fog, which covered the land and continued to do so for several days.

After the relative comfort and beauty of Crosby-on-Eden, Walcott found himself in a harsh landscape in spartan conditions, a rookie who was going to have prove himself in combat. But first he had to be declared operational by the squadron, which meant receiving his final training and assessment by his new colleagues. By now, 603 flew Spitfire VB aeroplanes. Although moved north to recuperate, it continued as an operational unit carrying out duties as and when required although the pace was much slower than in the south of England. With weather systems moving from west to east, the British were able to observe the weather conditions passing over their heads to forecast what might be encountered over Germany while the Germans had to carry out weather recces over Britain to find out what might be coming their way. A Heinkel He111 carrying out such duties flew regularly up the east coast of Scotland becoming known as 'Weather Wullie'. It became almost a matter of honour for 603 to intercept and bring down Weather Wullie, but they never managed! However, this and other operational sorties against the occasional bombers attacking shipping in relatively benign conditions helped to break in the new pilots. During the Battle of Britain, the shortage was of pilots as opposed to aeroplanes and as matters became more desperate, new pilots were thrown into the fight with fewer and fewer hours. On occasions, a young pilot would arrive on a squadron and be killed or seriously injured before having had the chance to unpack his kit.

Bud was promoted to flight sergeant on 25 March, but things did not go well for him. Two weeks after his arrival and the day after his promotion, 26 March, he and one of the more experienced pilots, Pilot Officer William Jones, collided over the airfield at 11.15 and Jones died. There are few facts available. Jones was flying Spitfire BL510 (XT-D), a new aeroplane that had been taken on charge on 27 December 1941. The weather on the day at nearby Dyce to the south was reasonable – 8/10 or 9/10 cloud above 3,000 feet with visibility of 20 to 30 miles except for some hazy patches where it fell to about 4,000 yards. There was a light northwesterly wind.[1]

Whether the two men were operating together or separately isn't known. They may have been in close formation and touched, or they may both have arrived independently over the airfield at the same time. Walcott survived; Jones died. Walcott's records make no mention of the incident, either to state that he attended the sick bay or that there was any comeback on him. No records of an inquiry have been found and no official blame attaches to Walcott, nor to Jones. It seems that Walcott could bring his Spitfire down while Jones's aeroplane was struck off charge, irreparably damaged. It is reported that it broke up in a dive.

Pilot Officer Jones was buried two days after the accident at nearby Longside Cemetery.[2] He was nineteen years of age, an American in the RCAF like Walcott. His parents lived in Kansas City, Missouri.

On the day of the funeral, 603 Squadron was classified as non-operational pending movement overseas, and another phase in its history and in Walcott's life came to an end.

If no official blame was attached to Walcott, for some within the squadron there was little doubt as to where the fault lay and little sympathy for the survivor. Long after the war, one commentator wrote that it would have been better if the result of the accident had been that Walcott should have been the one to die because he was to dishonour to the squadron in the future. With such sentiments, Walcott must have, at the very least, been able to sense a dislike from some in the squadron, and it can have done little to bolster his confidence and attitude to what lay ahead.

When squadrons moved bases, if the new base was within range of the squadron's aircraft, the pilots normally flew their aeroplanes to it while the ground crew travelled by road, rail or in transport aircraft. If going further afield, both the air and service echelons travelled together – on troopships if the new posting was to some distant land. But this move was different. It was all very secret, and it involved one highly unusual ingredient: the pilots would be travelling without their ground crews. After embarkation leave, they were ordered to report to RAF Abbotsinch near Glasgow at 20.30 on Sunday 12 April 1942 and then, in the dark, taken by bus to Port Glasgow on the River Clyde where they found the towering bulk of an aircraft carrier awaiting them. Unusually, it turned out to be American, the USS *Wasp*, and more questions were raised when 603 found that there was another group of pilots aboard – from 601 (County of London) Squadron. They were not accompanied by their service echelon either. The pilots boarded and were shown to their cabins, which many had to share. As it turned out, the service echelon embarked for a long sea journey around the South African Cape of Good Hope to Egypt whence it was intended that they would make their way to Malta and rejoin the pilots but in the end, this group of pilots never met up with their ground crews again.

Both squadrons needed to be reinforced. Pilots were posted in to replace those who had been transferred elsewhere and some joined their new units at Abbotsinch just as they were about to embark. This further diluted the experience and cohesion of the unit but in some cases the new arrivals brought valuable experience with them. Flight Sergeant Jack Rae, a New Zealander, was one of those who joined 603. He volunteered to join the Royal New Zealand Air Force on the outbreak of war and, like Walcott, did some of his flying training in Canada before being shipped to the UK. Posted to 485 Squadron flying Spitfires, he had forty-seven operational sorties under his belt and was credited with an FW190 'kill', four 'probables' and two 'damaged'.

The pilots would not have been human if they did not discuss what was happening. The circumstances generated rumour and speculation and not a little apprehension. The film star Douglas Fairbanks Jnr was one of the ship's officers, and this would lend a frisson of excitement to the proceedings – but of course the main concern would be to learn what was to happen to them. The ship remained docked overnight until, at 10.00 on Monday 13 April, it slipped its moorings and almost immediately touched a screw on a sandbank, requiring it to return to Greenock. Finally, at 06.00 on the Tuesday morning, it departed the Clyde.

Being vulnerable to attack, aircraft carriers are usually the centrepiece of a carrier group because they need to be protected. In addition to its escort of US Navy destroyers *Madison* and *Lang*, *Wasp* collected a number of Royal Navy ships – the battleship *Renown* and the destroyers *Inglefield*, *Echo*, *Partridge* and *Ithuriel*, with the carrier group becoming designated 'Force W'. Wednesday 15 April found the group steaming south through the Irish Sea in overcast and dank conditions, which at least would help prevent them being spotted by the enemy. By this time, if they had not already seen them for themselves, the pilots would know that the hangars of the carrier held a number of brand-new Spitfire VC aeroplanes – tropicalised and painted light and dark brown in the standard RAF camouflage pattern used for desert areas. But any uncertainty didn't last long. On 15 April, they were summoned to a briefing and told that their destination was Malta.

It is quite reasonable to argue that Malta is and always has been the key to the Mediterranean Sea. An archipelago of many islands, before the last ice age they were part of a land bridge connecting Sicily to North Africa. The group takes its name from the largest island, Malta, which lies at a latitude of 35° north and longitude 14° east, with Gozo to the north-west and the smaller Comino lying in a channel between the two. These three, the only inhabited islands, lie on a northwest–southeast axis with a distance of more than 26 miles from the northern tip of Gozo to the southerly edge of Malta, which on its own is 16.8 miles long and 8 miles across its widest point. But it is its position that makes it so important as a strategic base. It is 60 miles from the southern coast of Sicily, 1,000 miles from Gibraltar at the western end of the Mediterranean and 960 miles from Alexandria in Egypt at the eastern end. The main island is relatively flat with the highest point 830 feet above the sea near Dingli on its western side.

In ancient times, Malta was pivotal for the Greeks, Phoenicians, Romans, Egyptians, Carthaginians and, in later times, the British whose power centred on the great sea that provided the basic communications of the time – shipping. Trade, war and power flowed from the naval force of whichever empire possessed supremacy. Archaeological remains suggest that it was first inhabited by stone age hunters or farmers, who came across from Sicily about 5,000 BC but who disappeared about 2,500 BC having fallen victim to disease or famine, although curiously this is the same period that claims the disappearance of the mythological maritime city of Atlantis. The stone age inhabitants were replaced by another group of immigrants who lived on the islands until about 700 BC, when Greeks arrived, settling the area around what is now the capital, Valetta, to be joined 100 years later by Phoenicians, who lived in the area of Mdina and Rabat. The Phoenicians established a colony in North Africa at Carthage, near modern-day Tunis, and about 400 BC after the fall of Phoenicia, the Carthaginians gained control of Malta until 264 BC when the people rose up against their rulers to give the Romans control as part of the province of Sicily. It thrived under the Romans and in time became important to followers of Christianity as the site of the shipwreck of St Paul on his way to Rome to be tried. With the decline of the Roman Empire, control was taken by the Byzantine Empire administered from Constantinople until the ninth century although it is thought that during this period it fell briefly to the Germanic tribes. In 909, the Arabian dynasty of the Fatimids took control of Malta as part of the Emirate of Sicily, bringing improved irrigation methods and introducing new fruit and cotton. It was during this period that the distinctive small, low-walled fields that remain to this day were built. The custom of building these low walls would influence the battles of the Second World War – they would make it hard for an invader to land gliders but also for British pilots trying to land their damaged aircraft.

Rulers came and went, with the common factor of the link to Sicily continuing. In 1091, the Normans under Roger I conquered Sicily and Malta, and both became part of the Kingdom of Sicily, which extended from the archipelago in the south to the mainland of Italy in the north. Roman Catholicism became the official religion. But in 1194, Malta became part of the Germanic Holy Roman Empire after which its fortunes waxed and waned. Eventually, in the fifteenth century, it passed to the Aragonese and to the Spanish crown. Over the years, Malta was influenced by many different cultures, which can be seen in the differing forms and styles of architecture on the island, but for many of these years it was linked to Sicily, with resultant ties in family and culture.

In 1530, Malta was given to the Knights of the Order of St John in perpetuity and this was to become one the periods of its history most widely known. The Knights have their origins in an Order of Hospitallers established in Jerusalem during the eleventh century, providing care for sick pilgrims making the difficult journey to the Holy Lands. With the conquest of Jerusalem in 1099 during the First Crusade, it became a Catholic military order. Like many wars based on religion, little mercy was shown on either side and the fighting and its aftermath could be extremely brutal. As the Muslims recovered the Holy Land, the Order found itself pushed back to the island of Rhodes in 1310 where it remained until

1530 when, again, the Ottomans forced it further west to Malta, where it settled through the generosity of Charles I of Spain. But the Knights found little peace as the Ottoman Empire continued to expand and set its sights on Malta.

The Ottoman Empire replaced the Byzantines and lasted from 1301 until 1922 – one of the most enduring empires in history replacing another. Inspired by Islam and based on a strict Islamic warrior code, the Ottomans expanded over much of the eastern Mediterranean and as far north as Vienna. But the Ottomans took a pragmatic view in order to increase their power and influence, encouraging the co-operation of non-Islamic faiths and peoples while maintaining Islam as central to their philosophy. The Empire became very powerful, and, with a strong navy to dominate the Mediterranean, possession of Malta became desirable, positioned as it is astride the sea routes.

The Knights and the Turks had been fighting for many years during the Crusades – Christianity against Islam. In 1557, the Knights elected a new Grand Master, Jean Parisot de Valette, who, following the defeat of a Christian fleet in a naval battle off the Tunisian island of Djerba in 1560, ordered that the defences of the island should be improved in anticipation of an attack. Five years later, the attack came. Turkish forces arrived off Malta in May, landing on the island and over weeks capturing several of the Knights' fortresses. But de Valette was a cunning and wise commander and after a bloody and vicious campaign, the Turks lost heart and withdrew in September. Casualties on both sides were high but are difficult to quantify accurately. It is said that the Knights lost a third of their number, as did the population of the island. The siege became one of the most famous military actions in history; although it did not stop the expansion of the Ottoman Empire, it at least showed that the

Ottomans were not invincible. De Valette died in 1568. The present capital of Malta was named after him – Valletta.

The Knights controlled Malta for more than 200 years but as their power declined, they became unpopular and their autocratic rule became resented by significant numbers of the population and within the Order. Napoleon was asked to expel the Knights and in 1798, he captured the island and sailed on to Egypt, leaving a large garrison. But the French engendered such hatred by their religious attitudes and their pillaging to fund Napoleon's war that the people rebelled, and with the help of a Royal Navy blockade, the French were forced to surrender in 1800. The Maltese asked that the island become a British dominion and it served as a valued British strategic naval base until well into the twentieth century and beyond the end of the Second World War.

As in the past, it was Malta's position in the centre of the Mediterranean that made it so important to the British. With India the jewel in the crown of the British Empire, an unhindered passage through the Mediterranean to Egypt and the Suez Canal avoided the lengthy alternative voyage around the Cape of Good Hope. Combined with the naval bases in Gibraltar to the west and Alexandria to the east, Britain could exert power via the Royal Navy. In the years prior to the outbreak of the Second World War, the Mediterranean therefore seemed relatively benign as far as Britain was concerned. With France as an ally controlling North Africa, the northern and southern coasts were friendly. Italy's intentions were unknown but not overtly threatening, although Libya was under Italian control. Spain had a right-wing dictatorship sympathetic to Germany but not in itself a threat unless it allowed Germany the use of Spanish ports in the Mediterranean, which might swing the balance. To the east, Greece and the other states in the region were not perceived as threats. To reach the world's oceans from the Mediterranean, ships must either traverse the Suez Canal in the east or the Straits of Gibraltar in the west, and Britain could control them both from their naval bases at Alexandria and Gibraltar respectively. The development of aircraft helped countries like Britain project power more effectively and as far as Malta was concerned, air power became key.

But suddenly, the balance of power changed. With the surrender of France in 1940 and the creation of Vichy France as a supposedly neutral state, the western Mediterranean became a potential battle area. After the destruction of the French fleet at Oran, relationships between Britons and many Frenchmen became bitter.

Malta's population in 1940 numbered about 130,000, and while they had enjoyed a co-operative and friendly relationship with the British (English became the main language), there were family ties to Sicily 60 miles to the north, and indeed to Italy itself too. These ties created conflicts of loyalty for some when Italy declared war on Britain on 11 June 1940. The declaration came at a difficult time for Britain, whose main efforts were concentrated on events closer to home. The Italian dictator *Il Duce*, Benito Mussolini, judged that it was time to throw in his lot with Hitler and immediately started to bomb the island from his bases in Sicily. With the prospect of an invasion of Britain looming, Malta's defences were few and its air defence left to three obsolete naval Gloster Gladiator fighters, known as 'Faith', 'Hope' and 'Charity'. These were biplanes reminiscent of aeroplanes used during the First World War. They were also used by the RAF and, curiously, were the last RAF fighters to have fixed undercarriages and the first to have enclosed cockpits.

But there was more. Royal Navy ships had a series of engagements with ships of the Italian navy, and Italian troops moved east from Libya against the British in Egypt so that the deserts of North Africa became battlegrounds, with Malta the linchpin. For British ships traversing the Mediterranean east/west, it provided shelter and restocking. For Italian (and eventually) German shipping moving north/south to support the armies in North Africa, it became a vital British base to harry and attack by air and sea.

When Germany invaded the Soviet Union in 1941, there was a risk that they might push east and south through Middle Eastern countries east of the Mediterranean and join up with Axis forces from North Africa should they defeat the British in Egypt. This would then have exposed the routes to India, and once Japan entered the war in December 1941, the possibility of German and Italian forces joining up with Japanese forces coming through Burma exercised British military minds. Britain had to prevail in North Africa and it would be well-nigh impossible to achieve this without Malta. But 1941 brought with it the invasion of Greece by Italy and then the capture of Crete, driving the British to Egypt and leaving Malta even more isolated.

The bombing of Malta was unrelenting and not limited to military targets. Many of the old fortresses dating back to the days of the Knights were damaged or destroyed. The local population suffered dreadfully as well, with many killed or injured and their homes destroyed. But Malta endured, although the sympathies of some of the locals were, understandably, not with the British. For those with family links to Italy, the dangers and hardships they were enduring did little to further their lives or futures. Some resorted to sabotage – from time to time sugar was poured into the petrol tanks of RAF aircraft. Security was compromised; one pilot recounted being out with one of the local girls one evening who told him that they would be receiving new call-signs the next day – which they did. The airfields lacked strong perimeter fencing and it was found that silk was being stolen from parachutes. In some cases, the thief replaced it with brown paper, which of course meant that if a pilot needed to use it, it was useless. Several pilots said that each morning they would check that their parachutes were intact and then never leave them unattended during the day. Matters reached a head when the station commander at Ta'Qali, ordered that a gibbet be erected with a stark warning that anyone caught stealing parachute silk would be hanged – but once this became known in London, he was ordered to remove it. It is a rather unedifying aspect of the siege of Malta and in some contrast to the popular image of the brave little George Cross island. Axis intelligence-gathering was rife and often initiatives were known to the enemy in plenty of time for them to react. With airfields in Sicily only a few minutes' flying time away, the defenders on Malta were nearly always disadvantaged. Both the Italian air force, the *Regia Aeronautica,* and the *Luftwaffe* operated over Malta although their strengths varied from time to time – when Germany invaded the Soviet Union in 1941, *Luftwaffe* units in Sicily were pulled away to the Eastern Front.

The Italians gained a reputation for surrendering easily but this was probably a consequence of inferior equipment and not a lack of courage. Bob Sergeant flew on Malta with 249 Squadron (and with 603 Squadron over Europe in 1945) during the heaviest fighting and he commented that some of the Italian fighters performed very well and in the hands of competent pilots were a real match for the RAF and its experienced pilots.

Malta became more isolated; food and emergency supplies ran low. Convoys from Gibraltar and Alexandria, which attempted to fight their way through, were ravaged by the enemy – and both the civilian population and the military were living at subsistence levels. Conditions were dreadful. Many succumbed to a kind of gastroenteritis, which became known as 'Malta dog' or more simply 'the dog'. It was debilitating and unpleasant and clearly prevented the pilots from flying while afflicted.

Without air defences, sooner or later Malta would fall. During 1941 Hawker Hurricanes were the air defence mainstay but replacing losses posed a headache. For most of the siege, the nearest British airfields were Gibraltar in the west and Egypt in the east, well beyond the range of the single-engine fighters. For long-distance transport to other theatres, such aircraft were usually taken by sea in crates that contained the main components of a single aircraft already completed (fuselage, mainplanes etc.) and, in simplistic terms, ready to be bolted together. But with the high proportion of losses being suffered by the Malta convoys, sufficient aircraft could not be delivered to provide an adequate defence. However, a novel solution was found. Hurricanes were loaded on to aircraft carriers in British waters, which then sailed as secretly as possible into the western Mediterranean where, with long-range petrol tanks, they were flown off the deck and onward to Malta. The launching point was roughly north of Algiers, which brought the carrier within the Hurricanes' range of Malta and hopefully avoided the attention of enemy forces. It was enormously risky. The carriers did not possess steam catapults and the aircraft were not navalised – that is, they had no arrester hooks, nor were their undercarriages and wings strengthened to withstand a heavy deck landing. All this meant that, with the carrier steaming into the wind to maximise airflow across the wings, the pilot had to fly a heavily laden fighter off the short deck at full power. With insufficient airspeed, the fighter could fall into the sea in front of the carrier, which was likely to run it over and kill the pilot. A successful take-off meant a long flight with pin-point navigation to land short of fuel on an airfield that was more than likely under aerial attack. It also meant that once airborne, an aeroplane that developed a problem which would prevent it reaching Malta could not land back on the carrier; the options would be to fly to Gibraltar or divert to North Africa, where the pilot would be interned by the Vichy French.[3] But with courageous pilots, it worked. Approximately 350 Hurricanes were sent, with only about twenty not arriving at their destination – a remarkable record.

Despite this, by the end of 1941, the Hurricanes based on Malta were no real match for the modern aircraft being used by the enemy – particularly the *Luftwaffe* – and at the beginning of 1942, the Air Officer Commanding (AOC), Air Vice-Marshal Hugh Lloyd, was reporting to Middle East Command Headquarters in Cairo that the situation was in danger of becoming untenable. Fortunately, the AOC-in-C Middle East, Air Marshal Sir Arthur Tedder, recognised the warnings for what they were and ordered that a report on the situation on Malta be prepared with recommendations. Produced speedily, it confirmed that the Hurricanes were outmoded and found the systems for controlling the air battle to be inadequate. Although the morale of the pilots was said to be good, it was noted that they couldn't be expected to fight for long periods under the prevailing conditions.

At the beginning of 1942, it was cold and wet. The airfields bogged down and enemy aircraft roamed over the island almost at will. A convoy that left Alexandria in February failed to get through.

On 7 March 1942, the first fifteen Spitfires to operate outside mainland United Kingdom arrived on Malta, having departed the Royal Naval carrier HMS *Eagle* in the western Mediterranean early in the morning. An attempt to send Spitfires in February from HMS *Eagle* and HMS *Argus* had been aborted after problems with their long-range tanks, much to the embarrassment of the RAF. In two other operations later in March, a further sixteen Spitfires reached the beleaguered island. But they were not enough. What the air defences of the island needed were fresh, experienced pilots and Spitfires in squadron strength. One idea was to gather a large group of pilots by asking squadron OCs to nominate individuals, but it was pointed out that rather than nominate their best pilots, it would be those the OC wanted to get rid of who would be sent; this was the last thing Malta needed. It would be better to send full squadrons of battle-hardened and experienced pilots; 601 and 603 Squadrons received their orders to go. This was Operation *Calendar.*

But for 603 at least, many of those who were operational during the summer and autumn of 1941, and who had flown north to Peterhead to allow the squadron to recover from its losses, were posted elsewhere to be replaced by new, inexperienced pilots like Walcott. As a result, the 603 Squadron air echelon which gathered to go to Malta was not what it had been a few months before in terms of its experience and its operational capability.

Other problems arose. HMS *Eagle* couldn't be used because of problems with its steering gear; *Argus* didn't have the capacity and the lifts on HMS *Victorious* were too small to allow a Spitfire to be taken up to the deck from the below-deck hangars. One proposal was that crated Spitfires could be constructed in the carrier, but the size of the lifts made this unworkable. Where could a larger carrier be sourced?

Coincidentally, the much larger American aircraft carrier, USS *Wasp*, was making for British waters, and on 1 April the Prime Minister wrote to President Roosevelt asking that it be made available to transport the two squadrons to Malta. *Wasp* could accommodate about fifty Spitfires and had much bigger lifts. The President agreed, and the stage was set. Commissioned in 1940, *Wasp*, with a complement of 200 sailors, was about 700 feet long with a draught of 20 feet and a displacement of almost 15,000 tons. But, as was the norm for the time, there were no angled flight decks. By comparison, the flight deck of HMS *Argus* was 565 feet and HMS *Eagle* 667.

Rumour mills being what they are, it is quite likely that at least some of the pilots had concluded that Malta was their destination. The briefing they received certainly did not pull any punches. The officer in charge of the planning and organisation, Wing Commander John S. McLean, explained that the carrier would take them to a point roughly north of Algiers, where they would be launched. They would then fly east, hugging the coast of North Africa and, if at all possible, avoiding trouble until they reached Malta. Then Squadron Leader 'Jumbo' Gracie, who had already made the run to Malta, spoke about what the pilots could expect from their Spitfires with the extra fuel tanks, and described life on the island. It was not encouraging, and some of the pilots began to wonder if he was just 'shooting a line'. It became clear just how tough life was. With shortages of life's essentials, they stocked up with soap, tobacco, razor blades and other items so abundant in *Wasp* but soon to become luxuries. Officially they were allowed 10lbs of personal gear, but some took more, which meant that their already heavily loaded Spitfires would find it more difficult to reach flying speed on take-off. Each pilot took a sandfly net, a jar of Bamber oil, Sketofax anti-mosquito cream and a 'K'-type dinghy.

By the end of the briefing, it was clear that this would be no picnic. They were facing a highly dangerous future. The New Zealander Jack Rae, posted to 603 at the last minute, said later that he had not realised at the time just how dangerous it would be.[4] He noticed the lack of experience among the pilots, commenting that 'the entire squadron had no operational experience' and that Lord David was 'a magnificent man but straight out of Training Command'. Rae was concerned about the limitations on weight. Apart from being frankly nervous about the short take-off run, he said that he weighed his camera and found that it was 4lbs. As the voyage progressed, rumours built up about what was in short supply on Malta and he found himself surreptitiously going to his allocated aircraft, opening a panel and putting in tins of things like Spam. But this added to his nervousness, and he then started taking things out.

For those in positions of command, whether they felt apprehensive or not, they had to maintain an outwardly confident pose. Two days after the briefing, Flight Lieutenant Bill Douglas wrote to his parents in Edinburgh:

> Just a wee note to tell you that I'm alive and kicking and having one of the most interesting experiences I ever had. Unfortunately, everything is shrouded in official secrecy, and quite rightly, so I won't bother to try to hint at anything. I do know our destination now...

But he added:

I'm thriving, eating the best food I've ever had for quite some time, and basking a lot in a pleasantly warm sun.

He seems quite happy with his lot – perhaps he took the view that Malta was a fighter pilot's paradise, with a plethora of potential targets? Perhaps not – perhaps deep within himself he had doubts and concerns. And his letter was addressed to his parents, so he was hardly likely to tell them his true state of mind if he was concerned.

One of 601 Squadron's pilots, Denis Barnham, was a sensitive man – an artist and a writer.[5] Like Jack Rae with 603, Barnham joined 601 Squadron at the last minute in Glasgow but brought experience and, like the New Zealander, had a single FW190 on his scoresheet. Writing after the war and after surviving Malta, he is sombre and apprehensive about what the future holds. He looks at his fellow pilots:

Watching them drinking coffee, reading books, playing dice or cards they don't seem to think about what lies ahead. Frankly I wonder if they have any imagination whatsoever – perhaps they are better off without it. I only hope that I give the same impression of innocent calmness.[6]

He draws portraits of Squadron Leader Hughes, the engineering officer, and Gracie and compares the outlook and appearance of the two men. Hughes is enthusiastic and lively although Barnham makes the point that he will not be going to Malta but returning to the UK once the Spitfires have gone. Gracie, in contrast, is 'a sad hunched figure with the ribbon of the Distinguished Flying Cross', his face lacking its 'usual vigorous and forceful look, his expression betray[ing] his thoughts as he looked towards the horizon'. Barnham goes so far as to wonder about the 'impossibility of survival for long'.

Often, waiting is the problem. Warrant Officer Tom O'Reilly flew Spitfires with 603 Squadron much later in the war but commented that he found the worst part of any operation was sitting in the cockpit waiting for the order to start engines. Sometimes his aeroplane would be on a distant edge of the airfield and in the silence, while his apprehension grew, he could look at fields and see the birds and animals in them going about their daily routines. Occasionally he was tempted to jump out of the cockpit and over the perimeter fence to get away from the war, but he never did. Experience can be a double-edged sword. Experience of a difficult situation such as combat can help the individual deal with such situations in future, although knowing what lies ahead can also result in debilitating fear for those with active imaginations.[7]

Denis Barnham hoped that he was portraying an inner calmness. He commented with a suggestion of envy that Squadron Leader Hughes would not be going to Malta. Bill Douglas portrays what is almost enthusiasm for what is happening, which he probably did not truly feel. Any of the pilots with sense would have felt some apprehension, and Walcott would be no different.

Jack Rae found that conditions aboard *Wasp* were much, much better than in austere Britain. He commented on 'the immense luxury' of the ship, which had everything, including maple syrup and eggs over easy. It was beautifully comfortable and well equipped.

All of this might have affected Walcott's state of mind. As shall be seen, he was not a man to shy away from risky undertakings, and some of those who knew him considered him to be a bit of a risk-taker, but he was far from his home in Massachusetts. He had joined a squadron in the middle of winter in a bleak and miserable part of Britain, on an airfield that was lacking in comforts. And shortly afterwards, he had been involved in a mid-air collision in which the other pilot died. Disliked by at least some of the men he served with, who knows what he was enduring. There would be no counselling after the collision. He would just have to get on with things on his own, and if he was being blamed for the accident then it is quite possible that he fell into gloom or even depression. He had no combat experience. He was in a culture that was different to his own and was about to take a risky flight to one of the most dangerous places on earth. And on top of all of this, he was in an American ship surrounded by his countrymen and the trappings of his own culture, but was apart from it, a member of a foreign air force. If there were barriers against him in 603, there were also divides between Walcott and his fellow Americans in *Wasp*.

Down in the below-deck hangars, the Spitfires, all brand-new, were being readied. Space was at a premium, with some suspended from the deck-head, swaying uneasily as the ship rolled. The pilots visited to view the work going on. The long-range tanks still caused problems with sealing and the fighters all had new coats of paint applied. Black-and-white photos of the aircraft being loaded aboard on the Clyde show them as being in the standard desert camouflage scheme of light and dark brown on the upper surfaces and light blue on the underside, but experience on Malta showed that this was not appropriate because the fighters mostly operated over the sea, against which the brown stood out rather than the opposite. On 7 April, as the Spitfires for Operation *Calendar* were being readied, a request came from Malta that in future all Spitfires should be camouflaged for operations over the sea. Accordingly, during the transit to the Mediterranean, the top surfaces received a deep blue cover, crudely painted by hand. This is very evident in the photo of BR124 U-2 flown by Bill Douglas. The precise colour isn't known but it is likely to have been the blue used by the US Navy on their aircraft. Once on Malta, any paint that would do was used, crudely applied and easily scuffed by feet, weather and wear and tear.

At 03.00 on the morning of Sunday 19 April, Force W slipped through the Straits of Gibraltar. The transit of the narrow passage was purposely executed in the dead of night to try to prevent German agents and Spanish informants spotting the carrier and relaying the information to Axis forces who might intercept the ships and/or attempt to prevent the fighters reaching their destination. Dawn broke to reveal a clear blue sky and heat – a far cry from the gloom of the Clyde. The escorts made for Gibraltar to refuel, being replaced temporarily by others and acquiring the British cruisers *Charybdis* and *Cairo*. The pilots made their final preparations, writing letters, packing kit. Denis Barnham visited the padre but found the visit unsatisfactory and 'disappointing'. He gained little solace. Walcott also visited the padre. It would be a sombre and anxious night for them all.

The pilots were roused at 03.45 the next morning to a fine clear sky. Breakfast was scheduled for 04.15 with a final briefing thirty minutes later and the first engine start at 05.15. The Spitfires were to fly off in four groups, three of twelve and one of eleven. Having left many of its aircraft ashore to accommodate the Spitfires, *Wasp* retained a dozen Grumman F4F-4 Wildcats to act as air cover during the launch. They launched at 05.30 to give protection (and also more space on deck). The number of Spitfires on deck at any one time was limited to twelve so that as each group departed, the next was taken via the lifts onto the deck. 601 Squadron would leave first, which meant that the 603 aircraft would be in the hangars. Squadron Leader Douglas-Hamilton was to lead the first 603 group, Flight Lieutenant Bill Douglas the second. Walcott was in the first 603 Squadron group flying Spitfire serial BP958, that is, the third wave to leave *Wasp*. Flying Officer Tony Holland is said to have been the first of the 603 Squadron pilots to attempt the take-off. Holland was one of the pilots whose combat experience was limited but he nonetheless rose to the challenge.

The American carrier reached the launch point at 037°30'N, 003°20'E, a mere 15 or so miles due north of Algiers and about 480 miles due east of Gibraltar, turning into wind which was Force 4 from 245°, a relatively gentle breeze. Alongside taking off into the wind, aircraft have a range of lift-enhancing devices on their wings. On modern airliners these can easily be seen, particularly during landing, when various flaps and sheets of the skin move into the airflow accompanied by various whines and the occasional thump. Their purpose is to allow the wings to create more lift at the lower speeds required for a safe landing and to some extent for taking off. On the outboard trailing edge of the Spitfire's wings are the ailerons, used to bank the aircraft, and inboard are the flaps. To deploy them, the wing splits so that a section hinges down into the airflow. Depending on the amount of lift required, it can be set at a range of angles with the greatest being 90° so that it hangs vertically downwards. Unfortunately, the optimum angle for taking off from the carrier was not pre-set, so the flight crews cut sets of wooden blocks, which were held between the open flap and the wing while the pilot retracted the flap until it was stopped from going further by the wooden block. Once safely in the air, the pilot increased the angle to allow the blocks to fall away, then fully retracted the flap for normal flight. The 'Pilot's Notes'[8] for the Seafire I and II, which were 'navalised' versions of the Spitfire, include this procedure for a deck take-off, presumably without the assistance of a catapult:

> The Drill of Vital Actions is the same as that for normal take-off, except that the flaps should be lowered 18°. On aeroplanes in which Mod. No. 63 has not been incorporated, this flap setting is obtained as follows:
>
> a) Lower flaps fully, have flight deck crew insert wooden blocks, and then raise flaps.
> b) After take-off lower flaps fully at a safe height and then raise flaps.

All rather Heath Robinson-esque.

The first twelve Spitfires were already on the deck, 'spotted' at the stern to allow as long a run as possible, and they all took off safely. They were led by Squadron Leader 'Jumbo' Gracie, the man who had already made the run to Malta on a previous occasion and a very experienced airman who nonetheless made a rather uncharacteristic mistake in initially leading his group on the reciprocal course taking them west towards Gibraltar rather than east! The mistake was quickly noticed and the loose gaggle turned on to the correct course. The other Spitfires remained in the below-deck hangar until their turn to be taken up on the lift to the deck arrived. With engines running in the noisy, confined space, the whirling propellers needed to be treated with great care but one RAF airman, Sergeant Douglas Haig Preston, died after inadvertently walking into one of them. Sergeant Preston, only twenty-six years old and married, was taken back to Britain and is buried in Felixstowe New Cemetery in Suffolk. Apart from the tragedy for the airman, those who witnessed the accident were clearly affected by it and the dreadful image remained with them. In confined areas where many engines were running, such accidents were, sadly, not unusual. Corporal Bill Simpson, an airframe fitter with the 'Special Erection Party' on Gibraltar, witnessed something similar. His unit built up crated Spitfires for onward passage to Malta and for the invasion of North Africa at the end of 1942. He never forgot.

With the second group away, all of 601 Squadron had gone and the third group, 603 Squadron, made their take-offs. Relatively speaking, it was quite straightforward. With tail trim central, the throttles were pushed as far forward as possible, and at full power the brakes released and the Spitfire accelerated down the deck until it reached flying speed, which was at least 140mph Indicated Air Speed (IAS), with the undercarriage retracted as soon as possible. For some this meant a drop over the bow to pick up those crucial extra miles per hour before rising away and into the bright, clear sky. With a full load, the aeroplane had a tendency to swing, which the Pilot's Notes suggested countering by 'coarse use of the rudder'. Some disappeared out of sight below the ship's bow before struggling back to altitude again. None crashed into the sea.

It will be recalled that Jack Rae, like the others, had been stowing articles in the various panels of his aircraft and was concerned about the weight and how it would complicate his take-off. To his concern (and subsequent amusement), the night before departure, Lord David told Jack that he would be flying a different Spitfire and that the one which he had been filling with supplies would be taken by a Canadian pilot who, Rae recalls, had a rather nervous sniff. With no time to change over the illicit items, Rae told the other pilot that his Spitfire might be a 'bit overweight', which, he said, increased the frequency of the Canadian's sniff! He didn't have the heart to tell the other pilot just how overweight the Spitfire was.

With a safe airspeed, it was a climb straight ahead until reaching 400 feet when the revs were reduced to 2,400 at +2 lbs boost and an airspeed of 170mph. Once safely at 2,400 feet, the hood was closed and with the aeroplane trimmed for hands and feet off, there was a climb to 3,000 feet to rendezvous with the rest of the group. The group flew in a wide formation, avoiding the need for numerous throttle changes to hold a close formation and the accompanying demand on petrol. Once in formation, revs were reduced to 2,050 and there was a climb to 10,000 feet at an IAS of 160mph.

Lord David anticipated that the flight to Malta would take four hours and ten minutes and cover more than 667 miles. The navigation was relatively straightforward, more or less following the coast due east for 357 miles then dog-legging south and east to avoid the enemy-held island of Pantelleria before reaching Malta. If lost during the final stages, his plan was to fly north to find the southern coast of Sicily, and at its eastern end turn on to a course of 222° to find Malta. A final exhortation: 'Don't *Flap* or *Worry*.'

Squadron Leader Douglas-Hamilton's group, the first of the 603 aircraft, found the climb sluggish but they managed to rendezvous at 3,000 feet as planned before setting course for Malta and climbing to 10,000 feet where they found there to be a reasonable tailwind. Early on in the flight, Douglas-Hamilton noticed one Spitfire slipping back in the formation but apart from that, the flight was uneventful and, with the helping tailwind, took only three hours and twenty minutes. Flight Lieutenant Bill Douglas's group flew directly over Tunis and saw a French biplane, which rose to investigate but did not attempt to intercept them as it might very well have done. As will be discussed later, the apparent neutrality of Vichy France gave rise to another set of peculiar circumstances in which previously allied British and French airmen found themselves fighting each other in the skies. The sight of the four loose skeins of dark-blue Spitfires crossing the Mediterranean sky like so many migrating geese must have been exhilarating or threatening depending on viewpoint. Once over Malta, 601 Squadron landed at Luqa, which is now Malta's international airport, while 603 made for Ta'Qali, a basic airstrip in the centre of the island.

Keen to make a good impression, Douglas-Hamilton pulled his group into a tight formation and swung round to Ta'Qali. The local control warned that enemy aircraft were active but none were seen and the Spitfires picked their landing run on what was clearly a bomb-shattered airfield. One of the experienced pilots already on Malta, the officer commanding 249 Squadron, 'Laddie' Lucas, commented that the sight of so many Spitfires over the island at once was 'quite amazing' but the close formation seemed a rather foolhardy thing to do given the possibility of being attacked by the enemy. He thought it a measure of the newcomers' inexperience.[9]

As they climbed out of their cramped cockpits stretching arms and legs, the new pilots took in the devastation around them. The airfield was attacked several times a day but was rarely out of action for more than a few hours because of the heroic actions of airmen, soldiers and sailors who made emergency repairs. Nonetheless, it was a tricky place from which to operate. Bob Sergeant, with 249 Squadron, said that to land you picked what seemed to be a good line between the bomb craters and then hoped for the best. Often, the Spitfires, on almost empty tanks, were landing under the guns of marauding enemy fighters. Sometimes the first indication that the British pilot would have of an attack was when the airfield's anti-aircraft guns opened up – apparently firing at the Spitfire but actually at enemy attackers nearby. Later in the battle, Tony Holland experienced this and recalled quite vividly coming back from a scramble with the cockpit hood open, wheels and flaps down, just about to touch down when suddenly it seemed that an intense curtain of small arms fire was directed at him from below. Initially he couldn't understand what was happening but quickly realised that the fire was not directed at him but at a Bf109 that was following him with the intention of shooting him down. The firing made him aware of his imminent danger and he managed to take appropriate avoiding action without stalling his low and slow Spitfire.

The new Spitfires were refuelled and readied for action. The raggedy ground crews searched nooks and crannies for gifts from their colleagues in *Wasp* – canned fruit, small tools, Spam, soap; all the niceties of life. Jack Rae sought out the nervous Canadian flying the Spitfire originally allocated to him and found that he had arrived safely. Apparently the overloaded Spitfire had dropped down close to the surface of the water before slowly climbing to altitude. Unloading the tins and other articles, Rae felt obliged to give the other pilot half – which was probably not unreasonable under the circumstances!

The new arrivals were whisked off to their accommodation. This was reasonably comfortable for the officers, in the Xara Palace Hotel, on higher ground some way from the airfield, but a bit more basic for the NCO pilots, in tents and whatever billets could be found for them. It wasn't long before the enemy attacked the new arrivals. From the relative safety of the balcony of the Xara Palace on the hill, the officer pilots could see the dive bombers sweeping down and the bursting of the bombs on the already battered airstrip and on the newly arrived aircraft. Within a couple of days, of the forty-six Spitfires that made the flight on 20 April, only a handful remained in an airworthy state – six or seven at most. It was realised that the reception arrangements for the arriving Spitfires were inadequate, and for subsequent deliveries a much better system for guiding aircraft off the landing strip and into protected dispersal pens was instituted, improving the survivability of the aircraft.

For the officer pilots off-duty, watching the bombing from the balcony of the Xara Palace became a bit of a spectator sport. Bob Sergeant recalled that the Cisk brewery was near the airfield. It had a tall chimney that often was obscured by smoke and dust during bombing raids. Once the visibility improved, a great cheer would go up when the chimney could be seen to be still standing!

After some time, it was realised that one aircraft was missing – Bud Walcott's spitfire. His non-arrival attracted no comment in the sergeants' mess. Flight Sergeant Jack Rae knew nothing of it or the controversy until many years later.

If the NCOs knew nothing, the higher authorities were in little doubt that Walcott's absence was deliberate and not the result of enemy action or technical problems with his aeroplane. On 25 April, the AOC Malta sent a signal to the Air Ministry in London to report his 'desertion'.[10] It included the following:

SPITFIRE 958 PILOT SERGEANT WALCOTT DID NOT ARRIVE. O.C. 603 SQUADRON SAW HIM LEAVE FORMATION BUT THOUGHT HE WAS JOINED [sic]

FOLLOWING FORMATION. HE ALSO STATES THAT SERGEANT WALCOTT INTENDED TO DESERT. HAD PREVIOUSLY LANDED FOR NO GOOD REASON IN IRISH FREE STATE BUT NOT INTERNED. IN CONVERSATION ON VOYAGE STATED MALTA WOULD NEVER SEE HIM.

This is a serious accusation which leaves little room for doubt. But no evidence is given to justify the accusations that Walcott was deliberately intending to 'desert' or had flown to Dublin 'for no good reason'. And after this, little further action appears to have been initiated. The matter seems to have been dropped. Perhaps the authorities in London appreciated the lack of justification available. Perhaps other events overshadowed the issue. As shall be seen, the report seems to have been quietly forgotten.

But the affair did not end there. It has been reported and discussed at length since the war, with the suggestion that Walcott had disappeared in the most cowardly, dishonourable fashion, repatriated to the USA never to be heard of again.

The pilots of 603 Squadron fought bravely and against the odds over that summer of 1942, with nine being killed in action. Unfortunately for 601 and 603, their dangerous flight did not lead to an immediate improvement in the situation. It was noted that the preparations to handle the large number of incoming aircraft had not been adequate and had been a factor in the number damaged or destroyed so quickly. The Operations Record Book for Headquarters, Mediterranean[11] includes the following:

5. The fighter strength was reinforced on the 20th by the arrival of 46 Spitfires from U.K. It has not been possible to average more than 6 serviceable aircraft per day. Prior to the above mentioned

reinforcement there was a period when it was not possible to have any fighter aircraft airborne at all, due to unserviceability. It was very noticeable that with the arrival of the fighter reinforcements, the enemy preluded his bombing attacks with fighter sweeps and maintained fighting over the island even after the bombers had made their get-away.

6. During the period when the 46 Spitfires were necessarily grounded for refuelling and rearming and brought into a fully operational condition, many were damaged on the ground by enemy action. The inability to scramble our aircraft was due in the first place to the fact that minor details such as cannon testing were not done, and it would appear that the aircraft had come straight from a factory without being tested to see that they were fit to fly operationally.

The final remarks are interesting. Like any newly built piece of machinery, many Spitfires suffered teething problems not unlike those which might be experienced with a new car. Windscreens oiled up, the guns may not have been correctly zeroed in, the radios sometimes didn't work so that departing on this already risky flight might be compounded by deficiencies in the aeroplanes themselves. The number of hours these Spitfires had flown before taking off from *Wasp*'s deck was very low. Information suggests that the aircraft appear to have been checked between departure from the factory and arrival at the Clyde but clearly they were not perfect.

On 25 April, a Secret Cypher Message from 'HQ Malta'[12] notes the following in addition to leaking long-range petrol tanks:

4 COMPASSES SLIGHTLY OUT. 4 WIRELESS FAILURES IN 1 CASE DYNAMO NOT CHARGING AND 2 CASES FLAT ACCUMULATORS. ... AIRCRAFT SHOULD BE MADE FULLY

OPERATIONAL AND CANNONS AIR TESTED BEFORE LEAVING ENGLAND.

Further, the lack of experience of the new pilots did not go unnoticed. In another Secret Cypher Telegramme dated 27 April from the AOC Malta to HQ RAF Middle East and the Air Ministry in London,[13] this is raised:

FURTHER DETAILED ENQUIRIES INTO THE HISTORY OF PILOTS REVEALS THAT EXACT FIGURES ARE AS FOLLOWS 601 SQUADRON 12 PILOTS HAD UNDER 25 HOURS ON SPITFIRES OF WHICH 7 HAVE NO OPERATIONAL EXPERIENCE. 603 SQUADRON 13 PILOTS HAD UNDER 25 HOURS SPITFIRE FLYING OUT OF WHICH 9 HAD NO OPERATIONAL EXPERIENCE. IN THIS SQUADRON 17 EXPERIENCED PILOTS WERE POSTED AWAY FROM? [*sic*] SQUADRON WITHIN 2 MONTHS BEFORE LEAVING U.K.

The AOC-in-C Middle East, Sir Arthur Tedder, was soon raising his concerns with London, arguing that 'Malta was no place for beginners' and that only fully operationally experienced pilots should be sent.

And some pilots displayed their fear. One 603 pilot returned to the UK having been seen to leave a formation for no good reason but also apparently with no action being taken against him. Fighter Command and Bomber Command treated their aircrew differently. The airmen who flew with Bomber Command were all volunteers, and over the course of the war more than 55,000 bomber airmen were killed. A bomber crew was expected to fly thirty operations – a tour – before they were rested. They had a target number to reach, but the loss rate that prevailed for much of the war meant that statistically a crew was unlikely to achieve the thirty 'ops'. Those who did were celebrated, and after a rest many returned to carry out another tour. However, airmen who found that they were unable to carry on – those who were overwhelmed by the losses and the probability that they would not complete the tour – were treated in an extremely unsympathetic way that nowadays would be regarded as shameful. They were branded as 'Lacking Moral Fibre' and their personal files were stamped ostentatiously 'L. M. F.' to denote their status. Further, NCOs (aircrew were either commissioned or non-commissioned officers) were reduced to the lowest of ranks but had to continue to wear their flying badge. They were also given the most menial of tasks to perform so that it was very obvious that they were 'cowards'.

In contrast, Fighter Command did not operate to such rules. Pilots flew until for one reason or another it was deemed that they should be rested. Of course, this meant they might fly on operations for many months with no end in sight but also that a pilot who started to display problems with nerves – the twitch – would be treated more sympathetically than those in Bomber Command. During the Battle of Britain, fighter pilots spent much of their day sitting waiting for the order to 'scramble', which usually came via a telephone call. An orderly would pick up the phone and then shout out the order to go, and often ring a bell. Many of the pilots found the waiting intolerable. Some would be sick at the sound of the phone ringing, not knowing that it might be only for some mundane message, and some said that even after the war the sound of a phone ringing would make them feel sick. These men were heroes, but they were vulnerable human beings nonetheless.

Many of those airmen who had been rested or taken off operations spent time as instructors at the various flying training schools and found this to be a more stressful activity than operations! Later in his career, Walcott was an instructor and had at least one rather interesting experience with a trainee pilot.

Unlike the Battle of Britain, in Malta the shortage was of aeroplanes and not pilots. Squadrons shared aircraft. For those on Malta, servicemen and civilians, life was very tough. Virtually everything was in short supply, from food to fuel. And Malta Dog laid low many of the aircrew. The fighting continued to be intense. With matters becoming desperate, in August a last-ditch naval operation to bring two convoys simultaneously to Malta, Operation *Pedestal*, brought enough supplies to the island to break the siege – but at huge cost. By then, Lord David Douglas-Hamilton had been rested and command of 603 given to Bill Douglas on 20 July 1942. Lord David became a photo-reconnaissance pilot flying Mosquitoes and, tragically, was killed in 1944. Bill Douglas survived the war and returned to his family business in his home town of Edinburgh.

After launching the *Calendar* Spitfires, *Wasp* had returned to the Clyde for another load for Operation *Bowery*, which delivered sixty-four Spitfires, before heading for the Far East. In September, 250 miles north of Espiritu Santu, she fell victim to a torpedo fired by a Japanese submarine and sank. Fortunately, most of the crew survived.

603 Squadron has a proud history. Its members are conscious of all of those who went before them and of the sacrifices they made. In 1942 the pilots re-badged as 229 Squadron, which left the 603 service echelon at the eastern end of the Mediterranean without pilots. Eventually they were joined by aircrew to become a

Beaufighter unit, mainly carrying out maritime operations against Axis shipping. In January 1945 the personnel returned to the UK to Norfolk to fly Spitfires once again – rather to the surprise of the Beaufighter aircrew who were transferred to the Banff Strike Wing near Elgin. Coincidentally, the 603 Squadron service echelon was then joined by the pilots of 229 Squadron, who were based at Coltishall and reverted to become 603 again. The new 603 took part in dive-bombing operations against V2-related targets in and around The Hague, in Holland, until the end of March 1945, when V2 operations were overtaken and stopped by the advance of the Allied armies.

603 Squadron still exists. Still based in its original town headquarters in Edinburgh, it is no longer a flying unit. As with the other auxiliary squadrons, 603 was disbanded immediately after the war ended, but reformed again in Edinburgh in May 1946, flying later marks of Spitfires, then de Havilland Vampire jet aircraft. It disbanded again in 1957, but the town headquarters became home to 2 Maritime Headquarters Unit (2 MHU), which was heavily involved in intelligence and naval operations during the Cold War. With the break-up of the Soviet Union, 2 MHU in turn disbanded to be replaced by a regenerated 603 Squadron in 1999, with members of 2 MHU becoming part of 603 and preserving a strong historical line. Its new role is 'Force Protection', which essentially means helping protect airfield assets in Iraq and Afghanistan. At the time of writing, 603 has a dual role as an RAF regiment and police unit.

The Walcott incident has created a rare stain on the squadron's reputation and demands an explanation. So just what *did* happen to Walcott?

# PART 2

# WHAT HAPPENED TO WALCOTT

# 7

# NORTH AFRICAN ADVENTURES I

It is self-evident that without any type of flight data recorder – aircraft at that time did not have such technology – and in the absence of a wreck, the only source of information about what happened to a single-seat aeroplane flying solo is the pilot. There is no independent verification of what he or she says, but it is usually assumed that they are telling the truth. Accordingly, with regard to the immediate events surrounding Walcott's flight to North Africa, the only source available is Walcott's own account.[1] For later events in North Africa, and the rest of his life, there is some verification from the public domain in the form of books, newspapers, the internet and the testimony of some of those who encountered him. But the account of his flight on 20 April 1942 is his alone.

Walcott took off in Spitfire VB serial BP958. Built in Salisbury, it made its first flight on 19 March 1942 at Chattis Hill and the following day arrived at No. 6 Maintenance Unit to bring it to a combat-ready condition. Both to increase numbers and to avoid manufacturing being concentrated in a few factories vulnerable to enemy air attack, Spitfires were built in many locations including Salisbury. Such factories produced completed fuselage units and wings, which were taken to a nearby airfield for final assembly and initial test flying. Chattis Hill, about 6 miles south-west of Andover in Hampshire, was originally a landing ground for the Royal Flying Corps during the First World War but at the beginning of the Second World War was virtually a virgin site and was provided with only rudimentary facilities. The Spitfires going to Malta were tropicalised, the most noticeable difference being the addition of a Vokes air filter forming a chin immediately aft of the airscrew, designed to remove the dust and sand prevalent in the North African and Mediterranean areas. Further, the Spitfires were issued in the desert camouflage scheme with light and dark brown areas on the upper surfaces. These ones flew to RAF Abbotsinch, near Glasgow, on 10 April to await transport to, and loading on to, *Wasp*'s deck on the banks of the River Clyde. This involved a tortuous journey through the streets on low loaders. Once on board, they were taken down into one of the hangars for final adjustments – and repainting blue – in preparation for the flight to Malta ten days later.

Safely airborne, Walcott decreased the boost to +1 from the +12 employed to launch from *Wasp*, aiming to join Lord David's group – the third to depart but the first of 603 Squadron's two groups – at 3,000 feet as briefed, but the Spitfire could not generate enough airspeed to stay airborne so he increased the engine boost to +3 and made the climb successfully. However, he now found that he lagged behind the scattered formation and couldn't see it. He increased power and attempted to catch up with the others but concluded that extravagance with the fuel would result in the tanks running dry before reaching the destination, so he dropped back down to sea level, thinking that he would fly independently – after all, the flight was relatively simple in the clear air.

After some time he passed a small white ship, which he thought was a yacht, about 300 yards to port. At this point he found black smoke coming from his engine exhaust, and the cockpit filled with smoke. At the same time, the engine temperature increased dramatically. Anticipating that he might need to bale out, Walcott climbed to gain some altitude while turning towards the nearby coast. After several minutes at about 1,200 feet the temperature fell once again to a more normal level, but when crossing the coast the engine seized and he had to make an immediate emergency landing. If he followed the instructions, he would pull the propeller speed control right back and set the radiator flap to minimum drag to maximise the length of the glide. The recommended approach IAS in a glide was 95mph. For landing, the cockpit hood was normally locked in the open position and the emergency exit door on the port side of the cockpit set at 'half-cock' so that it could be opened easily to allow the pilot a speedy escape.

He spotted a road that would make a likely runway and lowered the undercarriage, but found that only one of the legs extended. He therefore decided to land alongside the road rather than on it. The landing was violent and damaged the Spitfire severely as well as knocking out the pilot. Often in such crashes, if the pilot did not have his straps as tight as possible, the sudden deceleration of the crash threw him forward to strike his head on the gunsight fixed on the top of the instrument panel. Walcott recovered consciousness about thirty or forty minutes later, he estimated, in a house about three-quarters of a mile from the crash site and it transpired that he had been pulled out of the wreck and taken there by some

*Gendarmes*. They treated him well – he said that none of his kit was removed, and they even let him retain his revolver.

He discovered that he had crashed not far from the town of Sétif, which is about 30 miles south of the Mediterranean coast. If he had lost power at about 1,000 feet, he could have glided only a short way before crashing. In total, he must have flown about 150 miles from taking off. Not long after he recovered consciousness, some French airmen turned up with an army officer whom Walcott found to be objectionable. Once recovered sufficiently, his captors took him back to the crash site where he protested that he was only a ferry pilot, and to justify this he pointed out that the cannons had not been fired – a moot point, perhaps, as they were armed, albeit only partially, to save weight for the long flight. There were machine-gun hits on the aeroplane, which surprised him and which he surmised must have come from the yacht, which he understood might have been an E-boat (a German fast patrol boat roughly equivalent to a British Motor Torpedo Boat or an American PT Boat). While the term yacht brings to mind a small ship with sail, it is also used to describe boats powered by mechanical means and used for pleasure. The small white boat he saw might very well have been an enemy ship.

The Frenchmen removed his kit and in doing so found his log book, which presumably confirmed the young American to be a member of the RAF. They asked where he launched from and if he had taken off from an aircraft carrier but Walcott claimed to have denied this, making the point that the Spitfire was a land-based aircraft not fitted for carrier operations. The French airmen present at the interrogation confirmed this to be true. But if the Spitfire had not taken off from an aircraft carrier, it is difficult to see where else it might have come from. With the nearest British airfield at Gibraltar, 600 miles away, there was no alternative explanation. If it was up-to-date, the last entry in his log book would have recorded a sortie in the north-east of Scotland.

Walcott was later entertained with lavish hospitality and what he interpreted to be attempts to get him drunk and talking, but to no avail. It is worth noting that other internees also reported that they were wined and dined in such a way as to make them think the purpose was to elicit information from them while they were tipsy.

After all this, they took him to a hospital in Sétif for treatment of his injuries, which included a wounded arm, and then to Algiers, from where he transferred to the internment camp at Laghouat (pronounced 'Lagwat'), a miserable, unpleasant and ultimately notorious place. Laghouat lies on the northern edge of the Sahara desert, just over 200 miles due south of Algiers and thus virtually south of *Wasp*'s position in the Mediterranean when it launched the Spitfires. The average temperature in July, which is marginally hotter than August, is 29°C (85°F) with a highest recorded temperature for that month of 48°C (120°F).

A small frontier town with a significant population, in 2005 Laghouat's inhabitants numbered 125,000. For those about to go into the desert it is the place to stock up with the essentials for survival; for those completing the journey and leaving the desert, it is the place to recuperate and recover from the rigours of the journey. It was a rough-and-ready town of square, thick-walled buildings covered with brown stucco exteriors to keep out the heat in summer and the cold of the winter nights. There were mosques and minarets, and a low range of dry, scrubby hills in the distance. The French conquered the town in the mid-nineteenth century and garrisoned it. Its barracks became home to, among others, units of the *Légion étrangère* – the famous French Foreign Legion – who sortied into the desert to protect their country's interests from nomadic Arab tribes.

The longest-held internees in the Laghouat camp were several members of the British Army. Left behind in France after the withdrawal from Dunkirk in 1940, they made their way to the south of France and then to French North Africa hoping to be repatriated to Britain, but were disappointed to be held as internees in a supposedly neutral country. Initially they were held in Aumale, about 50 miles south-east of Algiers; their numbers increased with the arrival, in dribs and drabs, of RAF airmen, many of whom had ditched their aircraft in the Mediterranean and spent miserable days in life-rafts before being either washed ashore or picked up. But by far the majority of the British were from the Royal Navy. As the numbers increased, the accommodation, such as it was, in Aumale became too cramped and the internees were moved to Laghouat – *Le Camp des Internées Britannique.*

One of the other airmen interned at the camp, Flying Officer James Douglas Hudson, recalled it in unflinching terms:

> The town was basically a filthy Arab Kasbah with a small French population and a Hotel Saharienne, used primarily for those French officers who were to run the prison camp. British prisoners occupied a section of a squalid barracks in a small compound that formed part of the garrison. This compound, encircled by a high triple fence of barbed wire, was surrounded by an even higher stone wall, encompassing the entire perimeter. Armed guards with machine guns were positioned strategically to ensure complete surveillance; their orders were to shoot any man who tried to escape.[2]

In the late summer of 1940, Hudson flew Bristol Blenheim Mk IVs from RAF West Raynham with 101 Squadron and was a member of two crews ordered to ferry Blenheims to Heliopolis in Egypt, near Cairo. The flight would be in two legs, leaving Britain from Thorney Island across neutral France with a refuelling stop in Malta. The crews asked that they might be allowed to make a first refuelling stop at Gibraltar before heading for Malta, but this was refused on the grounds that it presented a greater risk than the direct flight to Malta, which would require pinpoint accuracy and no course deviations if their fuel was to be sufficient. They left Thorney Island just after midnight on 27 August 1940 and crossed the Mediterranean coast at Marseille.

Nearing Malta, and with just sufficient fuel left, they encountered bad weather that required a detour but which left them with the only option of crash-landing on Cap Bon near Tunis. Initially they were treated well by the French and taken to Tunis to meet the American Vice-Consul, whose name was Springs. The Vice-Consul was in a difficult and rather odd situation. The United States, Tunisia, Algeria and Vichy France were legally neutral, and although the French did co-operate with the Germans and Italians in breach of their neutrality obligations, they had to ensure that they did nothing that might bring America into the war. The airmen were entertained with a formal dinner and promises that their aircraft would be repaired to allow them to continue their interrupted journey. However, this did not come to pass and within a few days they were taken to a fortified outpost at Le Kef. In Hudson's own words: 'Disillusionment and imprisonment had begun.'

It is worthy of note that although the British servicemen were legally internees, they regarded themselves as prisoners; once safely back in Lenox after the war, Walcott and others referred to their status in Laghouat as POW and not internee. This was because of the appalling conditions they endured under the French, which provided a stark contrast to the way the Irish authorities treated their internees at the Curragh. Another curious point about Walcott is that he was unfortunate enough to have been held as an internee by two supposedly neutral countries!

A naval airman, Charles Lamb, also endured Laghouat. Lamb had an active and distinguished career as a pilot flying Swordfish aircraft for the Fleet Air Arm. A biplane with a crew of three and an open cockpit, the Swordfish was primarily used as a torpedo attack aircraft. With a single torpedo slung beneath the fuselage, the mode of attack required the aircraft to approach enemy ships on the beam just above the water to release the torpedo, allowing it to slip cleanly into the water. The slow airspeed, low altitude and level flight presented the enemy ship's gunners with easy targets, and many Swordfish failed to return from operations. They did, however, have remarkable successes, including attacks on the Italian fleet in its base at Taranto in November 1940 and in May 1941 on the German battleship *Bismarck*, damaging its rudder and leaving it a sitting duck to be sunk by the gunfire of ships of the Royal Navy.

Lamb was posted to Malta and engaged in clandestine operations in North Africa. In September 1941, while delivering a civilian passenger, his Swordfish crash-landed and he found himself an internee of the Vichy French. Initially incarcerated in Sousse, Lamb's experience was identical to Hudson's. Kept in testing conditions and denied sleep, he too was introduced to Vice-Consul Springs, given a formal dinner and plied with alcohol. Lamb concluded that the French hoped he would let slip some incriminating comment that would demonstrate the illegality of his operations, but he was sure that Springs understood what was going on and was in fact on his side. Lamb also noticed that the French airfields were being used by Axis aircraft, in clear breach of their neutral status.

Both Lamb and James Hudson were initially in the charge of the same French Air Force officer, *Capitaine* Rubin de Cervans. It is worthy of comment that Walcott too reported that he had been plied with alcohol, presumably in the hope that he would make some incriminating remarks. In this respect, his account matches those of Hudson and Lamb, although he makes no mention of meeting American consular staff – of course by the time Walcott arrived, America had joined Britain as an ally, although an American consul and staff remained in the country, which was ostensibly neutral.

In October 1941, the internees held in Aumale were taken to Laghouat. Transported by train to Djelfa, about 75 miles north of Laghouat, the remainder of the journey was in trucks, bumping uncomfortably over the rough road across the open desert. Spirits sank and it became clear that any escape attempts were likely to be doomed to failure; indeed, this was confirmed the following day when a supercilious French officer, Lieutenant Martin, took them to a high point and with sweeps of his arm to the four points of the compass in turn called out, '*Regardez, le desert!*' and then made the point that the nearest railhead was at Djelfa but that any strangers appearing at the station would be arrested, with their identities checked thoroughly. Apparently, the only way to get to Algiers was by foot across the desert, which would be well-nigh impossible. In addition, the camp was guarded by Tirailleurs – sharpshooting infantry – and Spahis – light cavalry – recruited from the local Arabs, who knew the desert and how to survive in it.

The implication is clear – any escape from the camp would result in death or recapture, not freedom.

But why should the Vichy French treat the British internees as badly as they did? The reason has been mentioned previously: British actions following the French surrender in 1940. When France signed the armistice on 22 June 1940, about 200 or so French ships fled to British ports, with others at sea or in French ports. *Amiral de la flotte* (Admiral of the Fleet) François Darlan did not much care for the British, or probably more accurately the English, and he had no intention of allowing French ships to be used by the Royal Navy to prolong what he perceived as a pointless struggle by Britain against Germany. Further, by now the Germans held large numbers of Frenchmen as prisoners of war and their fates could be influenced by how the French military reacted – ceasing hostilities would help speed their release if French warships acquiesced by not turning themselves over to the British.

Darlan gave Britain assurances that the French fleet would not fall into the hands of the German or Italian navies, through which they might be turned against the Royal Navy and its allies, but the British took little comfort from this. Their preference was that the French ships joined those of the Royal Navy or alternatively sat out the war in a location where they could not be taken over by the Germans. With neither of these options accepted, the British acted simultaneously to commandeer those ships in British ports and ports under British control and to neutralise some of those in ports not under British control. The operation had approval at the highest level, from the Cabinet and the Prime Minister himself.

One of these ships was the submarine *Surcouf*. Launched in 1929, at the time it was the largest submarine ever built. When the Germans invaded France, *Surcouf* was undergoing refitting in Brest and limped across the English Channel to the Royal Navy base at Devonport, Plymouth, for sanctuary. A coded 'officer only' order that the French ships were to be scuttled arrived at dawn on Wednesday 3 July, but by the time it was decoded by *Surcouf*'s duty officer a sixty-strong boarding party from the Royal Navy had arrived. Half of the British sailors were submariners, with the remainder Royal Marines, and they were wearing steel helmets – the officers and petty officers carried revolvers.

*Surcouf* was moored outboard of the elderly French battleship *Paris*, which meant that a boarding party would arrive at the submarine either having first crossed over *Paris* from the dockside or from across the water of the harbour. Both ships were to be taken at the same time, and so the plan of attack was that *Surcouf*'s boarding party would land from the seaward side while *Paris* was boarded from the dock. But the hopefully peaceful takeover of the submarine was resisted by some of the French sailors, one of whom opened fire with a small-calibre pistol. Fire was returned by one of the Royal Navy chief petty officers using his .455 Webley revolver. These shots were significant in that they were the first to be exchanged between British and French troops since the Battle of Waterloo in 1815.

The fighting within the vessel escalated, with others becoming involved until eventually the French sailors surrendered to their erstwhile allies. The fighting in *Surcouf* resulted in the deaths of two Royal Navy officers and a rating as well as a French warrant officer. Others were wounded. The other boardings of French ships in British ports were bloodless, although many of the French sailors understandably felt enormous resentment at the treatment meted out to them.

But if the action in *Surcouf* was historically significant and created hatred and resentment, a far more significant and tragic incident was being played out on the Mediterranean near the French Algerian colonial port of Oran. The armistice with Germany allowed France to retain many of its warships to protect its colonies. When the armistice was signed, French ships in the Mediterranean had been seeking a confrontation with the Italian Navy. They quickly broke off their endeavours, and in short order half of the French fleet, including most of its larger warships, were in African harbours – Casablanca, Algiers, Bizerte, Dakar and Oran. Some others were in the Egyptian port of Alexandria, already bottled up by the Royal Navy.

At its height, the French colonial empire was second only to Britain's. It had substantial colonies in Africa and the Americas. One such colony was Algeria. Oran was one of the main cities on the coast, with a port at Mers-el-Kébir, about 4 miles to the west of the city. An ancient harbour dating back to Roman times, it had been a place of safety for all of the ships engaged in trade across the Mediterranean over the years, but now the Arab fishing boats shared these facilities with French warships. The local commander was *Amiral* Marcel-Bruno Gensoul, who was unhappy with the way that his ships were moored. He flew his flag from *Dunkerque*, the lead ship of the Dunkerque class of battleship, with a displacement of 26,500 tons, a length of 214.5 metres and a beam of 31.08 metres and with appropriate armament. In addition, her sister ship *Strasbourg* was there and two other battleships, *Provence* and *Bretagne*, and a seaplane tender, *Commandant Teste,* along with half a dozen destroyers: *Tigre, Lynx, Terrible, Kersaint, Volta* and *Mogador.*

The French had failed to dredge the channel and harbour, so the ships were compelled to tie up in such a way that much of their main armament could not be used against an enemy out at sea – a concern for Gensoul because he did not quite trust their former enemies, the Italians, to honour the ceasefire arrangements. His contingent of ships was powerful, but only single aft turrets on *Bretagne* and *Provence* could be trained seaward – a total of four heavy guns. The port was further defended by coastal batteries, but these were in the process of being decommissioned in accordance with the provisions of the armistice so his small fleet was vulnerable in the event of an attack.

For those French sailors in their ships in Mers-el-Kébir, the day was shaping up to be relatively uneventful – an almost peacetime routine was in place, although people were surely concerned about what would happen to them in the long term, and those with family in the occupied zone worried as to what had happened and what might be happening to loved ones. They did not appreciate that the Royal Navy was about to take actions that would reverberate around the world and cause friction for decades to come.

The sudden withdrawal of the French ships following the French surrender left a gap in the British naval forces, and in short order the Admiralty created Force H, based in Gibraltar, to help fill some of the gaps. Commanded by Admiral Sir James Fownes Somerville, who flew his flag from HMS *Hood* (the H in Force H), it was a powerful fleet, which in addition to *Hood* included two other battleships (*Valiant* and *Resolution*), two cruisers and ten destroyers.

The operation received the code name *Catapult*, and Somerville's orders were simply to ensure that the French ships were either voluntarily neutralised by their crews or destroyed. The three options put to the French were to join the Royal Navy and continue the fight against the Axis, to sail the ships to British ports with reduced crews, or to sail to French ports in the West Indies where they would be stripped of their weaponry or destroyed.

While Force H stood off the port, the destroyer *Foxhound*, with Captain Cedric Holland, who had developed a good relationship with *Amiral* Gensoul over the previous months, approached the harbour. Holland intended to deliver the ultimatum to the French Admiral, but the negotiations became protracted and difficult, with the French refusing to comply. Originally, the Admiralty instructed that the operation should be completed – one way or the other – by dusk, but Somerville decided that his deadline would be 15.00. In the event, the negotiations continued for another couple of hours until it was clear that the French were not going to agree to the British demands.

It's possible that Gensoul and Darlan did not, in their heart of hearts, believe that their recent allies would destroy the ships, but that is what happened. At 17.54, the Royal Navy's first shots boomed out and caused devastation to the French fleet. The French responded, firing on their attackers. The action dragged on for several hours. *Strasbourg* managed to escape the harbour into the open sea, where she was attacked by Fleet Air Arm aircraft; they in turn were intercepted by French Morane fighters, who destroyed several of the British aircraft.

Ultimately *Strasbourg* escaped, but it wasn't until 6 July, three days after it had begun, that Somerville regarded the operation as complete. It had been devastating. The bulk of the French fleet was destroyed or unusable, and their casualties were around 2,000 killed and 350 injured.

While the action at Mers-el-Kébir was uncomplicated in political terms – albeit tragic considering the relationship between the British and the French – another action later in the year demonstrated the complexity and bitterness in relationships between the two French factions – Vichy France and the so-called 'Free French' – and the British and Americans.

Dakar was part of French West Africa, positioned as far to the west as it is possible to be on the African continent. North of the equator, it is clearly well positioned as a jumping-off point for naval activity in the mid-Atlantic and as a springboard for offensive operations against central and southern America. Held by the Vichy French, it posed a potential threat should the Germans decide to occupy the port and use it as a naval base. While many ordinary Americans would not be aware of this, their planners were – and many of those Americans who wanted only to be left out of the war did not appreciate that America would not be allowed to remain uninvolved if the Germans prevailed in Europe.

When France surrendered, Hitler created Vichy France partly to avoid the need to tie up troops in occupation. If the French were willing to occupy themselves, then he was free to pursue his other conquests. But some Frenchmen and women were not prepared to submit to German domination, and resistance coalesced around Charles de Gaulle, a relatively junior army officer who nonetheless held the temporary rank of Brigadier General. De Gaulle's main desire was that France should regain its honour after its humiliation, and while he sought out the help of the British, he was an awkward ally and encountered some difficulty in attracting the support of fellow Frenchmen.

Some Frenchmen living in French West Africa had experienced German colonialism, and de Gaulle's cause attracted them. Plans were made for Free French troops to attack Dakar, but they did not have the resources to do this themselves and accordingly British support was requested. It was given, with the hope that landings on Dakar would be unopposed. But when the armada attempted to land in mid-September, the Vichy French defenders vigorously resisted. Ultimately, the combined British and Free French forces withdrew, partly because de Gaulle was unwilling to see Frenchmen fighting one another. In retaliation, Pétain ordered some bombing raids on Gibraltar by French aircraft based in North Africa, and honour was satisfied.

The consequences of these events were far reaching and would directly affect Walcott in 1942. While French ships may have been kept from use against the British, it wouldn't have been surprising if Vichy France had declared war on Britain. This didn't happen, but tension and ill-feeling against the British coloured relations for many years. And the fighting did not end here. Albeit in regions apparently not significant at the time, British and Commonwealth troops and airmen were in open conflict with their French counterparts. In Syria, for example, the French fighter pilot Pierre le Gloan, having been credited with the destruction of four German and seven Italian aircraft at the start of the war, shot down seven British aircraft. On the other side, Peter Turnbull, an Australian pilot, was credited with four downed French planes. Both were killed later in the war, by which time le Gloan was once again flying on the side of the Allies. The French campaigns were supported by the Germans – French Dewoitine fighters were refuelled on *Luftwaffe* airfields on their way to Syria, a quite bizarre co-operation and yet again an example of the unlikely alliances that spring up in international relations.

It is entirely understandable that many Frenchmen and servicemen despised the British for what they had done. In June, Churchill had proposed to the French Prime Minister that their two countries should unite against a common foe; now, barely two weeks later, the British Navy was perpetrating an act of war against its erstwhile ally, which resulted in the loss of thousands of French lives. Add to this the view of many Frenchmen that at Dunkirk in 1940 the BEF had deserted the French in their hour of need and it is no surprise that there were subsequent instances of fighting between French and British forces and a hatred on the part of some of the French of all that Britain stood for. This hatred would have consequences for Walcott in 1942.

The French servicemen were in an invidious position. They had just been fighting the Germans alongside the British, but now the relationship changed in a way that many found repugnant. The government to which they owed their allegiance and obedience was giving them clear instructions to cease fighting and co-operate with their country's conquerors – possibly even to fight alongside them against their erstwhile allies while their natural instinct would be to resist. The extent of the atrocities perpetrated by the National Socialists in Germany was not fully appreciated, and for many was not yet a factor. Nevertheless, some Frenchmen found the new situation difficult to accept.

Again, history intervened. In 1916, in the middle of the First World War, the British and French met quietly to agree how the Ottoman Empire should divided. They decided that France would receive Syria and the Lebanon, while Britain would control Transjordan, Palestine and Iraq. The significance for Britain was that this allowed overland access to India from the Mediterranean. Iraq had become a member of the League of Nations in 1932, and an independent but pro-British monarchy allowed Britain rights of transit and also air bases in the country – one of the biggest being Habbaniya, about 50 miles west of Baghdad, which opened in 1936. While the attitudes of the Iraqi politicians swayed with the prevailing international situation, in May 1941 a coup by four Iraqi colonels who called themselves 'the Golden Square' restored the deposed and pro-Axis Prime Minister Rashid Ali al-Gaylani. This precipitated the flight of the pro-British Emir Abdullah and his five-year-old nephew King Faisal II, and what followed was a distinctly anti-British national attitude and pressure for Britain to leave. The British responded by moving to reinforce their bases in Iraq. By the end of April, Germany and Italy had agreed to send aircraft to Iraq to help Rashid Ali get rid of the British. The help promised was substantial – Germany provided fourteen Messerschmitt Bf110s, which were twin-engine fighter/ light bombers, seven Heinkel He III bombers and a number of transport aircraft; Italy gave twelve CR42 fighters – biplanes, generally outmoded when compared with British fighters like the Spitfire and Hurricane. The German aircraft would wear Iraqi colours but would be manned by *Luftwaffe* crews.

In the meantime, Vichy France smarted from British naval activity in the Mediterranean. The Royal Navy blockaded French ships bringing goods into Marseilles and, in particular, rubber from Indochina. One estimate was that 167 ships had been seized.[3] A series of incidents occurred, some resulting in the boarding and confiscation of French ships – much to the annoyance of *Amiral* Darlan, who was by now deputy to *Maréchal* Philippe Pétain, who agreed to a German request that their aircraft be allowed to use French airfields in Syria to assist in their operations against the British in Iraq. In return, among other things the Germans would release French colonial troops held since 1940.

The fighting around Habbaniya increased significantly, and on 14 May 1941 a British Blenheim spotted German aircraft on the airfield at Palmyra in Syria, in clear breach of Vichy France's status as a neutral party. In response, the British opened a campaign against the *Luftwaffe* aircraft based in Syria. The attacks on the airfields resulted in casualties among Vichy French airmen and aircraft damage, and after a few days French Moranes were being scrambled to intercept the RAF attackers. On 28 May, a Blenheim of 211 Squadron was shot down by a French Morane over Aleppo and the three British airmen died. Crete at this time had been invaded by German airborne troops and had its Commonwealth forces ejected, albeit after costing the enemy substantial casualties. With Greece in the hands of the Axis, the possibility of an invasion of Cyprus and the clear use of Syria to support expansion, the British Defence Committee in London instructed General Archibald Wavell, C-in-C Middle East Command, to invade Syria.

Given the code name Operation Exporter, the British assault troops numbered about 35,000, comprising mainly Australians and Indians but with a large representation of British soldiers and some Free French. They attacked in three prongs – two Australian brigades and the 5th Indian Brigade Group – in the early hours of 8 June 1941, and if any had thought that the French might give up easily they were to be sadly disappointed, as bitter fighting ensued over the next five weeks on land, sea and air. When the truce came, it was seen as a British victory – but not entirely so. Final casualties numbered about 800 on the Allied side and more than 1,000 for the Vichy French. Roald Dahl, who became a famous author after the war, flew as a Hurricane pilot with 80 Squadron in Syria and expressed some bitterness about what he called the unnecessary deaths caused by the Vichy French. And there were other campaigns when the Allies fought the Vichy French – not least during 1942 in Madagascar.

As discussed above, it is understandable that some of the Vichy French would find their loyalties torn but would conclude that their duty as loyal Frenchmen was to their government and that they should fight – albeit with the assistance of the Germans. It is also understandable that some, having fought, should retain no lasting rancour against their erstwhile foes while others would. The aforementioned Lieutenant Martin had fought in Syria and, it was said, had been bombarded by ships of the Royal Navy, giving rise to a hatred for the British, and in particular the sailors now in his custody.

Martin had a cruel and vindictive streak in him. The inmates had adopted two stray dogs – 'Raf', who had been saved from a cruel life at Aumale by internee Wilbur Wright, and 'Wimpey', found in Laghouat. They presented no problems and became companions for the inmates. But for no good reason Lieutenant Martin had them shot, to the great sadness of the internees. Wilbur Wright was inconsolable. Lieutenant Martin first encountered the internees at Aumale and enforced a rigid regime imposed by the commandant there – a man who came to be hated and despised by the British troops because of the cruelties and difficulties he inflicted upon them.

But not all of the French officers hated the British. The commanding officer of the Premier Spahis, *Commandant* Jeunechamp, had been a prisoner of the Germans alongside the British in the First World War, losing an arm in the fighting. He tried to make life easier where he could, but at some risk to himself. Singing was banned, even at the Sunday church services, but the internees did not obey and incurred the fury of the guards on one occasion when they started to sing 'Eternal Father Strong to Save'. Matters escalated quickly, with the guards apparently about to open fire, but the situation was calmed by Jeunechamp who calmly walked to the rear of the prisoners and joined in the singing. He apparently had a son flying with the US Army Air Corps, and clearly his sympathies lay with the Allies, although his views made him a collaborator in the eyes of many of his Vichy French colleagues.

Officer internees were housed in a single block with a number of small rooms, sharing with one or two others, while the other ranks slept in dormitories. The dorms were intended to house twenty-five soldiers, but as the numbers of internees increased these were becoming more and more overcrowded, with up to fifty packed in. Apart from the natural hardships – the heat, sand and flies, along with the lice in the beds – the French contrived to make matters worse. Food was poor, and the water undrinkable unless boiled. Each man received a litre of coarse Algerian wine daily, but as it was from the last pressings it was rough and took some getting used to. With only three holes[4] in the ground for toilets, sanitary arrangements left much to be desired – dysentery was rife. And some of the French contrived to make life even worse. Food packages from the Red Cross intended to help the internees were left standing in the blazing heat – some of the captors even pierced tins of food with their bayonets to encourage the contents to spoil. Medical supplies were minimal. The internees also felt themselves forgotten by their government. There had been several exchanges of Vichy French captives and British internees since the fall of France in 1940, but somehow none from Laghouat had been included. The comparison of the treatment given to internees by the Vichy French and the Irish is stark.

In April 1942, the H class destroyer HMS *Havock*, with a complement of about 250, ran aground near Cap Bon. Built at

Dumbarton on the Clyde by William Denny & Brothers, she was launched in July 1936 and had an active service career including supporting the attack on Narvik and latterly the Mediterranean, providing gunfire support to the troops fighting in Syria. *Havock* sustained damage a number of times while escorting convoys to beleaguered Malta, and was on passage to the dockyard in Gibraltar, where permanent and substantive repairs could be effected, when it ran aground and the crew were interned. The influx of sailors from *Havock* increased the number of internees considerably from just over 100 to 360, and only exacerbated the issues of overcrowding and tense relations between the airmen of the RAF and the sailors of the Royal Navy.

With the majority of the internees being sailors, it was natural that the senior British officer should be a Navy man, Commander Richard Jessel, which resulted in the camp being run along Navy lines using Navy terminology, and, to the annoyance of the airmen, naval ranks were considered senior to the equivalent ranks of the RAF. The RAF men called the camp 'HMS *Laghouat* – the ship that ran aground in the Sahara'. Jessell, however, was a real leader of men and did his best for the internees. Alfred Surridge, a torpedoman in HMS *Havock,* said later that he would have followed Jessell 'to the ends of the earth'.[5]

One privilege accorded to internees and not available to POWs was that of being able to write letters home. On 23 May 1942, Lieutenant Commander G. R. G. Watkins, DSC, *Havock*'s captain, felt so strongly about the conditions in the camp and their treatment that he wrote to his Member of Parliament, Captain Victor Cazalet.[6] His letter[7] expresses several concerns but is somewhat petulant and not a little arrogant:

When we arrived here we found that the internees had had a pretty miserable time. Their rights were supposed to be catered for by the American Consul-General at Algiers (who has never visited any of the military camps) (this {*sic*} very inadequate Vice-Consul[8] has been twice in a year). Being young and full of 'go' they were of course a bit wrought but were treated vilely by the French. The Consul regarded them as a nuisance and reported to the British Government to that effect. It appears neither he nor the French can understand why Britons would like to escape and continue fighting for their country. As a result of the Consuls [*sic*] misrepresentations no effort was made to exchange the unfortunates here with the many French repatriated after Syria last summer. It is to be hoped that this unfortunate state of affairs will not be repeated when the time comes to repatriate the French in Madagascar which is the reason for my letter. We are treated like Prisoners of War exactly except we are allowed a wireless set, can write and cable as we like and are with our men. The latter being good for the men but not so good for the officers who have to keep them amused.

And then:

... we are guarded by Arabs, which is ignominious; there are very strict rules; our men are overcrowded: and we get insufficient to eat. In all fairness the French themselves do not get much to eat either.

And again:

If it is impossible to repatriate us – and I don't see why not – we badly need a Red Cross representative out here and I suggest the activities of the American Consul ought to be inspected. They appear to be pro-Axis and to be of a nature like a Middle-West Schoolmaster in his dealings with us.

Watkins expresses some very real concerns but his derogatory comments on the activities of the American consular staff contradict the treatment reported by Charles Lamb and James Hudson when they were initially captured, although it may not have been the same individual to which they were referring.

Another of the naval internees, Lieutenant M. A. Baillie-Groham, RN, made effective use of the privilege of writing letters and perhaps unknowingly recorded aspects of life at Laghouat for posterity. He wrote a number of letters home during the period of Walcott's incarceration and they quite vividly build up a picture of life at Laghouat. Extracts from some of these letters follow.

He describes the camp:

The buildings are set about with barbed wire. There are three main layers and on the inside the two lanes are filled up higgaldy piggaldy with odds and ends of it. The spaces between the wire and the wall are patrolled by the French and at each corner, and at intervals along the outside wall and on top of the buildings, there are sentry posts, each with a battery driven searchlight and gun.

The camp is set within the barrack walls, which are about 12 feet high, and in one corner there are two long low buildings, one storey each, the smaller of which is divided into small compartments, inter-communicating, and houses the officers.

With regard to food and supplies generally:

The food is filthy, but it is the same as everyone else gets. The place
is fearfully rationed! there is little or no meat, and no potatoes or
cabbage or any of the things we get in England. Sugar is unknown,
there is no petrol: cigarettes are local and obnoxious, chocolate or
sweets are unhear [*sic*] of. There are no matches. Our diet consists
of beans and lettuce at 1100, washed down with wine, and a rather
smaller quantity of the same at 1730. Nothing else. They vary the
beans by giving us macaroni, or lentils or carrots. Occasionally
a square of meat is added. We get about 9oz of good wholesome
bread each per day, and that keeps bod and soul attached.

Food was an ongoing complaint, as were the latrines and
cleanliness.

The sanitary arrangements are of the most primitive, there
being only 4 Arab type W.C.s (7 minutes per man per day) the
rest being trenches dug underneath the windows of the officers
quarters.

Even the lavatory stinks to high heaven and is crawling with
bluebottles etc. It is too hot to use the trenches except in the
evening, and I would rather use my cabin than squat on the ground
in front of an Arab sentry.

We are running out of Oy paper again. For the first two weeks in
cells and until we went back again we had none, and newspapers
were not then allowed into the camp. Then the consul sent up a
hundred packets and we had ¼ each. I have had diarrhoea for
10 days and have not been very happy! Everyone has it, and the
medical supplies aren't equal to the demand, so Doc. has had to
close down altogether.

Mattresses are of straw as are the pillows and there are not enough blankets; clothes are rationed and we are not allowed coupons. The sheets are old and soiled and usually split.

I have been having a frantic time dealing with lice. I picked them up from my bed in cells last time I think, and now all my clothes are full. We insisted on all our bedding being changed but have no disinfectants.

The officers were not the only ones to suffer from lice. Sergeant John Lewery ditched a Wellington bomber on the night of 7 December 1941 and ended up sharing a double bunk with Walcott. He remembered mattress-delousing sessions with Walcott in their dormitory. Insects were everywhere. Seaman James Brown from HMS *Havock* recalled that they stood the legs of the bunks in tins of water to try to stop the insects climbing up but it didn't seem to work. The bunks were bolted together, but the joints loosened with use. Brown remembered that when he climbed on to his bed the joints moved and squashed the insects which had gathered in the joint, their blood running down the legs.[9]

As well as lice, flies and the natural conditions aggravated matters. On 25 May 1942 Baillie-Groham wrote,

There is a sandstorm outside. The room is full of it and one's eyes and ears and beard also. There is a hole in the ceiling, and it comes rushing in through. We have no fly netting and they too are everywhere. Fly papers and Flit[10] etc. are unknown. They breed in thousands in the stables and then fly all over the camp.

On 30 May:

The flies are ghastly. It is pretty hot now, about 120 or 130 I think. Later it gets up to 160 or 170 in the sun, and about 130 in the shade. They say it is cool for this time of year. I hope it stays so!

The actions of their captors only added to the discomforts and frustrations.

At the moment I feel in the blackest of black moods ... The pettifogging nuisances showered upon us by the illiterate Arabs who ignorantly guard us, through their dumb stupidity and superior propaganda-fed outlook, do more to annoy us than any froggies. They turn on the light for the wireless 5 minutes after the news has started and switch off the water half an hour early in the morning so that we can neither wash nor make our tea. If we decide to stroll around the 'block' they shout at us and load their rifles. They count our bedding twice a week, and our furniture once and our utensils once, so that there is always some damned b.... nosey parker mucking around with the sheets or asking you to find your fork – which is dirty and puts you in a worse temper than before.

Such letters had some effect back in Britain, but little urgency was apparent regarding the situation. Lieutenant Commander Watkins' letter of 23 May to his MP Captain Cazalet was only forwarded to the Foreign Office on 31 August. Their reply, on 17 September,[11] is somewhat complacent:

The deficiencies of the camp are largely due to climatic conditions, and it is also to be remembered that as the interned men are not held by an enemy power, we cannot demand application of the Prisoners of War Convention.

The letter also praises the 'ungrudging work' of the American Consul-General.

In mid-September, the Senior British Officer at Laghouat managed to have a note sent to London baldly stating 'Conditions Very Bad', but the responsibility for action seems to have been passed from government department to department, as demonstrated by a series of manuscript notes on the page:

I don't think I said so. But French Dept are handling the negotiations by which we hope that the Laghouat p/ws will be exchanged.

French Dept.
I understand ... that you deal with prisoners on Vichy territory. Can I take it that any necessary action has been taken on this paper ...

On 3 October, the Prisoners of War Department commented: 'But you, not we, deal with conditions in N African camps.'

Some of the activity in September may have been stimulated by a visit carried out by Dr Wyss-Dunant of the Red Cross on 16 August 1942. He reported that at the time of his visit, the camp held 382 men: forty-five officers, sixty-six airmen and 271 sailors. He concludes that conditions could generally be worse. A summary of Wyss-Dunant's report dated 6 October 1942 comments that:

Accommodation for officers and men is as satisfactory as can be expected in circumstances. Steps are being taken to relieve overcrowding in men's quarters by installing tiers of bunks which are now in process of manufacture.

It states that the prisoners receive 'a sufficient diet' because of food reaching the camp from Canada as well the regular arrival of Red Cross parcels. The lack of adequate medical equipment and drugs is also commented upon, but little action follows.

The differences between the report and the letters of the internees is quite striking. The report paints a picture of hardship but perhaps nothing out of the way considering that the men are internees and the difficulty of providing better conditions in the desert location. The letters describe a quite different situation, with the calculated actions of the guards making life as difficult as possible for the internees – in some cases brutally so.

The appalling conditions are countered by the remarkable resilience of the internees, who, despite the virtual impossibility of successfully escaping back to British lines, set up an X organisation to plan escapes. POWs and internees being the sort of people they were, some took seriously the concept that escaping was a duty – although many others just settled in for the duration. In order to avoid multiple escape attempts being carried out at the same time, with the risk that they would compromise one another, many camps set up an X organisation. A senior officer was appointed as X, and, in conjunction with a committee, his job was to consider ideas put forward for escape attempts. Those that were approved would be allocated resources to help achieve the escape. Many of the escape attempts from German camps were very sophisticated, with escapees being provided with civilian clothes or even German uniforms, which were re-modelled from uniforms and identity documents and travel documents created by artists within the camps. Very few of those who escaped from the camps managed to get back to Britain, but the very fact that they were free in enemy territory tied up troops who would otherwise be available to fight on the front lines. The most famous escape of the Second World War, from *Stalag Luft III*, was of course immortalised in the film *The Great Escape*.

Later in the war, Jack Rae, who flew from the USS *Wasp* to Malta with 603 Squadron, was shot down and taken prisoner over Europe; he finished up at *Stalag Luft III*. He took part in the escape preparations but was in solitary confinement when the escape took place. He thought that this probably saved his life, as fifty of the escapees who were recaptured were shot out of hand by the Germans. He was in solitary because he and another prisoner had made a very risky but unsuccessful attempt to escape. Not long before the main escape took place, they noticed that at night the uneven ground of the compound provided shallow areas hidden from the camp lights and they worked out a path they could follow to the wire by crawling slowly. Reaching the wire, they planned to cut their way through it. One night, covered with darkened sheets, they put their plans into operation, moving carefully, expecting a bullet in their backs at any time. The attempt failed. Dogs found the two escapees and they were sent to solitary confinement – the 'cooler' – without any injury.

Virtually immediately on the arrival of the internees at Laghouat, a cellar was discovered underneath one of the blocks – ideal to be used as the start of a tunnel. One of the RAF internees, Squadron Leader R. C. Brickill, was a civil engineer. At first sight this may seem an unusual appointment, but the air force needed civil engineers to build, repair and maintain airfields. Brickill had been shot down on his way to Crete and rescued by the French. With his surveying and engineering expertise, he felt it was clear that a 180-foot tunnel could be built to the outside. Work started in mid-November 1941 and the tunnel was completed eight months later in June 1942. The digging of the tunnel is a remarkable story in itself, similar to the escape attempts made by POWs in German captivity – particularly the Great Escape – with limited digging equipment, ventilation problems to be overcome and the need to adequately shore up the walls and roof. Finally, on 6 June 1942, the breakout took place and thirty[12] officers and NCOs escaped. Walcott was not one of them. None underestimated the difficulty they would have in crossing the desert, and they went relatively well equipped, with 'Mae-Wests' (life jackets) full of water. Some managed to remain free for a number of days, but all were eventually recaptured.

The standard punishment for escaping was fifteen days in solitary confinement. Again, conditions were appalling – toilet facilities consisted of a metal drum that was rarely emptied and so stank to high heaven and attracted clouds of flies. It became known in British official circles that escapees at Laghouat were being given thirty days in solitary, and this prompted protests to be made via the American Consul-General, but it seems that while some did receive more than fifteen days as punishments, most recaptured escapees were only given fifteen. One result of the mass escape was the removal of the vengeful Lieutenant Martin, who probably faced a court martial for not preventing the escape. As another punishment, the gathering of groups of internees was banned; if any groups did form, the Arab guards would load and point their rifles as a clear threat.

While the tunnel occupied many, when opportunities to escape arose they were immediately acted upon, and Bud managed to escape by seizing one of these opportunities. From time to time, an ancient lorry came into the prisoners' compound; another American flyer in the RAF and a friend of Walcott's, Sergeant Bill Massey, managed to stow away underneath it one day in July and made good his escape, reaching Djelfa where he planned to get a train to the coast. Walcott claimed to have copied the escape the following day. The lorry had a cargo of sectional wooden parts for a new building (possibly one of those being built to help improve conditions) and seeing an opportunity, Bud attached himself to a working party detailed to unload the parts. In the general confusion he managed to stow away inside the large compartment underneath it intended to hold the spare wheel. He hoped to meet up with Massey and travel with him on the train, although this seems to have been a forlorn hope considering that the escapees were likely to be noticed – if for no other reason than that they did not have identity papers.

According to Walcott, he made his way to a Spanish internment camp in Djelfa the next day where he got some food and was told that a train would be leaving at 15.00. Massey hoped to be on it.

Meanwhile, back at the camp, the other internees caused sufficient confusion at the roll call the next day that the absence of one of the Americans went unnoticed – much to the amusement of the prisoners. Unfortunately, while making his way to the railway station Walcott was stopped by a suspicious Arab, who called the authorities; he was apprehended and taken to the local military HQ. He pretended to be an American ferry pilot but the authorities were having none of it. Coincidentally, the Laghouat camp commandant was in the building and was introduced to Walcott but failed to recognise him as one of his charges. However, after a couple of days, Bud's absence from the camp was noticed. He was re-arrested and returned to serve two weeks in solitary confinement. Massey failed also – in fact, all of those who managed to escape from Laghouat were recaptured sooner or later and none made it back to Britain or Allied lines. Accounts by other prisoners record the escape of only one American, not two, and their attempts to confuse the morning roll call the day after the escape. The question as to whether two Americans could escape on two consecutive days using the same *modus operandi* actually occurred without the authorities tightening up security after the first incident is a moot point. However, in an interview for the Imperial War Museum made in 1988,[13] Seaman James Brown of HMS *Havock* recalled just such an escape made by an American pilot who was known as 'Yank'. Yank was a magician in peacetime and entertained the other inmates with his tricks. which included hypnotising them – or rather squeezing a vein in their necks. Brown recalled that Yank made it to Djelfa but was recaptured and on his return to Laghouat received only a mild 'dressing down' from the Commandant. Brown's description of the hypnotism employed by Yank is virtually identical to the late Tony Holland's description of Walcott's hypnotising tricks, and it seems inconceivable that Yank and Walcott are not the same person.

Despite the conditions, the remarkable resilience and defiance of the captives shone through. Sergeant 'Tony' Randall, James Hudson's wireless operator, started producing a camp newsletter called *Camp Echo,* which became greatly anticipated. Charles Lamb started boxing lessons and competitions. There was a simple library and a debating group. Others started classes, which became known as the 'Laghouat University', and, as in most POW camps, the men laid on entertainments. James Hudson recalled that the last entertainment was given by a magician, and although he doesn't say who this might have been, with Walcott's experience and skill it might very well have been him.

Walcott and Massey seem to have retained their sense of fun and made good use of the letter-writing privilege. On Friday 16 October 1942, Walter Winchell's 'On Broadway' column of the *Burlington (North Carolina) Daily Times-News* included this snippet from the two would-be escapers:

> ... Budd Walcott and Bill Massey, two Yanks in the RAF, cable the colyum [*sic*]: 'Had two letters in six months. Please get some blonde to write to us.'

This was followed by the address of the camp.

The months passed. The Red Cross inspection in August recorded that the camp held 382 inmates, but this was about to increase significantly. On 13 August 1942, the Town class light cruiser HMS *Manchester* was torpedoed by Italian motor torpedo boats while taking part in Operation *Pedestal*, the attempt to force supplies through to Malta that ultimately broke the siege. Built on the River Tyne and launched in April 1937 with a complement of 750, *Manchester* had a short but distinguished war. She fought in the Norwegian campaign in 1940, and after service during the actions to find and sink the German ship *Bismarck* she operated in the Mediterranean, but was damaged in July 1941. After undergoing temporary repairs at Gibraltar, she sailed to Philadelphia for full repairs, which took until February 1942. She returned to Britain to take part in Russian convoy work before returning to the Mediterranean and *Pedestal*. A powerful vessel, 590 feet long, *Manchester* displaced almost 12,000 tons and could reach a speed of 32 knots.

With the ship severely damaged by Italian torpedoes, Captain Harold Drew decided to scuttle the ship, in part to prevent its highly secret radar technology falling into enemy hands. However, the British authorities believed that Drew's decision was ill-considered and premature, concluding that the ship could have been sailed to a neutral port. Controversially, Drew was subsequently court-martialled, found guilty and dismissed from the service. Many believed this to be completely unjustified, feeling that his actions were quite understandable. It was reported that the ship was listing at 45°, had lost one of its four engines and had little ammunition left to carry on fighting. Many believe that the captain made the right decision. But be that as it may, the sudden arrival of about half of Manchester's complement of 750 at Laghouat – the other half were picked up the Royal Navy – worsened the conditions almost to breaking point. The barrack blocks originally designed to hold twenty-five Arab soldiers now held 100 Allied servicemen. The conditions became so intolerable that one of *Manchester*'s petty officers lost the will to live and was found dead. He had previously made his feelings known. Another, Stoker 2nd Class Norman Greaves from Salford, tried to escape by giving his watch to one of the Arab guards as a bribe to turn a blind eye while he climbed through the wire. Having taken the watch, the guard waited until Greaves was making his escape then shot and killed him. This provoked outrage in the camp. Walcott claimed to be present during the incident.

Yet again, the overcrowding became the subject of correspondence between the British government and the American Consul-General. With winter approaching, the weather was about to change and the inmates did not have suitable clothing to deal with the anticipated cold. But although they did not know it, the course of the war was about to change dramatically – and instead of a miserable Christmas in Laghouat, they would be back in Britain.

On 8 November 1942, British and American forces invaded French North Africa. The authorities quickly surrendered, but not before some almost comical attempts by the Allies to secure the support of the Vichy French and their agreement not to resist. After the previous battles between the British and Vichy French, it seemed politically sensible that the North African landings should be primarily American as those French who might resent giving in to the British may not have had similar qualms about the Americans. The Americans, though, had yet to be blooded in this modern war and their lack of experience resulted in the attacking force being stiffened by British troops – some reportedly even wearing American uniforms. Overall command would remain American, with General Dwight D. Eisenhower being appointed. The Allies hoped that General Henri Giraud might provide a rallying point for Frenchmen. Giraud had fought the German invasion of his country in 1940 and been captured. In 1942 he escaped from Germany to Switzerland, subsequently slipping into Vichy France where he tried to convince Marshal Pétain that Germany could not win the war and that overtures should be made to the Allies. His appeals fell on deaf ears, but the Vichy French authorities refused to return him to his German captors despite his opposition to co-operation with the Nazis.

It was vital that the Allies knew how the Vichy French forces in North Africa would react to their landing, and in an attempt to achieve this, a few days before the landings General Mark Clark of the US forces surreptitiously landed on French territory from a British submarine to hold meetings with American consular staff to try to resolve the issues. In summary, they agreed that Giraud would make an appeal to the Vichy French not to resist the landings. Coincidentally, *Amiral* Darlan, who with his anti-British sentiments had enthusiastically thrown in his lot with the Vichy French, travelled to North Africa on 7 November to visit his injured son and was trapped there when the Americans took Algiers after their invasion on the night of 7/8 November. Giraud's appeals to the defending French troops not to take up arms against the Americans were ignored, and some sporadic fighting took place. However, with on 10 November the Allies encouraged the captured *Amiral* Darlan to order the French troops to cease fighting. His order was obeyed, and the Allies appointed him 'High Commissioner' of the French territories, with Giraud in command of the army. However, as a collaborator, Darlan was not acceptable to the Free French Gaullists as well as some of the Allied politicians and senior military officers.

Hitler and Pétain were furious. Hitler ordered German troops to occupy the Vichy French territory in France and Pétain ordered that the French in North Africa should resist to the end, although his order was ignored – thankfully for the Allies. The difficulties created by Darlan's collaboration were neatly resolved when he was assassinated several weeks later in December under somewhat mysterious circumstances.

Three days after the American landings in the west, on 11 November, British and Commonwealth forces launched the Battle of El Alamein in Egypt. While the outcome of the fight was not yet certain, the writing was on the wall for the Axis in North Africa.

The end at Laghouat came with theatrical – but potentially tragic – actions by the Vichy French guards. Their communications with Algiers were cut, and the internees learnt of the surrender of the city over their radio before the guards knew of it. They found it difficult to accept that what they were being told was true. Once they did, the commandant made a grotesque offer to the internees. He said that he would have to defend the camp should it be attacked by the Allies, but that the Arab soldiers were likely to shoot their former officers. Accordingly, he proposed issuing the British internees with weapons so that they could jointly defend themselves from the Arabs. Unsurprisingly, the senior British officers found this offer extremely suspicious, concluding that it was merely a ruse to allow the French to retain some honour. The French assumed that once armed the British would take over the camp and force a surrender. The offer was refused, and within a matter of days the internees were freed.

A Foreign Office note dated 11 November in reference to the conditions states, 'Happily, the news from North Africa makes all this past history now.' According to John Lewery, the internees left the camp on 13 November.

It was over.

# 8

# NORTH AFRICAN ADVENTURES II

The internees may have felt forgotten and frustrated at the apparent lack of urgency by British government departments to improve conditions, but the authorities responsible for their repatriation following the Vichy French surrender moved quickly. Within thirty-six hours, repatriation of the first batch – those who had been incarcerated the longest – began. On 8 November, in a signal to Gibraltar, Allied Force Headquarters in North Africa stated that they were aware of 2,609 detainees in French camps including 950 at Laghouat, composed of 850 Royal Navy and 100 RAF.

The Laghouat internees made a slow and uncomfortable journey in lorries along the rough road to the railhead at Djelfa; many found the jolting and swaying of the vehicles made them feel queasy and sick because it had been so long since they had travelled in this way. The newly freed prisoners also found that their stomachs had shrunk from the inadequate food, and they had to re-adjust to normal nutrition. Although they were technically free, the Vichy French continued to guard them for fear that some of the now ex-internees might take revenge on their erstwhile tormentors – a fear that was quite justified.

Arriving at Algiers, the first batch of returnees was taken from the train to the docks and boarded HMS *Kerens* – the former liner *Kenya*. Built in 1930 for the British India Steam Navigation Company, she could carry almost 2,000 passengers – 1,700 in second class. Pressed into service by the Royal Navy in July 1941 and initially named HMS *Hydra*, she was converted into service as an armed infantry landing ship with a change of name to HMS *Kerens*. Having been built to operate in the tropics, the ship had large areas of open deck. Charles Lamb recalled that on the evening before the ship sailed for Gibraltar, he stood on the boat deck gazing at the lights of Algiers and thinking over the whole experience of his captivity. He found one of his fellow 'long-termers' standing beside him. The other prisoner gave him a letter for his wife, with the request that Lamb post it once they arrived in the United Kingdom. When pressed, the other prisoner said that he had made a vow to cut the throat of the brutal commandant at Aumale and he intended to carry it out. Lamb tried to dissuade him, but the other would have none of it and dived into the water some 50 feet below. He thought that if the inmates complained about the treatment they had received at the hands of the Vichy French, they would be put to one side in the interests of rebuilding good relations between the two countries – and in this he was probably right. Yet again, the interests of nations and higher matters transcended the needs of individuals.

Walcott made the same journey as Lamb, but as one of those with a rather shorter imprisonment his departure was delayed for a few days. Finally, he boarded the SS *Arundel Castle*, another merchant ship requisitioned by the Navy as a troopship, for the voyage back to Britain. John Lewery also returned in *Arundel Castle*. Conditions in troopships tended to be poor, with cramped conditions and little to do, but after incarceration in Laghouat this was probably a great improvement for the ex-internees. Ironically, on 8 July 1942, Mr Benjamin Rile, the Member of Parliament for Dewsbury, asked the Parliamentary Secretary to the Ministry of War Transport whether he was aware that on board the SS *Arundel Castle* 'there is inadequate sanitation, shortage of fresh water, inadequate laundry provision and overcrowding; and will he remedy the shortcomings and prevent a possible outbreak of disease?' He was told that 'appropriate measures had been taken'.[1] Despite these comments, John Lewery was more than happy with the quality of the food; with the deprivations of the camp, however, he had to return to eating normal meals with caution.

*Arundel Castle* launched in 1919 and sailed with the Union Castle line as an ocean liner. Originally provided with the four funnels that usually indicated a transatlantic liner,[2] she and her three sister ships did not ply the north Atlantic. A refit in 1937 changed her configuration significantly, which included a reduction in the number of the funnels to two. Pressed into service during the war by the Royal Navy, she served mainly as a trooper in the Mediterranean and was on hand to transport the released internees back to the UK. With Walcott aboard, *Arundel Castle* sailed from Algiers on 15 November, arriving in Britain eight days later on 23 November; it sailed up the Clyde, from where Walcott had embarked almost eight months before. The change of temperature from the Sahara to autumnal Glasgow would have been noticed, although as November marked the start of the cold season at Laghouat it would all be relative. Typically, in November, the temperature in the west of Scotland is usually a few degrees above freezing while at Laghouat it was more than 10°C. The voyage would have helped them acclimatise.

Not yet allowed their freedom, Walcott and his comrades were taken under guard to a hotel and then to the now-demolished St Enoch's station in the heart of Glasgow and put on a train to London, arriving the following day. All British troops returning from captivity, whether having been released like Massey and Walcott or having made successful escapes from camps, experienced a debriefing by the Directorate of Military Intelligence 9, MI9, which only operated during the Second World War, being disbanded in 1945. Its broad remit was to gather intelligence and assist POWs and internees to escape, and in so doing tie down enemy resources. It encouraged the forming of the 'X' organisations in the camps. It ran a sophisticated operation and set up clandestine escape lines in occupied countries which successful escapees could contact so they would be helped to return to the UK, either directly or via neutral countries such as Spain. Of course, those agents and partisans operating the escape lines put themselves at tremendous risk and many were betrayed to the German authorities, tortured and either shot or sent to concentration camps where few survived.

As well as the lines, MI9 developed tools to assist escapees. These included items such as tiny compasses that doubled as tunic buttons, sports equipment sent to POW camps containing hacksaw blades and other tools, facsimile identity and travel documents to help once out of the camps, and all manner of other ingenious pieces of equipment. But they also gathered intelligence in the debriefing sessions with those who returned. At the end of 1942, MI9 used the Great Central Hotel in London, now The Landmark Hotel, on Marylebone Road as its headquarters, and this is where Bud and the others were taken on 25 November for debriefing. John

Lewery recalls they were taken to the Ecclestone Hotel in Victoria. In particular, the interview concentrated on the escapes by Bud and his friend Bill Massey in July and the shooting of Stoker Greaves in October. The relationships with the Vichy French would also have been discussed. James Hudson went through a similar process, but it was clear to him that the need for the Allies to regain the help and trust of the French surmounted any possibility of bringing to justice those responsible for the hardships placed on the internees.

Following the debriefing by MI9, and as a quite normal process, Walcott was debriefed again by the Air Intelligence section of the Air Ministry, who probed the circumstances of how the airman came to be lost. The report[3] that was produced received a limited circulation and included Fighter Command so Walcott's disappearance was treated like any other, with no reference to the accusation made against him in the signal from Malta on 25 April. He was just another pilot returned from captivity.

Routinely, the returning servicemen also received a medical examination. Walcott was suffering from the effects of his captivity. He weighed 153 lbs and had a pulse of 84. He commented to the examiner that he couldn't eat properly, having to take 'not much at a time'. The medical board concluded that he should be given sick leave and re-examined on 28 December – a month later. John Lewery had a similar experience and recalls that they were given extra food coupons and advised to drink Guinness.

No doubt Walcott was pleased to find that on 25 September, while interned, he had been promoted to Warrant Officer Second Class. But it mattered little, for on 8 December, almost one year to the day after the USA came into the war following the bombing of Pearl Harbor, he was formally discharged from the RCAF to join the United States Army the following day with service number

A0885686. He left with his honour intact and without a stain on his character – other than the contents of the Malta signal, which are not reflected in his service record and to all intents and purposes had been forgotten about.

By now, Americans in the RAF and other air arms of the Commonwealth and dominions were accepted into the American forces unhindered. The restrictions on citizenship imposed by the American Citizenship and Neutrality Acts were not applied (penalties were not formally removed by Congress until 1944) and many Americans remustered to their own colours. Even the so-called RAF Eagle Squadrons, 71, 121 and 133, passed over in entirety in September 1942 to become 334th, 335th and 336th Squadrons of the US Army Air Corps' 4th Fighter Group, still flying their Spitfires but with British roundels replaced by American stars. The majority, who had served independently, moved over to join existing American units or, as in Walcott's case, a new unit.

At the end of 1942, the RAF and the US Army Air Forces (and the US Army Air Corps) differed significantly in that the RAF was an independent air arm, and had been so for twenty-four years while the American air arm remained part of the Army and would do so until the United States Air Force (USAF) came into being in 1947. As far back as the development of the early hot air- and gas-filled balloons at the end of the nineteenth century, modern armies quickly realised that such lighter-than-air devices could give them an advantage in solving the age-old problem of seeing 'over the hill'. British observers noted the use of balloons during battles in the American Civil War and in 1862 reported this to the War Office in London – although it took sixteen years for the first official forays into this new medium under the auspices of the Royal Engineers, who ultimately formed a balloon section.

The development of heavier-than-air aeroplanes promised more advantages for the military, and although they were still primitive, the British Army regarded them as sufficiently advanced to warrant the establishment in 1912 of a new army corps dedicated to aviation – the Royal Flying Corps (RFC). The Royal Navy had also been aware of the new technology and carried out its own trials, but its air wing was subsumed into the new RFC, although as a specific naval wing that retained its particularly maritime aspect. However, in 1914, a few weeks before the outbreak of the First World War, the naval wing of the RFC returned to the full control of the Navy as the Royal Naval Air Service (RNAS).

As is always the case, war acted as a spur to the development of technology. On the Western Front, unarmed aircraft were initially used for reconnaissance purposes and the crews of 'scouts' from both sides cheerfully waved to each other as they went about their business. Soon they were firing handheld guns at each other, or trying to drop grenades into enemy aeroplanes, and before long each side was flying suitably armed machines designed for specific tasks – scouts to perform reconnaissance and bombers to hit the enemy's supply lines and vital installations behind the lines. Bombers needed to be protected from defending fighters, leading to more and more complexity in operations. More strategic missions were undertaken – particularly by the Germans, who used Zeppelin airships and bombers to attack targets on the British mainland. Although such attacks achieved little in themselves, they demonstrated what might be achieved. Britain, however, concluded in the 1930s that 'the bomber would always get through' and designed its bomber force accordingly. Those who promoted this concept saw its folly very quickly when British aircraft carrying out daylight raids at the very beginning of the Second World War were shot down in unacceptable numbers.⁴ The British concluded that the answer lay in bombing by night, but even with the development of radio aids later in the war it proved impossible to bomb with any sort of accuracy in the dark. Reluctantly, the concept of 'area bombing' came into being, justified by reasoning that indiscriminate damage to enemy cities contributed to damaging morale and industrial capability. The workers themselves were regarded as legitimate targets regardless of whether they were at home or in the factories.

While many in the various armies regarded aeroplanes as extensions of existing battlefield weapons and assets, others could foresee their strategic use and the desirability of having an air arm, independent of army control. Lengthy and sometimes bitter tussles ensued as proponents of each concept fought to retain control, although the sense of having independent air forces tended to win out. Britain grasped the concept quickly and in 1918, before the First World War had ended, the RFC and the RNAS combined to become the Royal Air Force. Initially, the RAF looked after the Royal Navy's air needs with the Fleet Air Arm being created in 1924 as part of the RAF but transferred to the control of the Admiralty in 1939.

In America, a similar development occurred but later than in Britain. At the beginning, the US Army's air power was provided by the Aviation Section of the US Signal Corps but in May 1918, this became the Air Service, finally being made a permanent arm of the US Army in 1920. In 1926, it became the US Army Air Corps (USAAC) until 1941, when the USAAC became the US Army Air Forces, although the two co-existed until after the Second World War ended and the United States Air Force became America's independent air arm and one of the most powerful air forces in the world. Of course, for the military of both countries, the army needed to have its own dedicated air arm to directly support ground operatons although this was also provided by their respective air forces. The British Army has an Army Air Corps currently flying attack helicopters in direct support of ground operations.

On the face of it, Walcott's transfer to the American forces happened seamlessly – one day he was a warrant officer in the RCAF, the next he was a 2nd Lieutenant in the US Army. However, there must have been a transition. Firstly, he would have had to undergo some training as to how to conduct himself as an officer, and he must also have received some refresher training as a pilot. Having not flown for eight months, and suffering the effects of his internment, he could not simply jump into an aeroplane and pilot it. It would have taken some time to be once more assessed as competent, and then there would be a conversion to an aeroplane different in many respects to the Hurricanes and Spitfires that equipped Walcott's units in the RAF. By April 1943, he was flying with the 346th Fighter Squadron of the 350th Fighter Group operating Bell P-39 Airacobras. (In the American nomenclature, 'P' signified 'Pursuit', which translated as 'fighter' to the British.)

In the autumn of 1942, American planners sought to create air units to cover the North African landings; the 350th was one of the groups intended to be used in this way, and with the situation of Americans serving in the RAF now normalised, nothing hindered their transfer to the US Army. To expedite its formation in time for the landings, unusually, the 350th and the air echelons of its three squadrons, the 345th, 346th and 347th, formed in Britain at RAF Duxford in Cambridgeshire rather than in the US at the beginning of October 1942 as part of the 8th Air Force, receiving some of the Americans now serving with the RAF. There were a number of P-39 Airacobras already in the UK and not in use. It seemed extremely logical to issue them to the new units, and clearly this would minimise the time needed to have them combat ready. The aircraft could not be delivered in time and so the group missed the actual landings at the beginning of November, but despite this they were still to operate in the North African theatre.

The Bell P-39 engendered mixed feelings. Already in service with the Americans before the war started in Europe in 1939, it proved to be a disappointment by not living up to its manufacturer's promises. They sold the aeroplane on the basis of its performance when unhampered by much of the hardware it needed to employ for combat, which added weight and drag. But like many aircraft, it had several variants with good and bad points. Under certain circumstances and altitudes, it proved more than a match for enemy fighters and also made an excellent ground-attack aircraft supporting infantry and armour. But it was not well thought of by the British.

Viewed in flight, it shared the same configuration as the British fighters Walcott was familiar with – single-engine, single-crew, low-wing monoplanes – but otherwise it was quite different. The designers wanted to create an aeroplane with excellent visibility for the pilot, but in attempting this they compromised the whole aeroplane. One Spitfire pilot commented that anybody who flew the P-39 'deserved a medal'. As a measure to help improve visibility, the Allison V-1710 engine was mounted directly behind the pilot, hard against the back of his seat, which meant the nose-mounted propeller required a long drive shaft to connect it to the engine. The drive shaft passed beneath the pilot's seat and between his (or her) legs, resulting in a cramped cockpit. It has been suggested that it was designed for a pilot exactly 5 foot 8 inches tall, which if true

Unchanged Lenox, Bud Walcott's home town in modern times. (Picture: Author)

One of the Berkshire 'cottages'. Spring Lawn was built by John E. Alexandre, a New York businessman. (© Detroit Publishing Co.)

The Tillotson Livery Stables. (Reproduced with the kind permission of the Lenox Historical Society)

Twin Maples, Bud Walcott's childhood home in Lenox. (Picture: Author)

Salvi Bassi

VIRGINIA TILLOTSON

*Above left*: Bud Walcott's class photo. (Reproduced with the kind permission of the Lenox Historical Society)

*Above right*: Virginia Tillotson's class photo on graduation. Virginia later became Bud Walcott's wife. (Reproduced with the kind permission of the Lenox Historical Society)

Roberta Tillotson

*Right*: Bobbie's class photo from the school year book. Roberta Tillotson was Virginia's older sister and later Walcott's sister-in-law. (Reproduced with the kind permission of the Lenox Historical Society)

Robert (Bob) Tillotson, Bud's father-in-law. (Reproduced by kind permission of *The Berkshire Eagle*)

Merian Cooper, an American who fought for Poland. The badge was subsequently used by 303 (Polish) Squadron of the RAF during the Second World War. The Polish cap and the stylised 'stars and bars' symbolises the links between the two countries.

Taken in 1940, this is Johnny Kent, a Canadian who flew with 303 (Polish) Squadron in 1940. Note the unofficial squadron badge. (© IWM. Image CH 1530. Reproduced with the permission of the Imperial War Museum)

The General Manager of the RAF Club accepts the 303 Squadron badge to hang with all the other squadron badges on the club walls.

Ed Tobin, 'Shorty' Keough and Andy Mamedoff trying out the Eagle Squadron patch. They fought with the RAF during the Battle of Britain. (© IWM. Image CH 1442. Reproduced with the permission of the Imperial War Museum)

*Above*: 71 Squadron scramble: American airmen of 71 Squadron run to their Hurricanes. (© IWM. Image CH 2401. Reproduced with the permission of the Imperial War Museum)

*Right*: An Eagle Squadron shoulder patch, displayed in the Smithsonian Air & Space Museum Washington, DC. (Picture: Author)

*Below*: The Eagle Squadrons of the RAF become part of the USAAF in the autumn of 1942. These Spitfires bear the markings of the former 71 Squadron but with British roundels replaced with American stars. (© IWM. Image FRE 2333. Reproduced with the permission of the Imperial War Museum)

Fleet Finch primary trainer. This one was built in 1940 but has now been beautifully refurbished by 'The Tiger Boys' and is still flying. (Reproduced with kind permission of Tom Dietrich and Bob Revell – 'The Tiger Boys')

## Course 32 "Y" Group

3. S.M. Scott 24. Salvatore Basso Walcott 25. + Alexander Duncan Melville .7603) 26. + William Charles Wigston 27. Ernest Arthur Glover (POW) J.S. DFC Korea) 28. J.A.L. Caron (J.7607) 29. William Richard Tew J.7597) (DFC) 30. Walter Edward Dunsmore 31. + John Lomer Kelly 32. + Ray Ormond Colquhoun 33. + Norman Clunie Pow 34. A.H. McLaren 35. M.C. Tucker (CT) 36. W.S. Howie 37. J.H. Ryan 38. + Henry Keith Lefroy J.7598) (DFC) 39. MacLean (CT) 40. Elden Eves 41. Orrin Charles Snell .2. Norman Charles Russell Howe (DFC) 43. Clarance Dickinson 44. Richard Lear Alexander 45. St. Cyrr

*Above*: Aylmer Course 32 'Y' Group. Bud Walcott is second from the left, in the back row.

*Right*: Bud Walcott at Aylmer.

The Harvard 3222 flown by Bud Walcott during training, beautifully restored and flying today with the Canadian Harvard Aircraft Association. (Reproduced with thanks to Shane Clayton and the Canadian Harvard Aircraft Association)

Operational Training Unit Hurricane. This Hurricane Mk X from 55 OTU is based at RAF Annan, about 30 miles north west of RAF Carlisle. This was similar to the aircraft Bud Walcott flew to Dublin. (© IWM. Image CH 9220. Reproduced with the permission of the Imperial War Museum)

Hurricane instrument panel.

The apron at Dublin Airport with its terminal building. The date of the photograph is thought to be 1945. This is the terminal building Bud would have seen on landing at Dublin. The Aer Lingus aeroplane is a DC3.

Officers of 602 (City of Glasgow) Squadron in 1937. This is believed to be the first occasion they wore the kilt as mess dress. (Reproduced with the kind permission of Professor Dugald Cameron)

603 (City of Edinburgh) Squadron's Town Headquarters. Taken recently, the building is virtually unchanged since it was acquired by the military in 1925. (Picture: Author)

A 603 Squadron Spitfire at RAF Turnhouse in 1939 or 1940. This is an early mark without a bullet-proof windscreen.

On 28 October 1939, Spitfires of 602 and 603 Squadrons shot down this Heinkel 111 near Humbie in East Lothian, to the east of Edinburgh. This was the first *Luftwaffe* aircraft to be brought down on British soil during the Second World War. (Copyright of and reproduced with the kind permission of *The Scotsman* Publications Ltd.)

603 Squadron pilots photographed at RAF Dyce in early 1942, just before Walcott joined the unit. The numbers on the picture identify unit members: 1. Squadron Leader David Douglas-Hamilton. 2. Flight Lieutenant Bill Douglas. 3. Flying Officer Tony Holland. 4. Sergeant Buckley. 5. Pilot Officer Jones, who later died in the mid-air collision with Walcott.

Probably taken during a press day at Dyce, these Spitfire Vs are the aircraft flown by 603 Squadron and Walcott before going to Malta.

A recent photo of Pilot Officer Jones' grave in Longside Cemetery. It is well tended by the Commonwealth War Graves Commission. (Reproduced with kind permission of the War Graves Photographic Project)

USS *Wasp* in British waters in 1942. It is likely that it is in the Firth of Clyde. (© IWM. Image A 9483. Reproduced with the permission of the Imperial War Museum)

603 Squadron pilots on the deck of the USS *Wasp*. Walcott is in the back row, bareheaded. Lord David is in front row, centre, with Bill Douglas on his right. Tony Holland is two away, on Lord David's left. (Official US Navy photo)

An elevation of one of the Spitfire VCs flown by 603 Squadron to Malta. This one was flown by Bill Douglas. (Reproduced with the kind permission of Richard Caruana)

603 Bill Douglas preparing his aircraft below deck for launching to Malta on 20 April 1942. Note the crude application of the blue paint particularly noticeable around the serial number. (Official US Navy photo)

A dramatic picture of a Spitfire of 601 Squadron crashed in North Africa later in the war. The rather unusual orientation does at least show the trailing edge split flap quite clearly.

*Above*: James Hudson.
(Reproduced with the kind
permission of Tucann Design
& Print and the family of the
late James Hudson)

*Left*: 603 Squadron Spitfires
taking off from the deck of
USS *Wasp* on 20 April 1942.
The pilot of the Spitfire just
launching is believed to be
Flying Officer Tony Holland.
(Official US Navy photo)

A postcard view of the town of Laghouat. Not a very inviting place for a holiday!

The French destroyer *Mogador* after being hit by Royal Navy fire during the attack at Mers-el-Kebir. (Reproduced with the kind permission of *Argunners Magazine*)

Vichy French air force aircraft stage through a *Luftwaffe* base in Greece on their way to Syria to fight the British. This co-operation was against international law.

*Above*: HMS *Ark Royal* in 1939, with Swordfish of 820 Naval Air Squadron. The ship was sunk in 1941 returning to Gibraltar by *U-81*. Captain Loben Maund would be court-martialled following her loss.

*Left*: Malta in the Second World War, seen from above.

*Below*: Oblique view of Malta during the Second World War.

*Above*: Destroyers patrol around a Malta convoy.

*Right*: Smoke screens were used to confuse enemy aircraft and submarines. This shows one being laid around a Malta convoy.

*Below*: The smoke of exploding bombs can clearly be seen in this photograph of a raid on Malta.

A very vivid artist's impression of a German air raid over the Grand Harbour, Valletta. The constant aerial bombardment took a heavy toll on both Maltese civilians and the British forces defending the island, 'the most bombed place on earth'.

Bomb damage in Kingsway, the main street in the Maltese capital, Valletta.

The siege of Malta was a long-drawn-out affair, the island being pummelled by German and Italian bombers. Even so the navy continued to use Malta as a base, particularly for its submarine fleet. On 15 April 1942 Malta was awarded the George Cross, the first time such an award had been made to a body rather than an individual.

*Above left*: A watchtower at the Laghouat internment camp. (With thanks to the Orion Publishing Group)

*Above right*: The wire at Laghouat. (Reproduced with the kind permission of Tucann Design & Print and the family of the late James Hudson)

A group of the internees at Laghouat. Walcott is in the front row, far left. (Reproduced with the kind permission of Tucann Design & Print and the family of the late James Hudson)

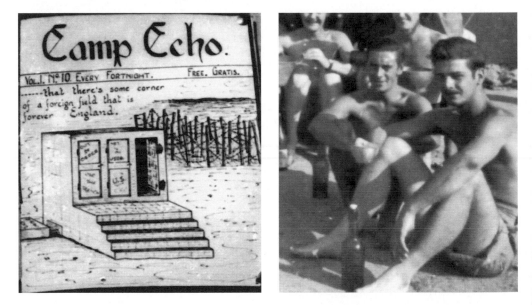

*Above left*: *Camp Echo*, the camp newspaper. This edition focused on the toilet conditions. (Reproduced with the kind permission of Tucann Design & Print and the family of the late James Hudson)

*Above right*: Bud Walcott in Laghouat.

*Right*: Another Laghouat group photo. Walcott sitting in front row, right.

*Below*: A boxing match in the camp. Note that the umpire wears a heavy Irvin flying jacket to keep warm. (With thanks to the Orion Publishing Group)

UNION-CASTLE LINE TO SOUTH AND EAST AFRICA.

THE UNION-CASTLE ROYAL MAIL STEAMER "ARUNDEL CASTLE" 19,216 TONS

A postcard of the *Arundel Castle*, the ship in which Walcott returned to the United Kingdom after being released from Laghouat.

A modern picture of what was the 'Great Central Hotel' where Walcott was debriefed on his return to Britain. (With kind permission from Squadron Leader Bruce Blanche)

This P-39 was flown by Hugh Dow, one of Bud's fellow USAAC pilots in North Africa.

A P-39 Airacobra on the runway. (Courtesy of the US government)

A P-39Q Airacobra. (Courtesy of Kogo under GNU)

Cockpit of the P-39. Compare the layout with the instrument panel of the Hurricane shown earlier.

The tunic of a former Eagle Squadron pilot who had transferred to the USAAC. Note the RAF wings. (© IWM. Image UNI 13853. Reproduced with the permission of the Imperial War Museum)

Bud's crashed Thunderbolt at Raleigh-Durham. (Courtesy of the US military)

The Tillotson family plot at the Church-on-the-Hill in Lenox. (Picture: Author)

CAPT. S. B. WALCOTT of Lenox, fighter pilot combat veteran of both England's RAF and the United States AAF, now in California.

Newspaper report of Captain Walcott's return to the Berkshires. (By kind permission of *The Berkshire Eagle*)

The Tillotson family home in Lenox where Bud and Virginia based themselves after the war. (Picture: Author)

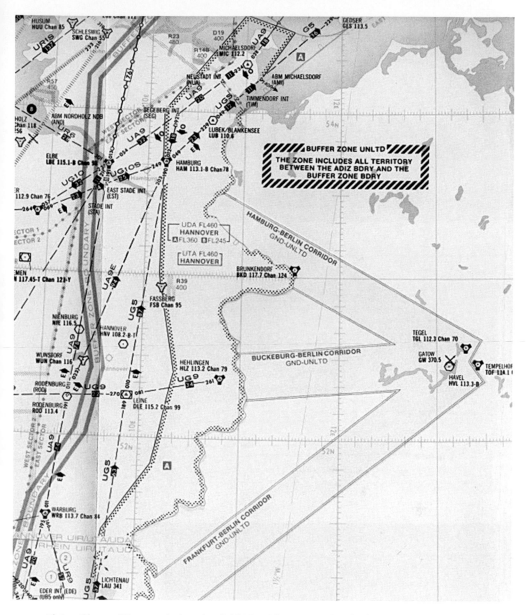

Flying Chart of Europe during the Cold War. There is no detail of East Germany other than the arrow-like airways pointing to Berlin for use by Allied aircraft.

Bud Walcott with the helicopter used by the Hunt Bros. circus for publicity purposes. 20 April 1956. (*Levittown Times*)

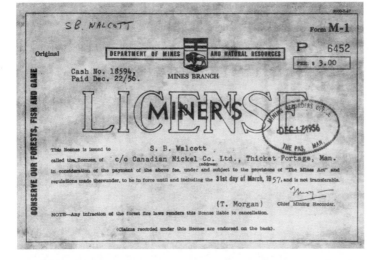

Bud's mining licence. (Reproduced with the kind permission of the Lenox Historical Society)

A U-18 built in 1965 by Air & Space Manufacturing and now held by the National Museum of Scotland at East Fortune near Edinburgh. (Picture: Author)

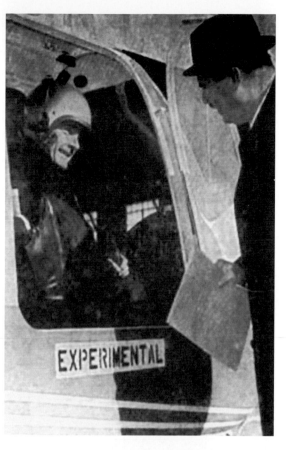

Bud at the controls of a U-18 during its demonstration flights in late 1959 or early 1960.

One of Bud's trial landings on the roof of the Old Colonial Theatre in Pittsfield. It was hoped to use this building as a base for feeder flights to New York and other cities, but this never came about. (By kind permission of *The Berkshire Eagle*)

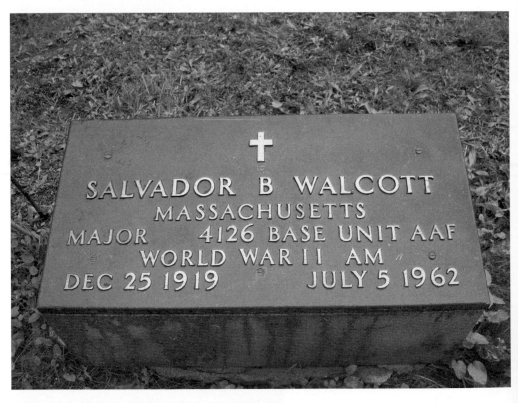

The application for a military veteran's headstone for Bud's grave in Lenox.

Bud's grave at the Church on the Hill in Lenox. (Picture: Author)

imposed severe limitations on those taller than this. A pilot over 6 feet in height could not squeeze in unless he dispensed with his seat-type parachute. And visibility was actually not much better than in other aircraft of the time.

Rotating at high speed, a slight imbalance in the long drive shaft created violent vibrations – one pilot commented that below 1,000 rpm 'the vibration was such the whole outline of the Airacobra dissolved into a shimmering blur'. In Britain, the Air Transport Auxiliary (ATA) delivered aircraft from factories and maintenance units to operational squadrons. These men and women flew many different kinds of aircraft, often piloting quite different types from day to day (anything from Spitfires to Lancasters), and were provided with a special set of 'Handling Notes' for each type – not unlike the 'Pilot's Notes' issued to operational crews, but giving only the essential information to allow them to ferry the aeroplane and deal with common emergencies. The 'Handling Notes' for the P-39 draw attention to several problems inherent in the aeroplane's design, including the vibration:

At idling speeds the whole aeroplane shakes violently. As a result the engine should not be run on the ground at less than about 1000 R.P.M., except when landing (to keep the landing run within reasonable length), and momentarily when necessary for manoeuvring.

And also,

The roughness is also evident in flight, but seems least at about 1800 R.P.M. A good guide is to watch the pitot-head shaft, which projects about three feet from the port wing-tip which responds to vibration in a lively manner.

But the American equivalent of the British 'Pilot's Notes', the 'Pilot's Handbook of Flight Operating Instructions', makes only a single and innocuous mention of the vibration problem. For 'Engine Warm Up' it states: 'The engine should be warmed up at a speed that is free from vibration, under 1400 r.p.m.' Clearly the British concerns were not shared or were being played down.

It also had brakes that tended to overheat. The British instructions noted: 'Owing to high landing speeds, the brakes tend to heat up considerably. If the brakes are "parked" while hot, they will probably seize ON, and remain on when next released. Therefore leave the brakes OFF for at least twenty minutes after landing or taxiing.' The brakes are, however, considered to be very effective.

Again, the American instructions are not as strong but do stress the point: 'During the landing run, do not lock the brakes or apply them continuously. It is recommended that they be applied, then released numerous times, this preventing severe wear on the tires and overheating of the brakes.' And the point is further emphasised in a separate note.

Another point of contention for the British was the cockpit doors, more like car doors than the normal canopy arrangement popular on many single-seat aircraft. The ATA Handling Notes commented:

Owing to their light construction, the doors are rather flexible. **It is therefore essential to wind the windows right down** before slamming the doors shut, or the windows may be broken by wracking.

There are three latches on each door, and these must be checked for engagement. This is done by ensuring that the **inside** door-handle is right home in the closed position. After slamming tight shut and checking that as mentioned, close the small safety bolt on top of each door. This is necessary to prevent the door from 'panting' at high speeds.

Again, the American handbook is much less dramatic:

Both cabin doors must be tightly closed and the auxiliary latch above each door securely fastened. This latch prevents the door from opening at high speeds.

Unusually for its time, the P-39 had a tricycle undercarriage – i.e. rather than a tail wheel it had a retractable nose wheel. This is common in modern aircraft and presents no problems for a trained pilot, but for Walcott it would present some different techniques to master. The cockpit layout did not include the basic flying panel common to RAF aircraft of the time so that a British-trained pilot needed to learn the individual configuration of the cockpit and its instruments; however, this should not have presented a major problem for a competent pilot.

Only one British squadron operated the Bell Airacobra: 601 (County of London) Squadron, which coincidentally flew to Malta with 603 Squadron from the deck of the USS *Wasp* on the day that Walcott crashed in North Africa. The squadron seems to be an almost integral part of Walcott's story! 601 received them in August 1941 but converted to Spitfire VB aircraft in March 1942, a few weeks before departing for Malta. They did not have a happy experience with the P-39. Regarded as unorthodox for the reasons set out above, 601 struggled with maintenance, having a poor availability and thus operational record. Only one operation was carried out in all the months that it had the P-39; a cross-Channel attack on Boulogne Pier and on some shipping. And over the period 601 suffered many casualties, including three fatalities. Morale plummeted, only to be revived when the change back to Spitfires came around. It is easy to blame the difficulties on the aeroplane, with its unorthodox characteristics, but it could equally be argued that the serviceability issues and casualties experienced by 601 may have been the result of poor maintenance and training, and not because of the aeroplane itself. The US Army operated the P-39 and its variants successfully in the Far East, the Pacific and, as shall be seen, in North Africa and the Mediterranean Theatre. It may be that the British developed some sort of institutional dislike of the type, hence the reputation it gained and the comments made about it. Suffice to say, as far as the British were concerned, the P-39s in their possession either equipped the new American units or made their way to the Soviet Union, where they found great success and affection in the hands of Soviet pilots in the ground-attack role as well as being a competent match for the *Luftwaffe*'s fighters.

From October 1942, the 346th Fighter Squadron of the 350th Fighter Group operated from RAF Coltishall in Norfolk just outside Norwich. Built at the end of the 1930s, Coltishall was a comfortable and typical RAF station operating fighters. It played a key role during the Battle of Britain in 1940 and would survive as an RAF airfield long after the Second World War ended, finally closing in 2006. No combat missions were flown by the 346th in England. The group moved to North Africa in January 1943, initially to French Morocco but then moving progressively east as the North African campaign developed. The pilots flew their aircraft for the long and dangerous flight from Britain to North Africa. They left from RAF Predannack and RAF Portreath in the far south-west of England not far from Land's End to minimise the distance, then flew across the Bay of Biscay to skirt the coast of neutral Portugal. Gibraltar was the nearest friendly port of call, but many of the Airacobras encountered problems and made forced landings in Portugal. The pilots were interned but in a reasonably short space of time were allowed to make their way to Gibraltar.

Although the Operation *Torch* landings in western North Africa resulted in the speedy surrender of the Vichy French in Morocco and Algeria and the release of the internees, the German *Afrika Korps* commanded by Erwin Rommel continued to fight fiercely. Success at the Battle of El Alamein allowed the British and Commonwealth Eighth Army to move solidly westwards from Egypt while American and British forces fought their way eastwards from Algeria. The fighting was hard. Repeated battles at the Kasserine Pass in Tunisia took their toll on the inexperienced American forces and the Eighth Army had a gruelling campaign to meet up with the Allied armies moving east. All the time, the advance squeezed the *Afrika Korps* into an ever-decreasing territory between the two Allied armies. By the spring of 1943, Malta had been relieved and continued to harry Rommel's supply shipping, making the continuation of the fight more and more difficult for the Axis forces.

The 350th Fighter Group and its squadrons supported the eastward advance. Ground attack and shipping protection took up most of their time, although the P-39s did engage in combat with *Luftwaffe* aircraft. Lieutenant Hugh Dow flew with Walcott's squadron, the 346th, and brought down two Messerschmitt Bf109s in aerial combat, proving that whatever reservations the RAF might have had about the Airacobra, in the hands of a good pilot it could match the aircraft of the enemy under the right circumstances. Dow's second victory came in Italy during April 1944 when he came across the enemy fighter at low level. Since his first kill, he had been able to test fly a captured Bf109 and knew that the P-39 could match the other aeroplane at low altitude – as he then proved. It is also of passing interest that Dow's second victory was probably the last of any P-39 serving with the US Army, as they were finally taken out of service shortly afterwards.

Unfortunately, the repository of the personnel records of American servicemen in St Louis, Missouri, the National Personnel Records Centre, suffered a major fire in July 1973, resulting in the destruction of many unique records – apparently including Walcott's – which has made it difficult to set out precisely what happened to him during his time with the US forces in the Second World War and subsequently. As will be shown, however, there is enough documentary evidence from other sources to be able to say definitively that he *did* transfer to the US Army with a commission and *did* fly P-39s with the 346th Fighter Squadron in North Africa.

In North Africa, the British Eighth Army started its final push, outflanking the German Mareth Line to meet up with the Allied forces coming in the opposite direction on 6 April. On the same day, soldiers of the Eighth Army fought and won the Battle of Wadi Akarit but suffered many casualties in the bloody fighting. On 7 May, the British entered Tunis while the Americans entered

Bizerte. Six days later, on 13 May, Axis forces surrendered – Rommel had already left North Africa.

By mid-April 1943, Bud had settled in to his new unit and its routines. Based at Es Senia just south of Oran, life consisted of patrols and seeking entertainment in the local bars or chasing American nurses from military hospitals in the area. There is an irony in Bud's return to North Africa and his changed circumstances – initially an internee suffering severe deprivations, he was now a member of a victorious army. Did he appreciate the irony? Did he harbour any thoughts of revenge like the unnamed inmate who swam ashore to take revenge on the French officer who had caused so much misery? Probably not. Bud was a freewheeling, optimistic sort of an individual who tended to look to the future, not dwell on the past. He was more likely to be grateful for his good fortune in surviving to become an officer in the US Army.

Towards the end of May 1943, the 346th Fighter Squadron moved to Maison Blanche, the airfield for Algiers. As soon as possible following the landings, the RAF moved aircraft there – many from Gibraltar – to support the ground troops, and within a matter of hours ground crew units known as 'servicing commandos' who sailed to the Mediterranean with the invading troops had marched 15 miles in full kit to the airfield to start the job of looking after the different aircraft that were arriving. Many were Hurricanes and Spitfires, well known to them, but the working conditions were primitive. Maison Blanche accommodated units from both Britain and America, and for the British this was also a major maintenance facility.

On 4 June, Bud's squadron deployed temporarily for a week-and-a-half to Monastir in Tunisia, about 440 miles south-east of Algiers and south of Tunis, before returning to Maison Blanche. Just at the end of the detachment, on the 13th, 2nd Lieutenant Walcott crashed one of the P-39s while attempting to land at dusk. The aeroplane in question was a P-39N1 serial 42-9401. He was cleared to fly from Korba on the coast near Tunis to Monastir, a direct distance of about 60 miles across the water using visual flight rules on a sea search mission lasting three hours. In Walcott's own words:

> I arrived over Monastir airdrome at 2050 hours. I made one pass over the flare path, turned down wind and placed landing gear electric switch in down position. I felt the trim of the aircraft change. I neutralized the electric switch and engaged the manual crank. I found I could make three one-quarter turns before the crank felt stiff. I turned onto the flare path, put flaps down and landed. I first realized my landing gear was not fully lowered when my belly tank touched the ground.

Unusually when compared with many other aircraft, the indicators for the P-39's landing gear were three pegs that stuck up, one from each wing and the nose, to show that the undercarriage was down. They retracted when the undercarriage was up. The pilot also had a cockpit indicator to show the position of the undercarriage. The flight handbook covers emergencies in lowering the undercarriage by instructing that the landing gear's electric switch should be off and the landing gear lowered using the manual crank. An investigation into the incident was carried out by Major John C. Robertson, who found that Walcott 'did not exercise full prudence in ascertaining that his wheels were fully lowered'. He commented that normally a single one-quarter turn should have been sufficient to lower the wheels and that Walcott should have been alerted that all was not well when he could turn the crank through three quarter turns.[5]

When the P-39 touched down, the landing gear was only extended by about a third – resulting in some serious damage to the landing gear struts, the starboard wing gear box, the engine and the propeller. While it was accepted that mechanical problems contributed to the problem, the main cause was put down to pilot error. In itself, pilot error is not always the absolute cause of the problem when aircraft crash. In some cases, the layout of the cockpit can be a factor as well as the presentation of information to the pilot and how it is interpreted. In a fatal airliner accident some years after the war, the design of the cockpit controls resulted in one part of the lift-enhancing devices being retracted accidentally during takeoff, causing the aircraft to stall and crash. There were several factors in this case: the aircraft captain was suffering a heart attack and was in considerable pain, and the co-pilot or first officer was very inexperienced and just starting line training. Although a third experienced pilot was in the jump seat, in the general confusion, the unintentional retraction was not noticed and none of the pilots realised what was happening. This accident resulted in the redesign of the control system to reduce the likelihood of the inadvertent retraction being repeated, but often this type of incident is attributed to pilot error and not faulty design.[6]

Bud's P-39 was written off.

When the accusations about Walcott became public after the war, his colleague in the 346th, Hugh Dow, by now a lieutenant colonel, was vociferous in Bud's defence, stating that the claims were unfounded and that if anything Walcott was a risk-taker – these words have also been used to describe him by his fellow internees at Laghouat. Given what is known about Walcott, it wouldn't be out of character for him to be behave recklessly when confronted with a situation such as that at Monastir. Combined with his risk-taking attitude, he had an impetuous streak to his nature and it would be quite within character for him to land without thinking through the full implications of what was happening.

The accident report notes that Walcott had 470 hours in his log on P-39s, with 120 on the P-39N1. His total flying time is also given as 470 hours, which clearly does not include his experience with the RCAF/RAF. It is likely that his RAF log book was confiscated by Vichy French authorities when he crashed on 20 April.

Although the battles in North Africa were over, the Mediterranean remained a battlefield, with the whole of its north coast in the hands of the Axis. Yugoslavia, Greece, Crete, Italy and France continued to suffer under fascist rule. The 346th subsequently took part in the battles for Sicily and then on the Italian mainland, converting to P-47 Thunderbolts in 1944. But by then Walcott had returned to the United States.

# 9

# BACK IN THE USA

Bud was based at Bradley Field in Connecticut as an instructor when he celebrated his twenty-fourth birthday in December 1943, but spent the holidays with his grandparents at Twin Maples. There are suggestions that he fell ill in North Africa, at one point having serious problems with his vision that may have been caused or exacerbated by the privations he endured at Laghouat, but this has not been confirmed.

There is an interesting and perhaps revealing article in the local newspaper, *The Berkshire County Eagle*, on 21 December 1943 reporting Bud's return from North Africa. In a nod to his skills as a magician, he is quoted as admitting that there may have been an element of magic in some of his escapes in the air, although this is hardly borne out by what actually happened. It is also interesting that in one newspaper article it is said that he flew combat missions with the RAF over France, which of course he did not. There is a suggestion of exaggeration and embellishment in these reports, which probably originated with Bud himself.

Bradley Field was built and opened in 1941, before the Japanese attack on Pearl Harbor on 7 December, as 'Windsor Locks', the town near it, but was renamed 'Bradley Field' early in 1942 in memory of 2nd Lieutenant Eugene M. Bradley, who died when his Curtiss P-40 Warhawk crashed during a training exercise not long after the airfield opened. He was the first of many trainees who lost their lives there.

Bud managed to visit the Berkshires, as the local newspaper reported, and in December 1943 a photo was published of him looking resplendent in his USAAF uniform. A close examination shows that he is wearing the RAF wings on his right breast. The badge itself appears to be slightly smaller than those issued by the RAF, and this, and the number of those pilots wearing them, suggests the practice was approved by the American authorities either formally or informally. RAF pilots who trained in the United States under the Arnold Scheme qualified with USAAF wings, and while some wore them on their left breasts until they received the RAF badge, the practice was stopped by the British as being illegal. However, many of the RAF pilots were proud of their American wings and retained them long after the war finished. Whether or not the wearing of British wings was acceptable to the US Army, Walcott was not alone in doing this and there are many photographs of American pilots dressed in such a way, although the practice did cease with the end of the war.

The by-now 1st Lieutenant Walcott experienced two crashes during 1944. On 28 March, while ferrying P-47C Thunderbolt 41-6127 from Orlando in Florida to Bradley Field, he crashed on landing at Raleigh-Durham air base in North Carolina.

When the Americans started their bombing campaign over Europe, their immediate experience was the same as that of the

RAF – bombers were vulnerable to attack by enemy fighters. At the start of the war, having suffered huge losses in small daylight raids, the RAF took a strategic decision to turn to night bombing, which would become controversial. The accuracy of night bombing was poor to say the least, and it was accepted that it was not possible to find and hit a target with pinpoint accuracy. Many bombs would fall far from the aiming point. Thus the concept of 'area bombing' was conceived – the attacking of whole cities or areas of cities that included legitimate targets such as factories or docks. But this meant that civilians would also suffer the bombing attacks. Part of the logic applied was that many of the civilians living near the legitimate targets would probably be employed there and thus could also be said to be legitimate targets. Of course, after the war ended, many considered these attacks to be unwarranted and some considered them war crimes. Bomber Command was rather shunned. There was no campaign medal. It did not seem to be appreciated by all that in 1941 and 1942, Bomber Command was the only arm of the British military taking action against the German homeland – or that it was the Germans who had first carried out indiscriminate raids against British target cities. Another factor was that these attacks tied up large numbers of German troops, guns, aircraft and other resources that might have been employed on offensive rather than defensive operations.

Despite the experience of Bomber Command, the Americans decided to pursue daylight bombing and this allowed Allied bombing of Germany to take place 'around the clock', although it was not without its problems. As an example, from the night of 24/25 July to 3 August 1943, the port of Hamburg was attacked and suffered heavy destruction. A mix of incendiary bombs and high explosive ensured that buildings would be set on fire and then totally destroyed. The fires needed oxygen, and their sheer intensity created such a demand that the suction of the air into the flames created what became known as firestorms. Apart from the flames and the destruction, some civilians who managed to make their way to shelters were suffocated because of the lack of oxygen caused by the firestorm. This concentrated attack marked the first occasion when British and American bombers operated in conjunction – the British bombing by night and the Americans by day. However, the Americans pulled out after two days because of problems caused by smoke from the night attacks obscuring their targets.

Four-engine Boeing B-17 Flying Fortresses and Consolidated B-24 Liberators formed the backbone of the USAAF bomber squadrons, largely based in the east and central areas of England. In particular, the B-17F became an iconic symbol of the 8th Air Force. Equipped with .50 calibre cannons in a number of turrets, with arcs of fire covering virtually the whole of the sky, the bomber could protect itself – in theory. For bombing raids they flew in large formations or 'boxes' designed so that the aircraft could all cover each other. One drawback of the rigid formation was that it did not allow an aircraft to take evasive action if under attack, and the loss of aircraft from the formation created gaps in the overlapping cover provided by the guns.

German pilots developed high-speed, head-on attacks from altitude. These were classic energy-conserving manoeuvres, converting potential energy (height) to kinetic energy (velocity) and then back to potential. American pilots were unnerved by the sight of the enemy fighters approaching fast and head-on. A bomber in distress, or a pilot who swerved to avoid a collision, could destroy the cohesion of the box and the mutually overlapping arcs of fire, creating more risk for the remaining bombers.

To start with, the bomber formations were escorted by fighters such as the Spitfire, but these did not have the range to accompany them to distant targets and back. And the Germans were no fools. They would leave the formations unmolested until the fighters turned back and would then carry out ferocious attacks all the way to the target and back until the bombers could meet up again with their protective fighters. There are some poignant accounts from bomber airmen describing their feelings as the 'little friends' departed and they awaited what was inevitably in store.

The answer was to develop fighters that had the necessary range, and the North American P-51 Mustang and the Republic P-47 Thunderbolt were two of the responses. Known affectionately as 'The Jug', the Thunderbolt was a huge, powerful fighter with a Pratt & Whitney radial engine. The Thunderbolt that Walcott was flying had the serial number 41-6127; the 41 meant that it was ordered in the financial year 1941, and 6127 is its sequential number. The C was an early variant, being overtaken in service by the D. It was thus relatively elderly, which might or might not have been a factor in Bud's accident. The Thunderbolt had a reputation for being a tough, rugged aeroplane that gave added protection to the pilot in a crash, and this may have helped Bud too.

The immediate cause of the crash was an engine failure due to a fire. Weather conditions were reported as good – cloud ceiling estimated between 3,000 and 6,000 feet with light rain but visibility 2–4 miles and a 15 knot wind. Bud was on the downwind leg when the engine failed. He immediately turned towards the runway, dropping the flaps and undercarriage. However, the port wheel did not extend fully, and although he managed to set the aeroplane down on the runway, it skidded off to the side and came to rest about 50 yards off the end. Bud is reported as having 'contusion of left neck'. The Thunderbolt sustained damage to the port wing, aileron and flap, as well as the damage to the engine caused by fire and to the propeller when it came down. However, Bud reported to the accident enquiry that he had experienced problems with the engine on two occasions on his way north from Orlando, and because of this the board opined that 'the pilot used poor judgement in attempting to continue the trip after encountering engine trouble on two previous occasions'. It also concluded that the locking down of the starboard landing gear probably reduced the damage that the aeroplane suffered.

There are similarities with the accident to the P-39 at Monastir, both criticising the pilot for essentially poor judgement. The aircraft was repaired.[1]

The report gives some revealing information about Bud. It states that he received his rating as a pilot on 9 December 1942, the day he was commissioned into the USAAC and the day after he was released from the RCAF. He did not have an instrument rating and his total flying hours are given as 800. He had flown fifty hours on P-47s, with thirty-five on the P-47C.

However, Bud is considered to be entirely blameless in regard to the second accident, which occurred on 14 June 1944 at Bradley Field. The aircraft was an RA-24B, serial 42-54797, a derivative of the Douglas SBD-5 Dauntless divebomber used by the US Navy but modified to operate from land bases, that is without a tailhook for deck landings. The Dauntless fought in the Pacific Theatre to great effect and started the war on 7 December 1941 over Pearl Harbor. The accident was quite straightforward. Bud was instructing a flight cadet on his first flight in the type; the cadet had just landed the aircraft and was taxiing back to the flight line. Walcott's statement reveals the sequence:

We flew around the local area for approximately thirty (30) minutes in which (*sic*) we then returned to the field. After receiving permission from the Tower, [the pilot] and I landed. We had completed our landing roll when [the pilot] stimulated the engine to clear the runway. After landing, I instructed [the pilot] to pull up his flaps which instead, he retracted his wheels. The ship therefore dropped on its' (*sic*) belly.

The trainee pilot's statement accepts his responsibility.

Landed at 1215 and after completing the landing run started to give the ship throttle to clear the runway. Lt Walcott instructed me to pull up the flaps, I reached down and retracted the landing gear. The right wheel collapsed first and the ship dropped on to its' (*sic*) belly. I cut all switches and got out of the cockpit.

The two statements are remarkably similar – even to the misspelling of 'its". And the investigating board placed 100% responsibility on the trainee pilot. However, it makes several recommendations, two of which relate to the cockpit layout. Firstly, the two levers for the flaps and undercarriage are very close to each other and it is easy to select the wrong one. Secondly, the retraction of the undercarriage requires only a single movement of the lever – it is recommended that it should be changed to require the pilot to make two consecutive movements, which would make the retraction more deliberate. An alternative to this would be to simply make it impossible for the undercarriage to retract while it bore the weight of the aeroplane.

This bears out the previous discussion about pilot error and shows similarities with the accident to the airliner mentioned on page 201. As discussed, it is easy but often dangerously superficial to simply blame the pilot, but in cases such as this, where a simple mistake, particularly under pressure, can be catastrophic, some causes of pilot error may originate in the layout of the cockpit or some other aspect of the design or operating regime of the aeroplane. The damage suffered by this aeroplane was sufficiently major to have it written off.[2]

Flying aside, 1944 proved to be significant for Bud in another way. On Sunday 2 April 1944, Bud married Virginia Tillotson in Suffield, Connecticut, while still a lieutenant. The marriage was announced in *The Berkshire Evening Eagle* by Virginia's parents. Suffield is local to the air base, but the couple lived in West Springfield.

The year 1944 also brought sadness, with the death of Virginia's father Robert on 4 December at the relatively early age of fifty-nine following a five-year illness. *The New York Times* published an obituary the following day – an indication of Tillotson's standing not just in the Berkshires but on the national political stage. By the time of his death the Walcotts were living in Wilmington, North Carolina, where Bud was now based. Robert Tillotson is buried in the graveyard of the Church on the Hill at the top end of Lenox Main Street in the secluded and peaceful family plot.

Early in 1945, Bud was posted to the Air Technical Service Command at Wright Field in Ohio after a reduction in the training programme for new fighter pilots. Then, in May of that year, Walcott, now a captain, moved again to become a test pilot with the 4126th Base Unit at San Bernardino in California. Working for a maintenance unit, the testing was not of experimental aircraft but of new aeroplanes making first flights and those that had been repaired. This was not without its dangers. Despite checking, test pilots doing this job occasionally found themselves having to react quickly to unusual situations. As an example, on one occasion the test pilot of an RAF Spitfire based at Maison Blanche near Algiers found that the aileron control wires had been reversed so that when he moved the stick to bank left, the aeroplane banked to the right. The pilot had to diagnose the problem in this highly dangerous situation then learn to fly the Spitfire safely back to earth. This required a high level of skill and excellent reactions.

Just as Walcott was moving to California, the war in Europe came to an end. As agreed with the British, American attention turned to the defeat of Japan in the Pacific. America (with Australian and some British help) had fought a bloody and brutal battle against a ruthless, cruel enemy in the Pacific islands. The Japanese were nothing less than fanatical and many fought until they were killed. Typical was Iwo Jima, a small island within striking distance of the Japanese mainland by US heavy bombers like the B-29, although it was earmarked as an emergency landing ground rather than an operational base. It was attacked by US Marines on 19 February 1945 and not finally taken until 26 March. The Japanese defenders constructed warrens of caves and tunnels with interlocking fields of fire, which made it extremely difficult for the Marines to prevail without large numbers of casualties. The Japanese fought to the death in many cases. The Marines had to resort to the use of flamethrowers to clear the defenders out of their warrens, inflicting horrific deaths. Even as the fighting went on, American bombers made emergency landings within earshot of the desperate struggle.

By this stage of the war there was little doubt that Japan would be defeated, but planners feared that a full-scale invasion of the Japanese homeland would incur huge casualties for both the Allies and Japanese. With fighting having ceased in Europe, Britain too was preparing to build up its forces to take part in the Pacific war, and the Soviet Union was looking to the east with a view to expanding its territory, much to the concern of the Western Allies.

Prime Minister Winston Churchill had little time for the Soviet Union or its dictator and had only become its ally through necessity. He distrusted Stalin and had grave concerns about Soviet desires for territorial conquest in Europe. In the European campaign Churchill had favoured quick, unexpected attacks on the enemy and feared that if the D-Day invasion failed then the opportunity to defeat Germany would be lost for many years – either that, or the Red Army would continue its advance across occupied Europe and arrive at the French Channel ports.

Since entering the war on the Allied side, Stalin had continually pressed Churchill and Roosevelt for the opening of a western front to reduce the pressure on the Red Army in the east. But it took time to build up resources and prepare for a cross-Channel invasion. and the date of the attack was pushed back and pushed back – partly because of Churchill's fear of the disastrous consequences of failure. This was much to the annoyance of the Soviet leader, who voiced his disgust at the lack of help coming from the Western Allies. To Stalin, it seemed that the Western Allies were allowing the Soviets to undertake most of the fighting, incurring large numbers of casualties – and they were. It isn't difficult to argue that the Second World War in Europe was won on the plains of the Soviet Union rather than in the West. As time went on, it became clear to Churchill and Roosevelt that if the planned invasion of

France did not take place soon, the war would end with the Soviet Union in control of much of Western Europe. With the relationship between the Western Allies and the Soviet Union less than ideal, an invasion would have to take place to restrict Soviet expansionism as well as to defeat the common enemy, Germany.

There were those in America and Britain who favoured embarking on a war with the Soviet Union once Germany had surrendered, by driving into Eastern Europe. Indeed, Churchill asked his planners to look into the feasibility of doing this with the help of the former enemy. using the defeated German soldiers and airmen as an additional resource. And while some commanders also favoured such an undertaking, it was never a realistic prospect. But it does demonstrate the concerns that Churchill harboured for post-war Europe. The decision by the Western Allies to allow the German capital Berlin to be within territory held by the Soviet Union also annoyed many of the soldiers and politicians in the West. Although Berlin would be divided into zones administered by each of the major powers, it would become a point of friction that almost resulted in another war – this time between the Western Allies and the Soviet Union. It would also have an effect on Walcott, who would be drawn into the situation once again, with his life affected by the machinations of politicians and international relations.

Thus, even before Germany had surrendered, the Allied coalition was cracking. Sadly, just before victory in Europe was achieved, on 12 April 1945, President Roosevelt died – to be replaced by Vice-President Harry Truman, who had to take critical decisions affecting not only post-war Europe but the international community. Whether or not the new atomic bomb should be used against Japan was one of those decisions. The concerns about the consequences of an invasion of Japan suggested that a demonstration of the dreadful destructive power of the new weapon in the American arsenal might encourage the Japanese to surrender; while its use would cause many casualties both from the immediate effects of the bomb and the long-term effects of radiation, it was felt it would save many more Allied and Japanese soldiers and civilians who would have been caught up in battles following an invasion of Japan.

The Soviet Union was not at war with Japan. It had been agreed that this would not happen until Germany had been defeated, and it wasn't until August 1945 that the Soviet Union declared war on Japan. It seems clear that it sought to expand against Japanese territory to its east, so use of the atomic bomb would be a clear warning to Stalin that his expansionist desires would be resisted and that America had the ability to inflict grievous damage on the Soviet Union, which at that time did not have 'the bomb', should Stalin decide so to act.

Accordingly, on the morning of 6 August 1945, an atomic bomb was dropped on the Japanese city of Hiroshima. Three days later, on 9 August 1945, a second was dropped on Nagasaki. Total casualties, including long-term effects of radiation exposure, amounted to about 200,000, with about 60 per cent caused by flash or flame burns. But the bombs made the Japanese appreciate that to resist further was pointless, and they surrendered. Over the years, controversy as to the rights and wrongs of the dropping of the two bombs has continued, with many claiming that it was an immoral act. In the author's opinion, if an invasion had taken place many more lives would have been lost, and on balance the use of the atomic weapons achieved the desired effect – later even serving as a warning of the dreadful consequences should the Cold War turn 'hot'.

Captain Walcott was discharged from the US Army and returned to Lenox. He and Virginia stayed in the Tillotson house at the other end of Main Street from the Church on the Hill and opposite the Town Hall with Mrs Tillotson and Bud's sister-in-law Bobbie. The family dynamics would have been interesting. Returning from the army, Bud was spared the immediate problem of finding a home for himself and his wife; as a junior officer he would not have been paid very much. But his wife and family were wealthy, which presumably proved helpful when it came to accommodation and financial resources, although Bud's grandmother might also have been a source of income for him too. He had little to offer a prospective employer; his main life skills were his training as a pilot in the military and his experience as a cabaret magician with a smattering of casual, low-paid jobs in the hospitality industry. For the locally influential Tillotsons, with Robert Tillotson's death only one year in the past, the prospect of Virginia's husband working in some menial and low-paid job would not be appealing. Bud loved to fly, and he tried to make his living as a pilot; however, with the army reducing in size, there were more pilots and aircrew seeking jobs than ever before.

International relations between countries intervened again, and on 20 August 1946 Bud was recalled to the army, sailing for Europe at the end of the year. In 1948 he found himself based in Berlin, with Virginia having joined him, but their lives were about to be disrupted by the crisis in relations with the Soviet Union that led to the Berlin airlift.

When the war ended in May 1945, the Soviet Union controlled more or less the eastern half of Germany, with the three Western Allies – America, France and Britain – occupying the remainder to the west, which they divided into three smaller zones over which each would exert control. Crucially, and against the wishes of many soldiers and politicians in the West, the Western Allies allowed the Soviets to advance west beyond Berlin so that when the fighting ceased Germany's capital city lay about 160 miles within what would become East Germany. However, agreements between the victors saw the capital divided into four zones so that each of the powers administered part of the city. The three Western Allies depended on the goodwill of the Soviets to allow them to travel overland to the city, but they enjoyed a legal right to fly to and from Berlin via three defined air corridors, which pointed like an arrowhead across the Soviet-occupied zone. This is clearly and depressingly illustrated by an RAF High Altitude chart of the Cold War period, with the Soviet/East German zone a blank area of white other than the three corridors.

After the destruction and misery Germany had inflicted on Europe during the war, some wished for it to be completely subjugated so that such events could never happen again. Meanwhile, others considered that an eventually independent and unified Germany with a strong economy would benefit the emerging world, and this view prevailed. After the First World War, the terms of the Treaty of Versailles had created resentment and played a role in bringing the National Socialists and Hitler to power. To avoid a similar outcome and to block the influence of the Soviets, America embarked on the Marshall Plan, giving aid to the ruined countries of Europe and starting the long process of recovery. But Stalin's objectives were different. He wanted to retain control of the lands taken during the fighting to act as a buffer between the Soviet Union and the West. Relations between the former allies deteriorated, and within a matter of months the relationship had become hostile. The Soviet Union had no wish to see another united and powerful Germany, and resisted the West's actions to achieve this by eventually setting up a separate state – the German Democratic Republic (GDR) – in 1949 so that there were two Germanys, known as 'East' and 'West' Germany.

Following the same philosophy as other countries, the United States decided that its interests were best served by having an air arm independent of its army, and on 18 September 1947 the strategic air forces of the US Army became the United States Air Force (USAF). This would make little difference to Bud other than that he would be wearing the blue uniform of the new air force rather than the brown of the US Army.

In 1948, Stalin wanted to oust the Western Allies from their sectors of Berlin. Initially the Soviets made life awkward for overland travel to and from the city by instituting what appeared to be petty restrictions. On 2 April, the Americans stopped their military trains making the journey and started to supply their units solely by air. This lasted ten days and is sometimes called 'the mini airlift'. As well as making life difficult for those making the journey, the Soviet interference began to affect the supplies West Berliners needed to carry on with their day-to-day lives. Trains and road traffic were held up while checks on their contents took place. Sometimes they would be re-routed to create delays and difficulties. Although the air routes remained sacrosanct, Allied aeroplanes flying on their legitimate business were harassed or 'buzzed' from time to time by Soviet fighters. This was dangerous and illegal, and resulted in a collision with a British Vickers Viking transport. All aboard the two aircraft died. On 9 April, the Soviets demanded the removal of Western personnel stationed in East Germany to maintain the radio beacons used by Allied aircraft to navigate the air corridors. This created another set of problems for the airmen, who knew that they might be shot down if they strayed away from the designated routes.

It became clear to planners in the West that the overland routes to Berlin might very well be cut at some point, which would mean that the city could only be supplied by air. Initial assessments concluded that this could not be sustained for any length of time. But as matters worsened, eventually the Soviets stopped all ground travel and also cut off utilities such as water supplies and electricity to the western sector of Berlin. It became clear that if West Berlin had any hope of survival, it would need to be supplied entirely by air. With the new political reality, the West could not afford to abandon West Berlin to the Soviet Union and ultimately the 'Berlin Airlift' started at the end of June. Yet again, the fickle changes in international relationships and alliances came to affect Bud Walcott, who now found himself helping those who had been his country's enemies only three years before.

An article in *The Berkshire Evening Eagle* of Thursday 16 April 1948 was headlined: 'Lenox Woman On Last Train To Leave Berlin':

> Mrs S. W. Walcott ... who is stationed with her husband, Capt. Walcott in Germany, was aboard the last train to leave Berlin before the Russians closed American rail traffic to and from the city.

Virginia reports that the journey proved uneventful but was full of tension, with the train guarded by American troops. This was during the 'mini' crisis of April, and the rail lines reopened within a few days; nonetheless it was a memorable experience for the young woman. Bud was based for part of the main airlift in the operations section at Tegel airfield in the French sector of Berlin.

A rocket-testing site during the war, it became a military training area in 1948 with the need for airfield resources to deal with the airlift; a runway and other facilities were hastily constructed to take the pressure off the other Berlin airfields, Gatow and Tempelhof in the British and American sectors respectively.

The operations sections were essential to the smooth, efficient organisation of the airlift. This involved the shuttling of a fleet of transport aircraft in and out of the city, down the air corridors twenty-four hours a day, seven days a week, if the city was to be sustained. Luxuries were few; the concentration was on the essentials for life such as coal and food. Flights could be disrupted by bad weather, and with different types of aeroplanes in use some travelled faster than others and could carry more cargo, leading to logistical problems both in the routing of them to avoid mid-air collisions and to ensure the unloading and turnaround on the ground was carried out efficiently and effectively. The crisis proved to be a rare opportunity for many British airmen who had been released from the RAF and were still seeking employment. With a glut of surplus military transport aircraft on the market, many took the chance to buy one of these aircraft and sign up to fly the airlift into Berlin for generous fees. Only four or five years previously some of these men flew with Bomber Command in raids against 'the big city', but now they were flying to it to provide help to those they previously hoped to defeat: one of the most striking examples of how the ebb and flow of international politics and relations affects the lives of individuals.

Regarded as a triumph and an undoubted snub to the Soviet Union, the airlift officially ended on 30 September 1949, although the Soviet Union actually ceased its blockade in May. Total tonnage delivered amounted to 2.3 million carried by in excess of 277,000 flights. About 100 airmen died.

Bud and Virginia returned to the United States from Europe in October 1949, at the end of the airlift, aboard *Henry Gibbins*, an army transport ship specifically fitted out for families and dependants. Immediately after the war, it operated as a 'GI brides' ship, transporting European women who had married American servicemen and their children to the United States to re-join their husbands. It operated a shuttle run from Bremerhaven to the east coast of the US and brought the Walcotts in at Staten Island, across the water from Manhattan. Facilities on board the ship included a formal dining room so it had a degree of comfort not usually associated with military transportation. From Staten Island, Walcott reported to Camp Kilmer in New Jersey for reassignment, which took him to Las Vegas. The couple spent an extended Christmas holiday with Virginia's mother in Lenox.

*The Berkshire Eagle* subsequently reported that Virginia's mother and sister Bobbie had returned from visiting Bud and his wife in San Antonio, Texas, at the beginning of April 1950.

Bud and Virginia led a peripatetic life both inside the military and in civilian life. They based themselves in Lenox in the spacious, comfortable Tillotson house on Main Street. Often they were separated, and Virginia lived at home with her mother and sister, and during these periods – as well as when Bud was there too – she took an active part in Republican politics with her mother and sister as they continued her father's work. In 1952, Virginia assisted in the campaign to elect Senator Robert Taft as President – but backed the wrong candidate when Taft failed to gain the Republican Party nomination. He was defeated by Dwight D. Eisenhower, who went on to win the presidential race. In October

1956, the three included their names in an advertisement urging others to vote for the Republican candidate in the forthcoming Massachusetts gubernatorial election, but they backed the wrong man again. Occasionally Bud took an interest in his wife's political activities, adding his support. They were a happy couple, sometimes seen driving around town in an open-topped sports car rather like a British MG, with two Boxer dogs whose exuberant and friendly demeanour matched Bud's own. Bud's happy-go-lucky outlook on life endeared him to his friends and neighbours and he was well liked in the small town in the Berkshires. Virginia went flying with Bud and commented that she felt as safe in the cockpit of an aeroplane with her husband as if sitting on a sofa beside him. Ten-pin bowling was a very popular sport in the United States in the 1940 and 1950s. Many local teams sprang up – each with their distinctive shirts – to compete in leagues. Virginia enjoyed bowling and took part in the sport regularly and was a serious and talented player.

Bud was released from the USAF on 5 November 1952 to become a member of the reserve.

Although the principles of rotary winged flight were known before the war, it wasn't until afterwards that helicopters came into more common use. The capacity for helicopters to land and take off vertically, without the use of long runways, provided significant advantages to military operations as well as having civilian applications. The US military, like the British, saw the potential in helicopters and started to employ them. Bud became an accomplished helicopter pilot in civilian life, and although it isn't known for sure, it is quite possible that he acquired this new skill with the air force.

Because they generate lift from air flowing over their rotor blades rather than over a fixed wing, the dynamics of helicopter flight are different from those of conventional aircraft – and the flying methodology as well. Instead of a control column, rudder pedals and throttle, a helicopter has a cyclic, a collective, anti-torque pedals and a throttle. The cyclic is in front of the pilot, rather like a conventional control column, while the collective is down at his or her left side. These two controls move the angle of the rotor blades in the air through which they are passing to change the lift produced by them, while the anti-torque pedals act in the same way as rudder pedals to change the direction. One of the basic laws of mechanics is that an action results in an equal and opposite reaction. Unless otherwise countered, spinning rotor blades will cause the body of the helicopter to rotate in the opposite direction, so to counter this helicopters conventionally have a small, vertical tail rotor to provide sufficient force to prevent the main fuselage rotating. Some helicopters use a jet of air to achieve the same effect.

Experiments in vertical flight started before the Second World War and continued through it, but it was in the 1950s that helicopters came into their own. The military in particular identified advantages to be gained from the helicopter's ability to hover and operate from small open areas rather than lengthy runways. During the Korean War, which ran from 1950 to 1953, the US Army employed Bell 47 helicopters in a casualty evacuation role (as seen in the film and TV series *M.A.S.H.*) evacuating about 22,000 casualties during that period. Without them, those wounded on the battlefield would have taken much longer to reach adequately equipped field hospitals and more would have died. And this has continued to the present day in Afghanistan, where fully equipped helicopters with medical teams lift seriously wounded casualties from the middle of the battlefield to fully equipped trauma hospitals within a few minutes – at no little risk to the airmen and medical staff who crew them. In the 1950s, military helicopters tended to be used for life-saving rather than life-taking activities but in more modern times helicopter gunships such as the Soviet Mil-Mi24 Hind or the American Boeing AH-64 Apache are ferocious and deadly firepower platforms, supporting forces on the ground. On the civil front, helicopters are valuable for lifting heavy equipment to otherwise inaccessible places – positioning staff, poles and equipment for power companies and energy companies in remote hilly areas as well as giving access to high buildings and the like, or to offshore oil rigs.

A competent fixed-wing pilot should be able to transfer to helicopter relatively easily. Many helicopter pilots start their flying training on fixed-wing aircraft. Bud would have little difficulty in making the change.

The first scheduled passenger helicopter service started in July 1953. New York Airways flew Sikorsky S-55s between the city's three main airports – LaGuardia, Idlewild and Newark. Later that year, Sabena initiated the first European and international service between Brussels and Rotterdam via Lille and Antwerp, and in subsequent years the use of commercial helicopters grew steadily. But they were not economical. In 1958, cost per capacity ton-mile of a helicopter was judged to be $7 (the equivalent of £2.50) with the equivalent cost for trunk airlines flying conventional airliners of 30 cents and about 50 cents for local carriers.[3] At that time, few companies operating helicopters possessed more than five machines, although in North America including Canada a total of more than 200 helicopters were being operated by companies with fewer than five machines – i.e., there were more than forty companies providing helicopter services.

Bud plunged into this exciting new area of flying with his usual enthusiasm. One resident, a boy at the time, recalled that in 1952 Bud landed a helicopter in the grounds of the high school to let the youngsters see it at close quarters. The downdraft from the rotors caused havoc but the kids enjoyed it. For the schoolboy, it triggered an interest in flying and he subsequently acquired a pilot's licence.

Many of the American civil operators of helicopters in the 1950s flew Bell 47s – the bubble-nosed skeletal aircraft used by the US Army in Korea – which became a workhorse, with roughly 5,600 being built, some under licence abroad, including in Britain. In 1946, it became the first helicopter to be granted a licence to fly in a civil role. The manufacturing company, Bell Aircraft Corporation, also built the P-39s that Bud flew in North Africa, and, being based in Buffalo, New York, it was only 285 miles from the Berkshires and reasonably accessible. It seems that Bud worked for Bell for a time – although this has not been absolutely verified.

In the middle years of the twentieth century, circuses were popular in Britain and the USA. Circuses arrived in towns with a parade to give a taster of what might be seen in the performances, and crowds lined streets to get a preview of the so-called 'romance' of the circus. The travelling shows toured cities, setting up their Big Top for a few days to give performances before moving on to the next town. Unlike modern times, exotic animals were objects of curiosity and were made to perform tricks; today this is regarded as cruel. The idea of keeping wild animals in bare, small cages is now regarded as unacceptable so many circuses now give performances without any animals.

In the United States, one of the best-known circuses was Ringling Brothers and Barnum & Bailey – a combined enterprise. In the early 1950s, it travelled the country and parts of Canada. It started its season in April, opening in Madison Square Gardens in New York City and finishing in Florida in mid-November. Another was the Hunt Brothers Circus; it tended to operate in the north-east of the United States. Owned by Charles T. Hunt, with Harry Hunt acting as manager, it based itself for the winter period in Burlington, New Jersey, but had a much shorter season. In 1955 it opened in Burlington on 23 April, ending in October, in Maryland. It generally covered the area from Maine in the north to Pennsylvania in the south, although in 1955 its activities in Pennsylvania were restricted pretty much to the northern environs of Philadelphia, in the south-east of the state. At the end of May 1955, both these circuses were operating in the Philadelphia area, with Hunt brothers in several of the little towns to the north – Flourtown on the 19th, Glenside on the 20th and Mt Airy on the 21st, with Ringling Bros Barnum & Bailey also in the area at that time. The following week, the two had gone their separate ways. On the 30th, Hunt Brothers was in Fort Dix, New Jersey, and Princeton on the 31st while Ringling Bros Barnum & Bailey was entertaining the families of Scranton on the 30th and Wilkes Barre on the 31st – both towns in Pennsylvania north of Philadelphia. Since then the popularity of circuses has much reduced, and at the time of writing Barnum & Bailey has announced that it will be closing for good.

Circus life was peripatetic and busy. The constant setting up and dismantling of the encampment and all that went with it left little time for resting. It was a seven-days-a-week job – hence the long winter breaks, which allowed for recuperation and avoided travel in the north-eastern winters. Overheads were high and owners were looking out for something new. As well as getting to the individual locations, advance promotions were important to ensure maximum income so advance parties visited locations days before the circus was due, to get publicity using posters, as well as radio and newspaper announcements. In 1955, advertising on radio was costly and the competition was affecting bookings. New ways of attracting attention were always being sought. During the war, Hunts owned a Piper Cub aeroplane, which they used to advertise by flying over forthcoming venues. A high-wing monoplane with seats for four, it was equipped with a sound system that was used to tell those on the ground about the circus. However, it was found that, with a minimum airspeed of about 75mph, it travelled too quickly.[4]

The advent of the helicopter did not go unnoticed, and on 12 March 1955 Hunts announced they had acquired one to be employed in the advertising role previously attempted by the Piper Cub. Equipped with a sound system and able to hover, it was expected to be more successful. The helicopter in question was a Bell 47G. According to the circus publicity, it was difficult to acquire a helicopter but for $36,000 they bought one based in Grand Junction Colorado, and then had to decide how to get it to New Jersey – to fly it or bring it by road. The engine had to be overhauled every 600 hours, at a cost of $4,500, so they were keen to minimise engine hours. They also estimated the annual additional cost to the circus would be $20,000, which presumably included the cost of the pilot. It was planned that circus venues would be covered by the helicopter, with its high-powered sound system, for six days prior to the show date, and it would be flying for four or five hours a day. Quite what those on the ground thought of the blaring sound from above goes unrecorded!

Flying for about four hours a day gave 150 days between engine overhauls – probably slightly less than the length of the season. *Billboard* magazine reported that Frank Horn, a pilot with ten years' experience of flying helicopters and 2,500 hours, had been engaged by the circus. In 1955 the season went well, with money rolling in. Hunts attributed their success to a combination of the helicopter and, rather bizarrely, a new gleaming 'comfort station'. The pilot at this time was Stuart Clark, said to be one of only sixty pilots in the US with more than 1,000 hours on helicopters. The circus tried to get a second helicopter, but demand in Europe and South America was high so they were unsuccessful.

The 1955 season finished on 27 October in Elkton, Maryland, and the circus retired to its winter quarters in Burlington, New Jersey – but by now with Major Bud Walcott as its pilot. Over the winter, Bud flew some 'Santa drops' and was there at the beginning of April 1956 when the circus gained some advance publicity in an article in *The Bristol Courier and Levittown Times* as the new season opened. There is a front-page picture of a serious-looking Bud Walcott dressed in dark flying overalls leaning against the helicopter, which has the name of the circus on it. He is described as a former fighter pilot and the circus's 'whirlybird flyer'. The newspaper reporter, Loretta Palermo, clearly enjoyed her 'whirling' experience!

The season continued, but in November 1956 the helicopter came down in bad weather on its way to Arnmonk in New York, causing significant damage to the tail structure. The cost of the repairs was estimated at $7,000.[5] It is also reported that the pilot and mechanic were not injured, but neither is named. The repair was carried out and the helicopter continued to operate throughout the 1957 season and into 1958. At the end of the '58 season, the

Hunt Brothers decided to sell it. They made a loss on the deal, losing $6,000, but they felt that in view of the hours flown this was not a financial disaster. Whether or not Bud was the pilot isn't known, but there is an intriguing possible link.

In the twentieth century, nickel became an important metal in the manufacture of aircraft, ships, electrical equipment and all manner of other manufactured items. In 1956, using airborne magnetometers, the International Nickel Company of Canada discovered large deposits in northern Manitoba and a new community sprang up, named after the company's former chairman and chief executive officer John Fairfield Thompson. Helicopters were very useful in carrying out this type of exploration and Walcott was part of it. Indeed, he applied for and was granted a miner's licence on 17 December 1956, a month after the Hunts' helicopter crashed. As will be seen, Bud's activities over the next few years were somewhat mysterious. His domestic situation as the husband and son-in-law who married into the wealthy and influential Lenox family may have put some pressure on him. It is quite within his capabilities to have decided that mining nickel in Canada might have been a way to make money as an adjunct to his flying, or it may be that, engaged in the mining industry, he was required by law to have a licence. Certainly he didn't make his fortune from the mining of nickel. His licence states he is connected to the Canadian Nickel Co. Ltd, of Thicket Portage in Manitoba. This is a tiny settlement in the north of the province and life must have been hard. The licence was only valid until 31 March 1957 so it was for a very limited period over the harsh winter season. It may, of course, have been renewed.

Whatever the result of his work in Canada, Bud continued to fly helicopters and in November 1958 created quite a stir in the Berkshires when, as a trial, he landed a helicopter on the roof of one the better-known buildings in the area, the Old Colonial Theatre in Pittsfield, to demonstrate the feasibility of a scheduled helicopter route to Boston. The Colonial Theatre is an important part of the local area heritage. It was built at the beginning of the twentieth century, with interior design by a famous theatre architect named J. B. McElfatrick, who was involved in hundreds of construction projects over the years, although the Colonial is one of only a few survivors. The exterior was designed by a local architect, Joseph McArthur Vance, who also had a hand in the design of many local landmark buildings. Critically, it had a flat roof. The interior had superb acoustics and a beautiful audience hall with quite remarkable plasterwork. It opened on 28 September 1903 and operated until 1934, when the general economic downturn forced its closure. In its time, it hosted performances by such greats as John Barrymore, Sarah Bernhardt, Eubie Blake, Douglas Fairbanks Jr (who, it will be recalled, was an officer in the USS *Wasp* on 20 April 1942 when Walcott flew to North Africa) and the Ziegfeld Follies, to name a few. It reopened in 1937 as a movie theatre, although some stage performances took place as well. It closed in 1951. It was bought in 1953 by George Miller, an enthusiastic entrepreneur who had moved to the area five years before. He turned the theatre into a paint store and converted an old police department ambulance into a delivery truck. With a 'can-do' outlook on life, Miller thought he saw the opportunity created by vertical flight and sought to open up routes connecting Hartford in Connecticut with Boston and nearby Albany, New York's state capital. His idea was to use the flat roof of the theatre as a landing pad and the interior of the building as the heliport centre.

As a spectacular demonstration of the possibilities, he arranged for a machine to land on the roof of the theatre in the afternoon on 15 November 1958. Having established that the roof would be strong enough to bear the additional load, despite some local opposition, he obtained a permit from the local zoning authority and the landing went ahead, to great local excitement and interest.

As reported in the local press, the pilot of the helicopter was none other than Bud Walcott, flying a Bell 47 variant from Boston, where he worked for I. S. Robie Co. From a hazy, overcast sky, the 'whirlybird' descended gently to hover just over the theatre roof before dropping on to it without 'a quiver'. Miller commented to the local press: 'It was like a feather dropping on a load of hay.' Walcott was quoted as saying that the facilities were 'adequate for regular service' – a fairly muted analysis.

There were six trial landings in all, with some concern about damage to the roof structure which seemed to be unfounded. If the service ever operated then it didn't last long, but the event says something about Walcott. Firstly, he needed to have good flying skills to carry out such a landing in 'hazy, overcast' conditions. He would also quite enjoy the publicity the incident gained, being a local boy and known to many of those watching. It also might have been an attractive job prospect for him as it was near his roots in Lenox, with Pittsfield only a few miles away.

Many in the area mourned the demise of the Colonial Theatre, but Miller continued to operate from it until, in 1997, it was allocated $2.5 million from the Commonwealth of Massachusetts. Designated a National Historic Treasure by the Save America's

Treasures Program of the National Park Service, the theatre was restored to its former glory, with Miller being credited for not destroying it – indeed helping to preserve it – during his period of ownership.

Bud seemed to be incapable of settling down into a career in aviation with a single company. The two stabilising factors in his life were Virginia and flying, and by the second half of the 1950s his flying concentrated on helicopters and similar aircraft. In April 1959, he flew with Helicol in Colombia on oil exploration work, again flying Bell 47s. Helicol was a joint venture founded in 1955 by Keystone Helicopters Coporation of Philadelphia and Avianca, the Colombian national airline. Keystone Helicopters was established by Peter Wright, a veteran of the famous American 'Flying Tigers' or the 1st American Volunteer Group, who fought on the side of the nationalist Chinese against the Japanese, commanded by Claire Chennault using Curtiss P-40s – celebrated for their shark-mouth paintwork.

Local laws required that commercial aviation companies operating in Colombia should be at least 51 per cent owned by a Colombian company, and Avianca fitted the requirement well. Keystone had signed a contract with Shell to carry out oil exploration in the northern part of Colombia. Starting with three Bell 47s, within a year or two the number operated by the company doubled. In recent years Colombia had been wracked by internal strife caused by the rivalry of the two main political parties and the assassination in 1948 of the Liberal presidential candidate Jorge Eliécer Galtán. But by the late 1950s, a more peaceful atmosphere existed. In April 1959, Virginia joined Bud in South America. They returned from Bogota to Lenox over a year later in September 1960, with Bud heavily involved in an exciting project to develop a relatively new type of aeroplane for vertical flight – the autogyro.

The concept of the autogyro was not new. As recently as the Second World War some German U-boats had used tethered autogyros to reconnoitre from height, but some aviation developers could see a future and the technology developed. As explained earlier, a conventional aircraft generates its lift by moving through the air, allowing it to flow across its fixed wings. To do this it requires a forward speed, provided by its engine(s). A helicopter requires lift, but this comes from the rotor blades, which provide both the forward speed and the lift needed for the machine to fly. An autogyro is a combination of the two: it has a conventional propeller-driven engine to create the forward motion or thrust and rotor blades to provide the lift, but for this type of aeroplane the rotor blades are not powered – in effect they glide or auto-rotate; a truly rotary wing.

Walcott worked as a development pilot for the Umbaugh Aircraft Corporation on his return from Colombia at the end of 1960. The company was developing an autogyro with a slightly different operating regime. For take-off, the rotors could be connected into the aircraft's engine to gain energy, which was released instantaneously on take-off. Normally the machine would have had a take-off run. This allowed it to jump into the air and into a normal flight regime where the rotors spun without power. On 19 December 1960, a newspaper in Nashville, Tennessee, reported the following incident at Berry Field, Nashville's airport:

Hundreds of cars lined the area around the north ramp near Capitol Airways hangar at Berry Field yesterday afternoon.

Other cars were parked along Murfreesboro Road to watch the demonstration.

S. B. Walcott of Lenox, Mass. one of five experimental test pilots for the Umbaugh Aircraft Corporation, took less than three minutes to warm up the 180-horsepoer Lycoming engine.

THEN SUDDENLY, Walcott changed the pitch of the blades – and the aircraft jumped 20 feet in the air, and was on its way.

Walcott circled the field several times, making two approaches. During one, the engine was cut down and the free-spinning rotors glided the plane to the ground at a speed less than half that of a parachute.

Walcott was quoted as saying that the aircraft was 'a real little dream to operate'.

The idea to develop and build the gyro-plane came from Raymond E. Umbaugh, a manufacturer of agricultural fertiliser, which provided him considerable personal wealth, but who possessed a real and personal interest in this unusual form of aeroplane. He set up the Umbaugh Aircraft Corporation in Florida in 1957 and engaged Gilbert Devore, a recognised helicopter engineer, to design an aircraft that would be cheap and easy to fly to satisfy the demands of the new markets emerging after the war. The first model, the Umbaugh U-17, flew in August 1959 but stability problems with the tail meant that several different arrangements were tried before a suitable one was found. Five development aircraft under the model name Umbaugh U-18, were built in 1960 and this model became known as the 'Flymobil'. In Bud's view, the autogyro was much easier to fly than a helicopter, with little that could go wrong. It didn't spin or stall. This particular type had a range of 200 miles with a cruising speed of 100 mph, a maximum speed of 125 mph and a slow speed of 25 mph. It could reach an altitude of 15,000 feet, which would have required pressurisation or the use of oxygen above 10,000 feet. It could carry two passengers with 200lbs of luggage at an operating cost of 6–7 cents per hour and a proposed capital cost of less than $10,000. A trained pilot should be able to become competent in two hours – an untrained novice in eight.

Umbaugh, as a wealthy entrepreneur, could fund the development himself and he entered into an agreement with Fairchild[6] for the development, and ultimately production, of the final design. He established a network of dealerships throughout the United States to obtain orders and service the new aeroplanes. The business model depended on having a large backlog of orders – presumably accompanied by deposits – to fund the construction by Fairchild, but a lack of manufacturing capacity resulted in lengthy delays in delivery, and in 1962 Umbaugh Aircraft Corporation ceased trading. Its assets were taken over by many of the dealers, who formed a new company, Air and Space Manufacturing Inc. of Muncie, Indiana. Unfortunately, this too eventually ceased trading but the rights to the design and manufacture of the gyroplane have been owned by several different companies over the years and there are still ambitions to build the aircraft in modern times. Only a handful of the original U-18s were built.

Walcott's demonstration flight in Nashville was not the only one. There are newspaper reports of others in Montgomery, Alabama; Phoenix, Yuma and Tucson, Arizona; and Winona, Minnesota, at the beginning of 1961. Bud Walcott gave 'a brisk and dramatic demonstration'[7] of the aeroplane's capabilities at Tucson's Freeway

Airport in February 1961. After taking off vertically, Bud stopped the engine at 400 feet and the aircraft auto-rotated slowly downwards before he restarted the engine and brought it down to land with a 15-foot run.

Although Bud's flying activities took him away from Lenox for much of the time, Dave Roche said that he always seemed to get back for the holidays. The Roche family, who had lived near Bud's family in the 1930s, coincidentally moved into a house just next-door to the Tillotsons and continued the family friendship with Bud. Dave was much younger than Bud, and attributes his own interest in flying – and his pilot's licence – to the encouragement he received from Walcott. Dave's first flight took place when he was about eight years old and was taken for a ride in a helicopter by Walcott. Dave said that he saw a great deal of Bud and that Bud would have magic parties for the local kids – he was particularly adept at coin tricks. Walcott encouraged the youngsters to join the military.

Walcott contributed to local affairs. He flew Santa Claus into town in a helicopter and helped Virginia with her political activities. He attended veterans' events and was always very smartly decked out in his blue air force uniform for any funerals of military veterans. He loved to fly and Dave considers him to have been a good pilot – although, interestingly, a poor navigator, which tallies with comments made about him during the war.

Another Lenox resident has similar recollections about Walcott, although he didn't know him well. He recalls that Bud flew displays at the nearby airfield at Westover. His speciality was contour flying – at very low level – and he would suddenly appear over the heads of the spectators with a great roar. Of course, contour flying is very risky, and after accidents at air shows in more recent times display pilots are forbidden to fly directly over the crowds or are instructed to fly in such a way that in the event of an accident any debris will land harmlessly away from the spectators. Others recall Bud as a likeable, 'swashbuckling kind of a guy'.

Although he was engaged in demonstrating the U-18, Bud's life was about to fall apart. The year 1961 was to bring the ultimate misfortune for Virginia and Bud, and sadly it marked the beginning of the end for them.

Firstly, Virginia contracted cancer.

It will be recalled that Virginia worked for some years as a young girl in the plant at Pittsfield manufacturing electrical transformers. Until being banned in more recent years, the oil used in electrical transformers contained poly-chlorinated biphenyls (PCBs), now well known to have carcinogenic properties. These were also used in the chemical and plastics industries. As with asbestos, prior to the dangers being clearly understood and before concern for the environment became a major issue for the more socially aware industrialised economies, waste products from manufacturing processes were often allowed to enter nearby rivers and watercourses. According to General Electric (GE) reports between 1932 and 1977, PCBs released by the Pittsfield plant reached the nearby Housatonic River and Silver Lake, but it wasn't until 1999 that the Massachusetts Department of Environmental Protection, the Connecticut Department of Environmental Protection and GE agreed a comprehensive cleanup plan. Indeed, the headline in *The Berkshire Eagle* newspaper on 27 August 1999 states 'RIVER DUCKS FULL OF PCBs, State set to issue a health advisory'. All of this created some local hostility towards the plant, but while the environmental issues were a major concern, the plant did provide employment and local economic benefits for many years, which may have been felt to counterbalance the environmental risks – although not the illnesses and deaths which the PCBs possibly caused.

It is a very tenuous possibility, and quite unverified, that this might have been the cause of Virginia's cancer. She was treated in Boston, but died on 31 December 1961 and was buried in the Tillotson plot in the graveyard of the Church on the Hill, near her father.

Bud seems to have been devastated. He had lost one of the two loves of his life. But as fate would have it, at this time, he also failed a flying medical and his pilot's licence was withdrawn. His life had been full; now it was empty. He had to come to terms with his losses. Unable to earn a living flying, he turned to more mundane activities. For some time he ran a gas station and garage in Pittsfield, but he decided to try his hand in the hospitality industry and bought the Stockbridge Inn in May 1962. But he couldn't take to this new way of life and became depressed. His friends said he had the opportunity to form relationships with other women but didn't do so. Life eventually became too much for him, and one morning he attempted to end it all but was prevented by his sister-in-law Bobbie.

He tried again, this time successfully, on 5 July 1962. He was forty-two years old.

His friends in the Berkshires reacted with shock that such a lively, likeable and flamboyant man should have resorted to taking his own life, but it was a measure of the despair into which he had sunk on losing both his beloved wife and his ability to fly within a matter of months.

He was buried beside his wife in her family plot and has a veteran's headstone.[8] On his death he was still a member of the

Air Force Reserve with the rank of major. Interestingly, it was his sister-in-law Bobbie who made an application to the Department of the Army for Bud to be provided with a veteran's headstone and a bronze marker. He was awarded the Air Medal. His obituary appeared in the local press.

Virginia's mother died in 1963, aged seventy-four. Bobbie, her only remaining daughter, survived until 1994. They too are buried in the family plot.

Sadly, there were no children to continue the Tillotson line and the once wealthy and influential family are now hardly remembered in the Berkhires other than by the gradually reducing number of people who knew them so many years ago. Despite enquiries, no descendants or relatives of the Tillotsons or of Bud and his family have been found. And this adds to the sadness.

One cannot help but see Walcott's life as tragic, with his tarnished reputation as an airman, his wife's untimely death and his suicide. It is unlikely that Walcott knew of the allegations made against him, and while in some circles he is regarded as unworthy, he is mainly remembered with great fondness by those who knew him in Lenox after the war as an ebullient and likeable man, full of life and with a zest for adventure and thrills.

This is the way he would have wished it.

# PART 3

# THE ALLEGATIONS,
# THE MAN AND
# THE ENIGMA

# IO

# ANATOMY OF AN ALLEGATION

With the aeroplane in question being a single-seater, and with no diaries or letters of Bud's to draw on to explain just what did happen, it is now highly unlikely that his reasons for leaving formation on 20 April 1942 over the Mediterranean will ever be unequivocally and definitively known. The accusation made against him is impossible to absolutely and totally refute. Barring the discovery of some documents belonging to Bud which state that he *did* go deliberately, the matter will never be finally settled. Although it is impossible to know for sure why Walcott turned away that day, there will always be lingering doubts over his integrity because of the mere existence of the accusation that he deserted. Such a claim will never quite disappear. This is despite judicial systems placing the burden of proof on the accuser; indeed, in Walcott's case no hard evidence has been found to support the accusation.

The signal from Malta after 603 Squadron arrived there is the first appearance of the allegation against Walcott.[1] This was from the AOC Malta to the Air Ministry, and it had a relatively wide circulation, including the Chief of the Air Staff. It was dated 25 April 1942 but it was 'Most Secret'. In its entirety it reads:

OPERATION CALENDAR MOST SECRET.
REGRET INFORMATION 47 CALENDAR SPITFIRES ARRIVED INACCURATE. ACTUALLY ONLY 46 ORIGINAL ERROR BY CONTROLLER UNDISCOVERED FOR 48 HOURS OWING TO CONTINUAL BATTLE IN PROGRESS. SPITFIRE 958 PILOT SERGEANT WALCOTT DID NOT ARRIVE. O.C. 603 SQUADRON SAW HIM LEAVE FORMATION BUT THOUGHT HE WAS JOINED (*sic*) FOLLOWING FORMATION. HE ALSO STATES THAT SERGEANT WALCOTT INTENDED TO DESERT. HAD PREVIOUSLY LANDED FOR NO GOOD REASON IN IRISH FREE STATE BUT NOT INTERNED. IN CONVERSATION ON VOYAGE STATED MALTA WOULD NEVER SEE HIM.

There are three key sentences which define the allegations: the final three. Of course, in such a signal, brevity was essential. Nonetheless, these three sentences deserve some consideration both separately and as a group.

The first reads, 'HE ALSO STATES THAT SERGEANT WALCOTT INTENDED TO DESERT.' 'He' is the 603 Squadron commander, Squadron Leader Lord David Douglas-Hamilton. There is no qualification expressed. The OC is reported to be stating – without any suggestion of doubt – that Walcott intended to desert. It does not say that Walcott 'may have been contemplating' desertion or express anything other than certainty that Walcott was going to deliberately leave.

The second reads, 'HAD PREVIOUSLY LANDED FOR NO GOOD REASON IN IRISH FREE STATE BUT NOT INTERNED.' This is meaningless. If Walcott had truly landed at Dublin 'for no good reason' then why report it? It almost suggests that he had flown to Dublin on a whim. There is nothing to report. If he had gone with the intention of deserting then that would have been worth reporting, but as has been shown, no evidence was found to suggest this; in fact, Walcott did have a very good reason for landing in Dublin: he was lost. But it is in the context of the other two sentences that the rather sinister implication is drawn out, and this explains why it was probably included in the signal.

The final sentence reads, 'IN CONVERSATION ON VOYAGE STATED MALTA WOULD NEVER SEE HIM.' This is discussed later, but again it is written in such a way that no room is left for doubt – and yet upon examination of Walcott's situation, it is clear that there was room for doubt as to just what Walcott intentions were.

If the three sentences are considered as a group, they can be interpreted in a way that is quite damning. The first makes the point that Walcott was intent on deserting. When read in conjunction with the second, which in itself is meaningless, it can be interpreted that Walcott had not flown to Dublin for no reason at all, but in the hope that he might be interned and ultimately sent back to the United States. And when the third sentence is added, the implication is that he was hell-bent on not going to Malta. So when considered as a group, one possible interpretation of the three sentences of the signal is that Walcott intended to desert rather than go to Malta. He had previously landed in neutral Eire in the hope that he might be interned and out of the war, but was returned to the RAF instead.

While the signal from Malta was 'Most Secret', the allegations about Walcott found their way into the public domain once such documents were opened up in the UK National Archives.

In 1981, the experiences of 603's OC Squadron Leader Lord David Douglas-Hamilton and the squadron on Malta were recounted in an excellent book written by his nephew, the then Lord James Douglas-Hamilton, now Lord Douglas of Selkirk. The Walcott affair is mentioned in brief, including the sentence:

> The thought that death might await him in Malta had preyed on his [Walcott's] mind, and he had chosen to desert in the face of the enemy.[2]

Quite how it is known that the thought of death in Malta was 'preying' on Walcott's mind is unclear – his mental state might have been in question, but to what extent is not known. The source of the information about Walcott included in three earlier editions of the book is given as a letter to its author dated 19 November 1979 from the late Tony Holland, who, it will be recalled, was one of Walcott's fellow pilots with 603 Squadron and who, it is believed, flew the first of the 603 Spitfires to depart *Wasp*.

The issue of the quality of the evidence against Walcott was raised with Lord Selkirk, and in later editions of his book (the 4th edition, published in 2006 onward) the paragraph about Walcott has been altered to take account of the information that has come to hand and to remove the allegation.

In 1992 the late Wing Commander 'Laddie' Lucas, who was already on Malta with 249 Squadron and who witnessed the arrival of 603 and 601 Squadrons, published another excellent account of the air war over the island, which included a discourse on Walcott's disappearance.[3] He initially describes Walcott's non-arrival as an 'inexplicable defection', referring to the unplanned landing in Dublin as having 'no particular reason' but perhaps being a sign of what was to come.

But he then provides an extensive quotation from Tony Holland, who says that Walcott was noticeable for his cropped haircut and 'eyebrows that met over his nose'. Holland claims that Walcott was a hypnotist who would seek volunteers to be the subjects of a trick whereby the American would press on a blood vessel or nerve on the back of the volunteer's neck, and although he doesn't report the outcome of this it is suggested that it would have been 'highly dangerous' for pilots waiting to fly. Holland also recalls that Walcott shared a cabin with Sergeant Buckley and that Buckley had told his commanding officer, Lord David Douglas-Hamilton, that during the voyage to the Mediterranean Walcott had 'confided' that he would not go to Malta and that he had arranged to see the padre but was told that the padre could not help Walcott change what lay ahead.

Holland later found himself in hospital in the United Kingdom with a broken leg, and in conversation with another pilot he heard that an American pilot crashed south of the Atlas Mountains and made his way to a US consulate in Algeria, where he convinced them that he was a civilian pilot and eventually was returned to the United States. However, Holland also reports that there were stories that one of the sailors from HMS *Manchester* in a French detention camp said that Walcott was there and had managed to escape by stowing aboard a provisions lorry on its way out of the camp. He thought Walcott had managed to find his way back to America.

It is interesting that the original signal about Walcott describes his action as an attempt to 'desert' while Lucas calls the disappearance a 'defection'. The difference in meaning of the two words is quite significant. To desert is to leave or run away without permission; to wilfully abandon a legal or moral obligation. To defect is to transfer allegiance from one country to another.[4] While it is not possible to state unequivocally that Walcott did not desert, i.e. deliberately leave, there is absolutely no evidence or any suggestion that if indeed he did desert then he also intended to defect. The two are quite different. Assuming he was minded to defect, he must have known that he would be landing in Vichy French territory and not German – would he wish to throw in his lot with the Vichy French?

Tony Holland states that Walcott 'was instantly distinguishable' by his cropped hair and joined eyebrows. None of the photographs of Walcott give this credence – quite the contrary. In particular, photographs of him taken on *Wasp*'s deck and then in the internment camp and at home in his uniform show him as a good-looking young man with a full head of hair. Holland's remark creates a grim appearance in the reader's mind, and it is surely inappropriate to make comments about Walcott's supposed appearance in order to portray his character. Once returned home to Lenox, many of the ladies thought that Bud was handsome and quite a catch.

Holland also suggests that Walcott put his fellow pilots on readiness at some risk by practising his tricks on them, and yet he states that Walcott only carried out tricks on willing volunteers – so why should Walcott be blamed? If he did put his fellow pilots in danger, why did his officers not stop the practice?

Holland also mentions Walcott's visit to the padre and discloses what took place – but how did he know? According to Holland,

Walcott's cabin-mate Sergeant Buckley made the disclosure to Lord David. But such meetings are supposed to be confidential. How did Holland, as a junior officer of the squadron, come to learn of it? Did he have sight of the signal sent to London following the arrival of the Operation *Calendar* Spitfires?

The accusations made against Walcott probably would not stand up in a court of law, nor in a court martial if this should have ever have come about. If Walcott had been behaving incorrectly, no one had done anything to stop him nor taken any steps to prevent him deserting if this intention was suspected, as is suggested.

In investigating historical subjects, it is easy to accept work which has been researched by others and published. Since the allegations about Walcott appeared in the public domain they have been repeated in other books, but changes have been made in editions published later to correct matters.

A history of 603 Squadron published in 1989 takes a particularly harsh view of Walcott's non-appearance on Malta.[5] Although published privately, this book is in the public domain. Recounting the mid-air collision with Pilot Officer Jones over the airfield at Peterhead, the author states that it would have been better if 'the result had been reversed for ... Walcott was to bring dishonour to the Squadron'. This is a breathtaking sentiment regardless of whether or not the allegations against Walcott are true, and considering that nothing has been found to apportion any blame for the accident, nor any evidence that Walcott did 'dishonour' the squadron, it is remarkably intolerant. The death of Pilot Officer Jones was a tragedy and his family would have been devastated, but to suggest that it would have been preferable for Walcott to have died is a sentiment that would not sit easy with many.

With regard to the chapter covering 603's time on Malta, which includes the disappearance of Walcott, it is noted that 'additional background has been provided by Tony Holland DFC' and with regard to the previous chapter and the accident at Peterhead that one of the eighteen sources for the contents of the chapter was Tony Holland. Whatever the truth or otherwise as to why the accident happened, it is sad that a statement should be made wishing death on a man whether or not the accusation of desertion is true.

Another source is my own interpretation in another history of 603 Squadron, published in 2003.[6] Without independent evidence, I reported the matter in terms of the allegations previously made and speculated, also without evidence, that Bud's actions might have been caused by his mental state after the mid-air collision with Pilot Officer Jones and the way that he then found himself in the familiar American cultural environment of *Wasp* but could not be a part of it.

It has been alleged that he made for North Africa, flying across the Atlas Mountains to force land his Spitfire in scrub. Quite what happened to him after that isn't clear, other than that he managed to get back to the US. The most quoted outcome is that after landing, he made his way to the office of the US Consul in Algeria, claiming that he was a civilian pilot who had been forced down and that he was subsequently re-patriated.

I mention the possible sightings of Walcott in the internment camp but conclude that his departure discredited the squadron. However, I also acknowledged that he was a volunteer fighting for another country.

But I too, like 'Laddie' Lucas, incorrectly refer to Walcott's action as defection.

Despite all of this, I was uncomfortable with the lack of evidence about Walcott's departure and that everything was apparently based on rumour, speculation and hearsay – hence the years of research and this book to correct what has been said before.

The accusation of desertion is founded on four pillars.

Firstly, it is implied that during training he deliberately flew his Hurricane to Dublin in Eire in the hope of being returned to the USA.

Nothing has been found to suggest that this flight was anything other than what it was – a trainee pilot becoming lost in poor weather and straying into the territory of a neutral country. According to the report produced by the Irish authorities, he did not ask for asylum or to be returned to America. There is no suggestion of any reluctance on his part to return to British territory, despite his knowledge that he would likely be in trouble with the RAF for his error. And if he was disappointed that the reaction of the Irish authorities was to fill up his Hurricane with petrol, feed him, give him a bed for the night and then send him packing, he could easily have crashed his aircraft in some remote field in neutral Eire and made his way to the American Embassy in Dublin on his own rather than fly meekly back into the war. Further, both during his training and after the war, a specific observation about Bud is that his navigation skills were poor. And of course, the Irish report states that he had no map. Again, if he had intended to fly to Dublin surely he would have taken a map by which to navigate?

There is no mention of the flight to Dublin in Bud's service record, even as a simple recording of the fact, so how it came to be known and interpreted in the way it has been is unclear. The flight itself would have been recorded in Bud's log book, and it was common practice for a new pilot arriving on a squadron to be interviewed by the squadron commander, so Lord David might very well have been aware of the flight to Eire and asked the new pilot about it. But the log book would show only brief facts and not include any comments about Bud's possible motives. If Walcott had intended to desert to Dublin, he is hardly likely to have confessed this to his new squadron commander. (The log book was with Bud when he was captured by the Vichy French so was probably either confiscated or lost.) And if he had gone 'for no good reason', it seems likely that he would have been sanctioned in some way by the RAF authorities.

The flight to Dublin can only be seen as a mistake.

Secondly, the comment made to his cabin-mate Flight Sergeant Buckley that 'Malta would never see him'. This is interpreted as evidence of his firm intention and is mentioned in the signal from AOC Malta to the Air Ministry dated 25 April 1942.[7] But can this be taken as a serious statement of his intent to desert or to defect? The whole operation to fly the Spitfires to Malta under the code name Operation *Calendar* was fraught with danger and risk. The take-off from the carrier itself and the subsequent long flight, requiring accurate navigation while running the gauntlet of enemy aircraft, with a final landing on an unknown, bombed-out airstrip, possibly under air attack, mitigated heavily against success and by extension the pilots' survival. If they arrived safely then they faced some of the most dangerous air combat situations of the war, with the expectation that their safe return to their loved ones might never occur.

Of twenty-four pilots who left with 603 for Malta, Walcott was one of those with no operational experience – specifically no offensive operations in his log book, nor any operational hours. In fact, he had a mere 260 flying hours in total; only six of his fellow pilots had fewer, the lowest being 190. Several pilots were well experienced, having taken part in forty or fifty offensive sorties, and four had been credited with the destruction of enemy aircraft in combat. Flight Sergeant Jack Rae headed up this list with two confirmed destroyed, four probables and one damaged. Lord David Douglas-Hamilton was by far the most experienced pilot with over 1,000 hours in his log book, but only thirty hours were operational and he had only experienced four offensive sorties. Tony Holland flew to Malta with 980 hours in his log book but only twenty of these were operational and he had no offensive operations as part of his experience. Nine pilots had flown no operational sorties and a further six had flown fewer than ten.

The problem of safely gaining operational experience is a thorny one. Newly trained aircrew arriving in a combat zone are vulnerable because of their lack of experience, and the consequences of mistakes are often fatal. In many conflicts, trainees could only gain the necessary experience in real combat. If an RAF Bomber Command crew could survive their first ten operations during the Second World War, they had a good chance of completing the tour of thirty. During the Vietnam War it was discovered that most aircrew were lost while gaining combat experience during their first ten operations, and to mitigate this the USAF Red Flag and US Navy Top Gun programmes were designed and instituted to give pilots experience that was as close as possible to the real thing. Students in these programmes flew realistic simulated missions. The defenders used anti-aircraft equipment and radars that simulated those which might be encountered in reality, plus F-5 aircraft designated as aggressors. The aeroplanes were painted up in Warsaw Pact-type camouflage schemes and the pilots used tactics employed by enemy air forces to make their 'attacks' as real as possible. Apart from these programs, which took place in California and Nevada, USAF aggressor squadrons also operated elsewhere. In Britain they would bounce NATO aircraft on exercise, giving the pilots reason to be fully alert and on their toes. For aircrew deployed to Vietnam, the training proved successful and the losses of new aircrew markedly reduced.

The general lack of experience of the Operation *Calendar* pilots (both 603 and 601 Squadrons) became a source of contention. A cypher telegramme dated 28 April 1942 from AOC Malta to HQ RAF Middle East[8] complains that in 603 Squadron '13 pilots had under 25 hours Spitfire flying' and that '17 experienced pilots were posted away from Squadron within 2 months before leaving UK'. And all this in response to a request for experienced pilots capable of taking on the battle-hardened Italian and German units 60 miles away in Sicily.

Many years later, one of the very experienced 603 Squadron NCO pilots who flew to Malta said that he had not heard of the allegations made against Walcott and that they were certainly not a subject of discussion in the mess when he was on Malta. Interestingly, he also commented that if Walcott had deliberately decided to not to go then he couldn't blame him or feel anything other than sympathy for him, with discretion being the better part of valour. He took the view that sending such inexperienced pilots into the cauldron of air fighting that was Malta amounted to irresponsibility and should never have happened – indeed, the discovery that many of the pilots were so lacking in experience was to result in some recriminations.

Having been briefed as to what was to be expected of them, it is hardly surprising that some of the men would say to their friends,

'I won't be going to Malta.' It's the sort of comment most people have made at some point in their lives when learning of something difficult or unpleasant that will have to be endured, and it isn't usually taken literally. If the information available refers only to one passing comment and not a series of conversations with Buckley or anything else to suggest that there was a real intention to 'desert', then it is worthless. On the other hand, if Walcott declared his intention in a debate or in a series of conversations, then shouldn't Sergeant Buckley have reported it?

Certainly, what may have been a throwaway remark should not be taken as an explicit intimation of serious intent. If it was Buckley's summary of a conversation or a series of conversations then it could be alleged that Walcott was minded to desert, but even if he was so minded this in itself doesn't mean that he did. This is the only potentially credible piece of evidence, but it is less than firm. And who is to say that Walcott did not have engine trouble? If it is impossible to say with certainty that Walcott had no intention of deserting, it is equally impossible to say for sure that he intended to do so.

Thirdly, it was suggested that he had visited the ship's padre the evening before take-off in the hope that somehow he might be excused, only to be disappointed.[9] As mentioned above, discussions with a padre are usually considered privileged or to be kept confidential, so the obvious question is that if this happened, how did it become known generally? Did the padre break the confidence? According to Tony Holland the information came to light when Sergeant Buckley was interviewed by Lord David, but how did it become generally known?

Furthermore, why should the act of visiting the padre be considered a sign of weakness or cowardice? After all, the reason that fighting units of all the branches of the services have padres is to help the unit's members in just such situations. One pilot who flew from *Wasp* to Malta with 601 Squadron that morning, Denis Barnham, also visited the padre the evening before:

> Spiritually I feel dreadfully alone. The visit was a great disappointment. I was told all the usual stuff designed to make a fighting man fight. I was told that I should fight the enemy because of his barbarity. I was told that this was the war to end all wars; that the future would be rosy and glorious … I was not satisfied and asked more questions.
> … but of God himself, … the Padre did not talk.[10]

Hardly comforting. This pilot served with distinction on Malta in the following months and nothing untoward is implied by his need for spiritual guidance.

Fourthly and finally, it is said that Walcott was never seen again – that he just disappeared back to the USA and nothing more was known of him.

This is quite untrue. Walcott returned to the UK and London at the end of 1942 on his release from internment in the Laghouat camp and transferred to the US Army with a commission. But crucially, he could only transfer after being debriefed by the British intelligence agency MI9, responsible for working with POWs and internees. MI9's report signally fails to suggest any suspicion on the part of the debriefing officer that Walcott had 'deserted' and his forced landing in Vichy French territory is seen as just that – a forced landing. The contents of the signal from Malta to London suggesting that Walcott had deliberately departed were not connected with the man who returned from Laghouat to be debriefed by MI9 and the RAF – or if they were, the implications were quietly dropped. It is of course possible that at the time, with Americans in the RAF transferring in numbers to the US Army, the British authorities decided to ignore the allegation either to get rid of a potential problem or to avoid stirring up any problems with their ally. Or both.

Rather bizarrely, one historian commented that if Walcott had nothing to hide then why, on his return to Britain, did he not seek out his Commanding Officer, Squadron Leader Lord David Douglas-Hamilton, to explain himself and his actions? But why should he? Many other fighting men from all branches of the services became separated from their units – many for years – but were not obliged to seek out and explain to their unit OCs why they had disappeared when they went missing. Why should Walcott be expected to act differently? Even if he wished to do this, it is unlikely that he would have been allowed to do so. By the time Walcott was returned to Britain at the end of 1942, the aircrew element of 603 Squadron had rebadged as 229 Squadron and Lord David had departed from Malta and was carrying out other duties. In any case, with 603 represented only by the ground crew element, then based in Cyprus, it's unlikely that Walcott could have managed to track down any of the squadron officers to offer his explanation.

To be quite fair, it is also said that there were possible sightings of Walcott in a French internment camp[11] but overall the emphasis is on his alleged attempts to leave the war and return to the United States, and of course the implication is that nothing was heard of him again.

Having criticised the lack of evidence to support the allegations made against Walcott, it may be foolhardy to indulge in more speculation. The 603 Squadron the young American joined in March 1942 still observed the old pre-war social conventions and divisions between officers and other ranks, and the arrival of a cocky young Yank NCO might have created friction and dislike within the squadron. With the exception of some of his colleagues in 603 Squadron, Walcott seems to have been well liked throughout his life. During training his magician skills were applauded – one instructor said, 'Get him to show you.' At Laghouat he seems to have been respected, and his attempt to escape by stowing away in a lorry certainly enhanced his reputation. John Lewery, who shared a bunk with Bud, claimed to be surprised at the allegation made against the American and said he saw nothing in his behaviour to justify such an allegation – in fact, he considered Walcott a 'bit of a risk-taker'. This view was shared by Hugh Dow, a colleague in the Army Air Corps. James Hudson, who also knew Walcott in Laghouat, 'strongly refuted' the allegations when told of them, saying that based on the character Bud displayed he could not accept that the man was a coward.[12] After he returned to his home in Massachusetts Bud was well liked, and popular as a bit of a character. One eighty-three-year-old lady when asked if she remembered Bud straightened her back and, with a twinkle in her eye, said, 'Oh my. He was a fine-looking man!' He is remembered in Lenox for his good-natured generosity, not least in holding magic parties for the local kids. Another of those who knew him in Lenox after the war wrote:

All the time I knew Budd I never once heard him utter one word of profanity, drinking only socially and with a neat appearance. Budd was one of the most decent persons I have ever known. The same goes for Virginia, they were two peas in a pod. I consider myself lucky to have known them both.

The whole business about Walcott's so-called desertion/defection is not based on hard fact. It was mentioned above that one risk in historical research is that previously published 'facts' are unthinkingly accepted. The essential source of any fact should be checked to ensure that it is reliable, and ideally the same fact should be found in different sources. Three of the books which condemn Walcott most strongly draw much of their information from Tony Holland – in one case directly quoting him in the others, drawing on information contained in communications with him.

Walcott claimed he flew to North Africa because of technical problems with his engine, but after what he had experienced his state of mind might have been a factor. He was in a different country and culture. His first operational posting in Britain was to a bleak and unwelcoming airfield in the middle of winter shortly after Christmas. He had quickly been involved in an incident in which he might have been killed and another man had died, and he would receive no psychological help. He was inexperienced in combat and yet was about to be sent to what at the time was one of the most dangerous places on Earth – if not *the* most dangerous – due to the ferocity of the fighting. He was in an American ship, surrounded by his own culture and people, but was not a part of it.

On top of all of this, he is disliked by at least some of his squadron companions. If indeed Walcott did desert, then it is very possible that the decision was made while he was not of entirely rational mind. But while interned, he behaved quite normally; he tried to escape and a fellow prisoner who shared a room with him found nothing unusual in his behaviour, and nothing to suggest that Walcott was a coward or wished to defect. Quite the opposite.

But this too *is* speculation, and it is easy to make the same mistake as was done originally – to attribute motives to his actions that are wrong.

The final and overall conclusion is that no firm evidence whatsoever has been found to justify the allegation that on 20 April 1942 Walcott deliberately flew his Spitfire to North Africa for reasons that were less than honourable.

When 'Laddie' Lucas described Walcott's so-called defection as inexplicable, he unwittingly stated the truth. It *was* inexplicable, because there is no evidence to explain that it was a defection or, for that matter, a desertion.

# I I

# THE MAN AND THE ENIGMA

This book is written with two clear main objectives: to demonstrate that there was (and is) no evidence to justify the allegations that Walcott was afraid of going to Malta in April 1942 and deliberately deserted; and to show what happened to him on his release from Laghouat and how he led his life. But in starting the research, there was a third, unstated hope, and that was to try to tease out the character of the man and what made him tick. The machinations of the human mind are very private. Most will display a face to the world that does not necessarily reflect true feelings and emotions. Work colleagues see one face, family members another, and so on. The Salvi Bassi recalled by schoolmates was different to the Bud Walcott recalled by colleagues in the RCAF during his training in Canada, who was yet still different to the man who served in 603 Squadron – and the man seen by his friends in Lenox after the war was different to the husband who loved Virginia.

The act of banking his Spitfire to starboard on that fateful morning of 20 April 1942 in the western Mediterranean would prove to be one of the defining moments of Salvator Walcott's rather tragic life.

Giving rise to the accusations of desertion and defection, it would colour his wider reputation and that of his squadron. Although he ultimately took his own life, there is nothing to suggest that Walcott even knew what was being said about him – the various accusations were only made publicly after his death.

Concluding that there is no evidence that Walcott deliberately defected is not quite the end of the matter. As mentioned before, with the allegation having been made, even in the absence of evidence it is in the nature of things that there will always be a lingering suspicion that he might have left the formation as a conscious act to avoid going to Malta, afterwards making up the whole story of what happened to him and his Spitfire that April day in 1942.

Warrant Officer Tom O'Reilly's fears were discussed earlier. There is another story – possibly apocryphal – about a Lancaster crew that returned from a bombing operation to find that their rear gunner was missing. It transpired that he had done what Tom O'Reilly had not. Faced with another gut-wrenching operation, he had succumbed to his fears and left his turret before the Lancaster took off. Of course, the possible consequences were much more serious than for a single-seat aircraft. Without a rear gunner, the Lancaster would have been in considerably more danger of being attacked and shot down by a night fighter, so in succumbing to his fears the gunner put the lives of the six remaining members of the crew at serious risk.

Walcott enjoyed being in the limelight – almost literally when he performed as a cabaret magician before the war. He continued to perform magic. His instructors in Canada commented on it and said that he was very good. He performed while with 603 Squadron at Peterhead, and although Tony Holland may have disapproved of his tricks, clearly others enjoyed them, or else why would they allow him to continue? He performed magic entertainments in the internment camp. Back in Lenox after the war finished, he put on magic shows for the local kids.

He drew attention to himself as a pilot when he landed at Pittsfield in an Air Corps aeroplane while ferrying it to Bradley Field; he landed an early helicopter in the grounds of the elementary school in 1952; he flew as Santa Claus when he arrived by helicopter on several Christmases. He and Sergeant Mitchell wrote to an American newspaper from Laghouat seeking to correspond with some American girls. He may not have seen the result of the letter, but it certainly drew attention to the two internees and their plight in an amusing and sympathetic way.

In Lenox he wore his major's uniform with pride when attending the funerals of veterans and on various commemoration days, and his wartime exploits would add to his status locally, although they seem to have been embellished somewhat. An article in *The Berkshire Evening Eagle* in May 1945 notes that 'in the English (*sic*) RAF ... he was flying Spitfires over and around England by December, 1941, as a sergeant pilot', something that is quite untrue. His obituary makes similar comments and adds that 'serving as a sergeant pilot, he did much low-level strafing over the French coast'. But Walcott flew no operations with the RAF, so where did the information come from if not from Walcott himself or from his family? It is quite possible that Bud exaggerated his activities. Or it may have been just a fabrication by the press. He was the local hero returning from the European war thousands of miles away. It was exactly the kind of story a local journalist would embellish for effect.

With regard to his escape attempt from Laghouat, James Hudson was aware that an American had attempted an escape but did not know the escaper's name. In his book[1] Hudson describes only one attempt to escape in this way, but if Walcott's account is to be believed, there were actually two, on consecutive days – the first by Sergeant Massey, the second by Walcott. And while Hudson describes in some detail the actions taken by the remaining inmates to confuse the roll calls to cover up the escape, the description is for only one escape. However, the recollections of Seaman Brown of HMS *Havock* make it virtually impossible to doubt that Walcott's claim to escape was genuine.

Walcott increased his social standing when he married into the Tillotson family, and snippets of information about him and Virginia and their activities appear relatively frequently in the local press. One has the impression that Bud probably quite enjoyed all this. Even after Robert Tillotson's death in 1944, Virginia continued to be an active worker for the Republican Party and the Walcotts thrived under the Tillotson name and reputation. Captain Walcott's new postings were reported in the local press, as were his wife's political activities. He was given a substantial obituary in the local press.

Walcott was impetuous – a trait that is not necessarily an advantage for a pilot. He is described several times as 'a risk-taker' by those who knew him, and some of his escapades suggest that he made decisions on the spur of the moment rather than taking calculated risks. A citizen of Lenox remembers him flying down the street in an aeroplane on its side with its wings vertical; if this actually occurred it could either be described as dangerously irresponsible or a fun prank, but the potential consequences for him and anybody caught up in an accident could have been catastrophic. The landing at Pittsfield while transiting to Bradley Field was probably a snap decision to bring some fun into his life and entertain his friends. His crashes in the P-39 at Monastir and the P-47 in North Carolina were caused in part by his own actions. He failed to think through the indicators he was receiving about what was happening to his aeroplane, with the result that he was considered responsible in whole or in part for serious damage to two aircraft. However, no blame was attached to him when the Harvard he was flying in Canada suffered an engine failure, and he brought it down safely.

There is a saying in aviation circles that there are old pilots and bold pilots but no old, bold pilots. Fighter pilots in particular often have a live-for-the-moment attitude to life, but that doesn't mean that they should not be careful. Accidents in aeroplanes can be unforgiving and, yes, Walcott did survive at least four incidents, including the mid-air collision with Pilot Officer Jones at Peterhead. And with regard to that incident, no detailed accident reports or court of inquiry results have been found. Only the bald facts are known – that there was a mid-air collision over the airfield resulting in the death of Jones. If Walcott had been flying in an irresponsible manner that resulted in the collision it would explain why he attracted ill feeling in 603 Squadron, but nothing to suggest this has been found.

It is said that he wore his uniform with pride in Lenox after the war and that he was always very smart, on occasions remonstrating with others who were not as smart, and yet in the photograph of him during his recruit training in Canada his uniform is not particularly neat, and in the photograph of the 603 Squadron pilots taken on the deck of USS *Wasp* he isn't wearing a hat – a heinous crime in the British military! It really is quite extraordinary that this formal photograph was taken without Walcott's headgear. Perhaps it had just blown off as the picture was taken!

During his training he was sanctioned on several occasions for overrunning periods of leave, and in general he appears to have been less than enthusiastic with regards to authority, and yet in Lenox he appears to be the perfect veteran. It could be argued that the charges he faced demonstrated that he had spirit and a sense of adventure. They might also be the result of impetuosity, but they no doubt contributed to the decision not to grant him a commission when he completed his training in Canada.

In the few photographs of Walcott that exist, it is noticeable that in those taken before he transferred to the US Army at the end of 1942 – his class photo, the pictures taken in Canada while training and with 603 Squadron on the deck of the USS *Wasp* – he appears solemn, and distinctly unhappy in the latter one, as do many of the others who are also in the photo. In contrast, those taken afterwards, and which appear in the local newspaper, show a happy young man resplendent in his officer's uniform – the ideal war hero.

He had two major loves in his life – his wife Virginia and flying – and it is significant that his self-inflicted death came soon after he lost both of them in quick succession. The ebullient, popular, good-looking war hero the residents of Lenox could see masked something different.

Of course, there would be nothing easier than to speculate on his motives for almost all his actions. Why did he join the RCAF? What was his relationship with the Tillotsons? Why did he fly to Dublin? Why did he force-land in North Africa? Why did he commit suicide?

It is easy to fall into the trap of attributing to Bud motives for which there is no evidence – as has been done in the past, resulting in him being accused of desertion and cowardice. Better to consider the known facts rather than speculate about what is unknown. This is the enigma. And it seems unlikely that it will ever be explained.

The key and final comment has to be that he has been unfairly accused of being a coward and a deserter. And that is unacceptable.

# AUTHOR'S NOTE AND ACKNOWLEDGEMENTS

Much of the research for this account was carried out by my friend and colleague Squadron Leader Bruce Blanche RAuxAF Ret'd, who was also intrigued by the enigma of Sergeant Walcott and felt that the young American had been poorly treated. Squadron Leader Blanche was a co-author of *The Greatest Squadron of Them All*, the history of 603 Squadron that we wrote with David Ross, and was a serving member of the revived 603 Squadron in the early years of the twenty-first century. This biography could not have been completed without his help, but any errors are mine.

In researching the enigma of Sergeant Walcott, I had two objectives: to find out just what did happen to him, and to establish the reasons why he went to North Africa. I think I have achieved the first. We know what happened to Bud after he departed from *Wasp* and pretty much what he did with his life. With regard to the second, I am disappointed that I have not been able to discover with absolute certainty the reasons why he left.

I am aware and disappointed that I have not been able to find any documents originating with Bud himself – no diaries, letters, or even his log book. That does not mean to say that nothing exists. It is quite possible that there is a dusty trunk full of Bud's papers lying unopened in a basement somewhere that would shed much more light on his motives and feelings, but if such papers exist, I have not found them. What I believe I have been able to show is that there is no available evidence on which to base the allegations that he flew to North Africa because he was frightened to go to Malta or that he deliberately 'defected' to the enemy; I hope I have shown that such allegations were unjustified. I use the word 'were' deliberately. As has been stated previously, Lord Selkirk and others who wrote about Bud, including me, have changed their views having been made aware of the lack of evidence to support the allegations and have accordingly reflected this in reprints of their books. I am grateful for this. I am fully aware that the research does not remove the possibility that he *was* frightened to go to Malta and flew to North Africa having made a conscious decision to do so, and I do not believe it will ever be possible to completely remove the question mark over his motives.

Once made, the allegations are almost impossible to refute. Indeed, absolute certainty will only be achieved if a document emanating from Walcott himself is found, which states persuasively that he did go there deliberately. Even if documents are found, without any reference to his motives there will always be doubt. And if he did go for the reasons he gave to the British authorities on his return at the end of 1942, he might be covering up the truth. I fully accept that.

It is remarkable that, considering the influence of the Tillotsons in the Berkshires in the first half of the twentieth century, I could find no descendants of Bud. His family and his in-laws seem to have left nothing behind. Again, it may be that some descendants or distant relatives live yet, but I could not find any. When I reached the point when I wanted to try to find relatives of Bud and Virginia in Lenox, I made my approaches very cautiously. I did not wish to recklessly damage the local image that Bud had. Happily, although those that I met in Lenox did not know about the allegations, no one seems to have given them much credence and I do not believe my research has damaged Bud's reputation.

I am, of course, always interested in learning more about Bud if more information comes to light. I would be delighted to be made aware of it. And if any of his relatives do hear about this book, I would be very pleased if they would contact me.

In addition to Squadron Leader Blanche, I have been helped by many others.

Martin Gleeson is an Irishman who has an interest in the German, British and American airmen who fetched up in Eire, and over the years he has been a great help and source of encouragement in our joint researches into the case of Sergeant Walcott. Certainly this book could not have been written without his consistent, quiet help, which I have valued enormously. He commented on my account of the history of Eire and its relationship with Britain during the Second World War.

Once made aware, Lord Selkirk of Douglas, the former Lord James Douglas-Hamilton, has unhesitatingly accepted that no solid evidence exists to prove that Walcott deliberately flew to North Africa and I am grateful to him for this and for his willingness to change the comments about Walcott in the fourth edition of his book *The Air Battle for Malta*. I am also grateful to Lord Selkirk for generously giving his permission for me to quote from the earlier editions of his book, despite the fact that the quotation no longer represents his views.

Victoria Salvatore, Curator of the Lenox Historical Society, has been a great help and encouragement. She has trawled the society's archives looking for material about the Tillotsons and the Walcotts and arranged for me to meet Dave Roche and Jim Chague when I visited the Berkshires for my research. I am grateful to Dave and Jim, and to Tom Bosworth, another resident of Lenox, who spoke to me about Bud. Others in Lenox who helped were Susan Strong at Lenox High School and Lynn and Emily Watson, who found Bud's grave.

Amy Lafave, Music/Reference Librarian, Lenox Library Association, was one of my first contacts in the Berkshires and helped the whole process get started. Jill Mitchell provided encouragement and help from an American perspective.

In Canada, I was helped in my research by Mrs Joan Whiston, a researcher with Air Forces Heritage & History, 1 Canadian Air Division Headquarters. She sent me much information about Americans in the RCAF and the work of the Clayton-Knight Committee and this was invaluable. Also Wally Feydenchuk, who has a fund of knowledge about the legal position of Americans who joined the RCAF.

The late James Hudson and John Lewery were both internees in Laghouat with Walcott, and both shared their memories of him and of the dreadful conditions they endured in the camp. They are brave men who served our country well in its hour of need. I am grateful to Tom Cann of Tucann Design & Print and the family of the late James Hudson for giving me permission to use some of the photographs in the book. The late Jack Rae flew to Malta with 603 Squadron from *Wasp*; he discussed the experience with me and his views on the Walcott controversy. A courageous and accomplished fighter pilot and POW, he had no reservations in his defence of Walcott, saying that in his view inexperienced pilots should never have been sent to Malta at that time. I was fortunate to meet Jack on Malta in 2005, and it was a privilege to have his help and friendship. The late Bill Vine was another pilot who flew Spitfires from Malta and was shot down in flames in January 1943 over Sicily. Taken prisoner, he finished the war in a camp in Poland and was one of those who made the winter marches to Germany as the war was ending. Although he did not know Walcott, Bill provided me with background material about Malta and about the handling of Spitfires and Hurricanes. I valued his friendship.

Gordon Leith, Curator, Department of Research & Information Services at the RAF Museum, was helpful in searching for information about the mid-air collision over Peterhead airfield.

David Martin is chairman of the Fairlop Heritage Group, which seeks to remember those who served at RAF Fairlop (on the east side of London) during the war as well as being a vehicle for education about the Fairlop area and its history (www.fairlopplaintimes.com). 603 Squadron was based at RAF Fairlop in the autumn of 1941 when it suffered the losses that precipitated its move north to Dyce and Peterhead. He prepared the maps for me and I am grateful to him for this and his support over the years.

I have been researching Walcott for many years and it may be that some of those mentioned have forgotten the help they have given! Nonetheless I am grateful.

I need to thank those who have helped me with permissions. I have made some effort to identify owners and get their permission to reproduce pictures and quotations. I must mention Richard Caruana on Malta, Kathleen O'Connor at Lasell College, Hannah Goodman at Orion, Kevin Moran at *The Berkshire Eagle*, Steve Rogers of the War Graves Photographic Project, and Shawn Wylie and Shane Clayton of the Canadian Harvard Aircraft Association for their help in researching the Harvard which Bud force landed during his training and for Shane's photo of it in modern days. Tom Dietrich and Bob Revell of 'The Tiger Boys' kindly allowed me to use their photograph of the restored Fleet Finch aircraft, which they fly currently. With regard to quotations, I am grateful to Lori Jones at Pen & Sword and John Davies and his colleagues at Grub Street for their help. Also, Commandant Stephen MacEoin OIC the Military Archives of the Defence Forces Ireland and his staff members Captain Daniel Ayiotis, Noelle Grothier, Hugh Beckett and Lisa Dolan, for permission to reproduce the report into Walcott's landing at Collinstown Airport. I would like thank Emily Dean, customer sales and services executive at the Imperial War Museum, for her help with the images used in the book which are owned by the museum. Finally, my thanks to Sonja Marshall and *The Scotsman* Publications Ltd for giving me permission to use the photograph of 'the Humbie Heinkel'.

I have not been able to find the copyright holders of a few of the illustrations. If any happen to read this book, I would be happy to acknowledge their ownership in any future editions should they contact me.

If I have omitted anyone, I apologise.

Lastly, I thank my wife Marion once again for her forbearance as I lost myself in history.

Bill Simpson
Edinburgh

# Appendix

# IRISH MILITARY REPORT ON WALCOTT'S LANDING AT DUBLIN

Landing of British Aircraft at Dublin Airport

on 28th January, 1942.

A British aircraft first sighted 8 miles N.W. L.O.P.
Dunany, Co. Louth, moving west at 15.36 hrs. on 28th
January, 1942, was subsequently sighted west of L.O.P.
Cardys Rocks, Balbriggan, moving S. and was finally
observed circling low over Collinstown aerodrome at 15.51
hrs.    At 15.52 hrs. the aircraft landed safely on the
aerodrome and the single occupant was held by the A.A.
personnel on duty at the Airport.

The aircraft proved to be a Hurricane Mark I fighter
armed with eight Browning guns.    The machine bore yellow
marks on the fuselage which usually denotes a training
machine.

The pilot who was clad in R.A.F. uniform with 'U.S.A.'
on shoulder straps, was R.79006 Sergeant Salvatore Walcott,
Hotel Tudor, New York City.    (Next of kin (grandmother)
————————————————————————, Providence, Rhode Island,
U.S.A.).

Walcott stated he had been stationed with the R.A.F.
at Crosby on Eden, Cumberland and had been in England for
the past three months.  He stated that he had been on a
local flight from Cumberland from 14.15 hrs. and had lost
his bearings.    He also stated that he was running short
of petrol, (there was approximately 12 gallons left in the
tanks at the time of landing and the tank indicators were
already pointing to zero) and suffering from the severe
cold when he landed at Dublin Airport.

The airman was detained overnight and after refuelling
was permitted to depart at 10.20 hrs. on the 29th January,
1942, from Collinstown Aerodrome.

# NOTES

## Chapter 1
1. Signal 25 April 1942 AOC Malta to Air Ministry (AIR2/7698).

## Chapter 2
1. From Walcott's birth records.

## Chapter 3
1. Hosking, Geoffrey, *A History of the Soviet Union 1917–1991* (London, Fontana Press, 1992) p194
2. Solzhenitsyn, Aleksandr, translated from the Russian by Thomas P. Whitney and Harry Willetts, abridged by Edward E. Ericson Jr. *The Gulag Archipelago 1918–56* (London, The Harvill Press, 1999) p342.

## Chapter 4
1. Britain did more than give the South moral support. It clandestinely supplied weapons and ships to the Confederacy and it has been estimated that this may have lengthened the Civil War by up to two years. It is reported that there was a low-profile base for Confederate agents to obtain the weapons in the small town of Bridge of Allan near Stirling. See *The Independent* of 23 June 2014.
2. A dominion was one of the larger countries in the British Empire (e.g. Canada, Australia) possessing a rather greater degree of autonomy than a colony.
3. Personal correspondence Wally Feydenchuk 2011.

4. Goodson, J. A. & Franks, N, *Over-Paid, Over-Sexed and Over Here*, (Canterbury, Wingham Press, 1991) p15.
5. Mason, Francis K. *Battle Over Britain* (St Albans, McWhirter Twins, 1969) p500.
6. The Auxiliary Air Force became the Royal Auxiliary Air Force (RAuxAF) after the war.
7. *The Creation of a National Air Force The Official History of the Royal Canadian Air Force Vol II* by W. A. B. Douglas published by the University of Toronto Press. Page 635.
8. Aircraftman Second Class.

## Chapter 5

1. *ABC of the RAF* edited by Sir John Hammerton.
2. Leading Aircraftman.
3. Churchill, Winston S. *The Second World War Vol III*, (London, Cassell & Co 1950) p359.
4. *Flying* Magazine (USA) December 1946 via Martin Gleeson.
5. Report 'Landing of British Aircraft at Dublin Airport on 28th January, 1942.' Courtesy of Military Archives Cathal Brugha Barracks, Rathmines, Dublin 6 (File numbers G2/X/0961 and ACF-S-113)
6. It was only as recently as 2013 that the 'deserters' were pardoned by the Irish government.
7. Dwyer, T. Ryle, *Strained Relations: Ireland at Peace and the USA at War 1941-45* (Dublin, Gill and MacMillan Ltd, 1988) p27.
8. From files in the Eire Military Archives ref G2/X/0961 and ACF/S/113 via Martin Gleeson.
9. Eire Military Archives ref G2/X/0961. Report 'Landing of British Aircraft at Dublin Airport on 28th January 1942'.

## Chapter 6

1. RAF Dyce Fighter Sector Operations Record Book UK National Archives AIR 28/235.
2. The author visited Pilot Officer Jones' grave in August 2005. It is one of about a dozen wartime graves at the far wall of the cemetery; well kept and with flowers.
3. On one occasion during a later delivery, a Spitfire with a problem did manage to land back on to the carrier from which it had just launched. It was a remarkable piece of airmanship on the part of the pilot.
4. Interview for Imperial War Museum 2005 catalogue 27813.
5. Barnham wrote an account of his experiences on Malta called *One Man's Window* and at least one of his paintings is on display in the Imperial War Museum in London.

6. Barnham, Denis, *One Man's Window* (London, New English Library, 1975) p37. Reproduced with kind permission of Grub Street.

7. As an ex-sport parachutist, the author was told to enjoy his first jump. It would be the best because he didn't know what to expect and this proved to be correct!

8. All aircraft flown by the RAF were accompanied by a set of 'Pilot's Notes', which gave information essential to flying the aeroplane, e.g. settings and drills for take-off, landing, emergency landings etc. Relatively simple for aircraft of that era, aircrew manuals for modern day aircraft are voluminous and complex.

9. Apart from being a highly successful and competent fighter pilot, Percy 'Laddie' Lucas was a renowned left-handed golfer. He was born in the old clubhouse of the Prince's Golf Club at Sandwich Bay in Kent and maintained strong links with the club until his death in 1998. He was awarded a DFC and DSO and Bar for his gallantry during the war. Leaving the air force in 1945, he became the Member of Parliament for Brentford and Chiswick, but did not stand again for the 1959 General Election. He wrote prolifically about the Royal Air Force during the Second World War and was heavily involved in promoting golf as an amateur. His wife Jill was the sister of Thelma, the wife of the famous fighter pilot and golfer Douglas Bader. He was made a Commander of the Order of the British Empire in 1981.

10. UK National Archives AIR2/7698.

11. UK National Archives AIR24/908.

12. UK National Archives AIR2/7698.

13. UK National Archives AIR2/7698.

## Chapter 7

1. UK National Archives AIR40/258. 'Repatriated from North Africa Statement by Sgt S. B. Walcott'.

2. Hudson, James D., *There and Back Again, A Navigator's Story* (Lincoln, Tucann Design & Print, 2004) p76. Reproduced with kind permission of Tucann Books and the family of the late James Hudson.

3. Smith, Colin, *England's Last War Against France,* (London, Phoenix, 2010) p169.

4. One account states 4 holes.

5. Imperial War Museum Oral History Ref 11455.

6. Cazalet was killed on 4 July 1943 while travelling in the same aircraft as the Polish General Sikorski when it crashed under mysterious circumstances on taking-off from Gibraltar.

7. UK National Archives FO 916/415. Internees in Laghouat Welfare.

8. The American diplomat is not named.

9. Imperial War Museum Oral history ref 10504.
10. A popular fly killer of the time.
11. UK National Archives FO 916/415 Internees in Laghouat Welfare.
12. One account states that the number was 29. Hudson, James D., *There and Back Again, A Navigator's Story.* (Lincoln, Tucann Design & Print, 2004)
13. Imperial War Museum Oral History ref 10504.

## Chapter 8

1. Hansard 8 July 1942 vol 381 cc 775–6.
2. RMS *Titanic* followed this tradition although her fourth funnel was a dummy.
3. UK National Archives AIR40/258 'Repatriated from North Africa Statement by Sgt. S. B. Walcott.
4. In 1957, similar muddled and disastrous thinking by the British concluded that missiles represented the way forward and that the day of the manned aircraft was over. In executing this philosophy, the Conservative administration of the day and the Minister of Defence Duncan Sandys MP helped destroy the British aircraft industry, at the time competing with the best in the world.
5. From US Army report.
6. The accident referred to was the Papa India Trident crash of 1972. Even in modern aeroplanes, pilots can be distracted by warning horns, vocal warnings, multitudes of flashing lights, which can result in poor analysis of a situation and inadequate responses. Sometimes it is not possible to switch these devices off once they are activated. These are design issues, not the fault of the pilot.

## Chapter 9

1. Information from US Army Air Forces 'Report of Aircraft Accident dated 4 April 1944'.
2. Information from US Army Air Forces 'Report of Aircraft Accident dated 16 June 1944'.
3. *Flight* magazine 21 March 1958 'Helicopters in Civil Operation'.
4. *Billboard* magazine 19 March 1955.
5. *Billboard* magazine 10 November 1956.
6. Fairchild Engine and Airplane Corporation based in Hagerstown, Maryland.
7. *Arizona Republic* 12 February 1961.
8. The headstone gives Walcott's date of birth as 25 December 1919. His birth certificate and RCAF records clearly show it to be 24 December 1919.

## Chapter 10

1. UK National Archives AIR 2/7698.
2. *The Air Battle for Malta* by Lord James Douglas-Hamilton (now Lord Selkirk of Douglas). The comment is in the first three editions of the book but the 4th, which was published in 2006, is amended to report the changed circumstances. The quotation is reproduced with the kind permission of Lord Selkirk and Pen & Sword.
3. Lucas, P. B. 'Laddie', *Malta: The Thorn in Rommel's Side* (Stanley Paul, 1992)
4. *Chambers Twentieth Century Dictionary* (Edinburgh, W. & R. Chambers 1977)
5. Ross, Wing Commander A. E. *The Queen's Squadron – The History of 603 (City of Edinburgh) Squadron 1925–1957* (Edinburgh, published privately 1989. Copy available for viewing in the National Library of Scotland, Edinburgh.)
6. Ross, D., Blanche, B. & Simpson, W., *The Greatest Squadron of Them All, Vol II,* (London, Grub Street, 2003)
7. AIR2/7698.
8. Ibid.
9. Quoted by Tony Holland in *Malta: The Thorn in Rommel's Side.*
10. Barnham, Denis, *One Man's Window* (London, New English Library, 1975) p37. Reproduced with kind permission of Grub Street.
11. Lucas, P. B. 'Laddie', *Malta: The Thorn in Rommel's Side* (Stanley Paul, 1992)
12. Conversation with the author 27 March 2013.

## Chapter 11

1. Hudson, James D, *There and Back Again, A Navigator's Story* (Lincoln, Tucann Design & Print, 2004)

# SOURCES

## Published

Barnham, Denis, *One Man's Window* (London, New English Library, 1975)

Delve, Ken, *The Source Book of the RAF* (Shrewsbury, Airlife Publishing Ltd, 1994)

Douglas-Hamilton, Lord James, *The Air Battle for Malta, Third edition* (Edinburgh, Mainstream, 1981)

Douglas-Hamilton, James, *The Air Battle for Malta, Fourth edition* (Barnsley, Pen & Sword, 2006)

Dwyer, T. Ryle, *Strained Relations: Ireland at Peace and the USA at War 1941–45* (Dublin, Gill and MacMillan Ltd, 1988)

Goodson, J. A. & Franks, N, *Over-Paid, Over-Sexed and Over Here* (Canterbury, Wingham Press, 1991)

Hillmer, Norman, *The Creation of a National Air Force: The Official History of the Royal Canadian Air Force Volume II* (Toronto, University of Toronto Press)

Hosking, Geoffrey, *A History of the Soviet Union 1917–1991* (London, Fontana Press, 1992)

Hudson, James D., *There and Back Again, A Navigator's Story* (Lincoln, Tucann Design & Print, 2004)

Jefford, C. G., *RAF Squadrons* (Shrewsbury, Airlife Publishing Ltd, 2001)

Lamb, Charles, *War in a Stringbag* (London, Cassell 2002)

Lucas, P. B. 'Laddie', *Malta: The Thorn in Rommel's Side* (Stanley Paul, 1992)

Mellinger, George, Stanaway, John, *P-39 Airacobra Aces of World War 2* (Oxford, Osprey Publishing Ltd, 2001)

Ross, Wing Commander A. E. *The Queen's Squadron – The History of 603 (City of Edinburgh) Squadron 1925–1957* (Edinburgh, published privately 1989. Copy available in the National Library of Scotland, Edinburgh.)

Ross, D., Blanche, B. & Simpson, W., *The Greatest Squadron of Them All, Vols I & II* (London, Grub Street, 2003)

Shores, Christopher, Cull, Brian & Malizia, Nicola, *Malta: The Spitfire Year 1942* (London, Grub Street, 1991)

Smith, Colin, *England's Last War Against France* (London, Phoenix, 2010)

Tusa, A & J, *The Berlin Airlift* (Staplehurst, Spellmount, 1998)

## Archives
### Eire Military Archives
G2/X/0961 Report 'Landing of British Aircraft at Dublin Airport on 28th January 1942'.

### UK National Archives
AIR 2/7698 Telegramme 25Apr42 From AOC Malta to Air Ministry Whitehall and HQ RAF Middle East

AIR 2/7698 Telegramme 27Apr42 From AOC Malta to HQ RAF Middle East

AIR8/980 Telegramme Winston Churchill to President Roosevelt

AIR/27/945 133 (Eagle) Squadron Operations Record Book

AIR28/4 RAF Abbotsinch Operations Record Book

AIR28/18 RAF Aldergrove Operations Record Book

AIR/28/235 Dyce Fighter Sector Operations Record Book

AIR28/637 RAF Peterhead Operations Record Book

AIR28/637 RAF Fraserburgh Operations Record Book

AIR28/653 RAF Prestwick Operations Record Book

AIR 28/807 RAF Takali (sic) Operations Record Book

AIR29/684 RAF Crosby-on-Eden Operations Record Book

AIR40/258 'Repatriated from North Africa Statement by Sgt S. B. Walcott'

FO 916/415 Internees in Laghouat Welfare

### Imperial War Museum
Oral histories

10504 James Arthur Brown, HMS *Havock*

11455 Alfred John Surridge HMS *Havock*

11328 Maurice Albert Cutler, HMS *Havock*

22361 John Larraway, HMS *Havock*

27813 Jack Rae, 603 (City of Edinburgh) Squadron

### Others
Attempted Escape by Sgt WALCOTT, S. P., RCAF 603 Sqn. Fighter Command, RAF 21 December 1942 MI9. (This British report was obtained privately, and its original source is not known.)

# INDEX